The Complete Idiot's Co...

My Favorite Personal Fin...

➤ **www.quicken.com** Quicken.com can easily be your first stop for any personal finance topic: planning, savings, debt reduction, banking, investments, insurance, and just about anything else. Quicken's Debt Reduction Planner and insurance-related Family Needs Planner are the best specialized online tools available.

➤ **www.vanguard.com** The Vanguard Group Web site provides great online planning tools and a full self-paced financial curriculum, as well as online mutual fund and brokerage services. The Vanguard Group is known for its great low-cost mutual funds.

➤ **www.fpanet.org** If you want a certified financial planner to help you with your financial plan, use the Financial Planning Association PlannerSearch tool.

➤ **www.estrong.com** The Strong Funds Web site is another well-rounded offering, with planning tools, great educational material, online fund access, and brokerage services.

➤ **www.getoutofdebt.org** Debt Counselors of America offers self-help publications as well as interactive services if you want help getting out of debt. Its one-pay service pays your creditors while you make one payment to DCA each month—rebuilding your credit history in the process.

➤ **www.gomez.com** Gomez Associates ranks numerous types of e-commerce companies, including banks, brokers, and even pet supply stores. It also offers lists of firms that satisfy different customer profiles.

➤ **www.bankrate.com** BankRate.com can help you find the right deals for most financial products, including online banking, CDs, money market accounts, credit cards, mortgages, and more.

➤ **www.hsh.com** HSH Associates provides a great education in mortgages and other loans, tools to identify the loan for you, and a preview of available loans. A complete report of available loans carries a modest charge.

➤ **www.investorguide.com/insurance.htm** InvestorGuide provides links to help you educate yourself on insurance. You also can use online insurance calculators, get online quotes, purchase insurance online, find company ratings, and more.

My Favorite Personal Finance Web Sites

➤ **www.priceline.com** At priceline.com you can bid for airline tickets, rental cars, mortgages, and even groceries—at the price you want to pay. If a vendor is willing to meet your price, you could save 60% or more! Priceline.com can tell you recent successful prices and the probability of your price being accepted.

➤ **www.shoppinglist.com** ShoppingList.com lets you electronically search for sales on the items you want at the stores in your area.

➤ **www.collegeboard.org** The College Board Web site helps students find and apply to the schools they want, while helping their parents figure out how to pay for tuition.

➤ **www.better-investing.org** NAIC provides education, tools, software, and a helpful online community when you want to learn about fundamental stock analysis.

➤ **www.investorama.com** Investorama provides great investment education, thousands of investment links, and samples of investment publications.

➤ **www.wsrn.com** Wall Street Research Net provides lots of information to make your stock research and portfolio management a snap.

➤ **www.fool.com** The Motley Fool is an educational and fun site for financial education at all levels. Fools around the world create a good community for succeeding in the market and with all-around personal finance.

➤ **www.siliconinvestor.com** For in-depth data, news, and discussions on technology stocks, head to the Silicon Investor Web site.

➤ **www.yahoo.com** The Yahoo! Finance Web site has lots of investment resources, message boards, and online investment clubs.

➤ **www.annualreportservice.com** Annual reports are key to fundamental stock analysis, and you can find almost all of them at the Annual Report Service Web site.

➤ **www.bigcharts.com** When you need charts, the BigCharts Web site provides charts that are easy to read—and you can email them to yourself or your investment buddies on a set schedule that you define.

➤ **www.morningstar.net** Morningstar publishes definitive reports on mutual funds. Its online portfolio X-Ray can show you the true asset allocation and other features of your portfolio, whether you own stocks, mutual funds, or both.

➤ **www.about.com** You might find yourself at about.com no matter what topic you want information about. Check out its links to online financial glossaries.

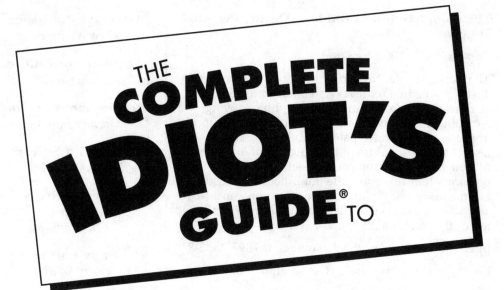

THE COMPLETE IDIOT'S GUIDE® TO

Online Personal Finance

Bonnie Biafore

A Division of Macmillan USA
201 West 103rd Street, Indianapolis, Indiana 46290

Trademarks

Warning and Disclaimer

Associate Publisher
Greg Wiegand

Acquisitions Editor
Angelina Ward

Development Editor
Gregory Harris

Managing Editor
Thomas F. Hayes

Project Editors
Casey Kenley
Tricia Sterling

Copy Editor
Sossity Smith

Indexer
Kelly Castell

Proofreader
Jeanne Clark

Technical Editor
Ken Little

Illustrator
Judd Winick

Team Coordinator
Sharry Gregory

Interior Designer
Nathan Clement

Cover Designer
Michael Freeland

Copywriter
Eric Borgert

Production
Darin Crone
Steve Geiselman

Contents at a Glance

Table of Contents

Part 2: Using the Internet for Personal Finance 71

About the Author

Bonnie Biafore has written and taught classes on technical subjects to technical and non-technical audiences alike since 1984. A self-proclaimed computer illiterate during her college years (there were no PCs then!), she was introduced to computers with Computer Aided Design in the engineering firm where she worked as a structural engineer. Soon, she began teaching courses and short seminars on CAD systems, programming, and software development to other architects and engineers just beginning to use computers.

As a director on the Denver Chapter of the National Association of Investors Corporation (NAIC) since 1995, she has written and taught classes on basic finance and investing, stock analysis, computerized stock analysis tools, and online investing. With classes for adults, Bonnie likes to start with why the subject is important and follow with clear, easy-to-follow instructions on the "how-to." She frequently speaks at investor fairs about stock analysis, Internet investing, and computer basics.

Dedication

To my husband, Pete, who has always graciously answered my never-ending requests for advice.

Acknowledgements

There are a few people whose help cannot go without recognition. Thanks to John Hedtke for getting me the opportunity to write this book. I am eternally grateful to Pat McVey-Ritsick for her insight on explaining the Internet and personal finance clearly. I can't thank Jane Bryant Quinn enough for her comprehensive, clear, and entertaining book, Making the Most of Your Money. *I devoured every page, and my own personal finances benefited tremendously.*

Tell Us What You Think!

As the reader of this book, *you* are our most important critic and commentator. We value your opinion and want to know what we're doing right, what we could do better, what areas you'd like to see us publish in, and any other words of wisdom you're willing to pass our way.

As an Associate Publisher for Que, I welcome your comments. You can fax, email, or write me directly to let me know what you did or didn't like about this book—as well as what we can do to make our books stronger.

Please note that I cannot help you with technical problems related to the topic of this book, and that due to the high volume of mail I receive, I might not be able to reply to every message.

When you write, please be sure to include this book's title and author as well as your name and phone or fax number. I will carefully review your comments and share them with the author and editors who worked on the book.

Fax: 317-581-4666

Email: consumer@mcp.com

Mail: Associate Publisher
         Que
         201 West 103rd Street
         Indianapolis, IN 46290 USA

Introduction

In the past century, we have gone from the Industrial Revolution to the Computer Age; the horse-drawn carriage to the space shuttle; and a Dow Jones Average of less than 50 to more than 11,000. We would have to be idiots to not want to use technology to grab some of this prosperity for ourselves.

But technology and the financial markets can be pretty confusing and downright scary. If you're a novice at one or both, you might think you're better off without them. In reality, you only have to learn a little about technology and finances to put them to work for you. Some common sense and a healthy dose of skepticism are enough to avoid the pitfalls.

The twenty-first century won't let up. More and more technology will hit us faster and faster. To make matters worse, everyone wants us to take responsibility for our own financial futures. Retirement plans are quickly switching from the company-funded pension plans to 401(k) plans, where the employee has to make his or her own investment decisions. Parents are kicking us out of the house. (Well, at 40 it's about time!) Is Social Security secure?

How do we choose from the thousands of company stocks and mutual funds available today? How do we sort out all the products pitched to us: affinity credit cards, reverse mortgages, whole and universal life insurance, derivative securities, and tax strategies? Whose recommendations can we trust? How do we choose the right products? Do we have to be financial experts to survive?

You don't have to be a financial expert to be a financial success. You can build a good financial plan using basic financial products. But, you must plan! Dwight D. Eisenhower once said, "In preparing for battle I have always found that plans are useless, but planning is indispensable." Financial plans can change with the stages and events of your life. But, when you build your financial plan, you find out what is important: what you want and need from your money. A financial plan acts as a target. It is much easier to get where you want to be when you know where you are! You also can make informed choices about all those financial products thrown at you.

As you learn more, you can always apply your new knowledge to fine-tuning your plan. Conventional mortgages, term life insurance, and plain checking and savings accounts all work well as long as you look for good rates and the services you really need. Later, you might decide an adjustable-rate mortgage is just the ticket, or that whole life insurance or money market funds better suit your needs.

Relax! You don't have to learn everything at once! There's nothing wrong with learning about different areas of personal finance as the need arises. Learn about mortgages when you buy your first house. Learn about life insurance when you get married or have children. Start learning about investing as early as you can. And remember that you have the rest of your life to master this!

There is a good reason for handling your finances well. Personal finance can save—or make for you—more money than you will earn in your career. Decreasing your life insurance premium by $200 a year would save $5,000 over 25 years. Lower credit card interest rates, or better yet, keeping no balances on your credit cards, can save tens of thousands of dollars in interest. Even better, lowering your mortgage rate 1.5% on a $250,000 mortgage would save you almost $100,000 in interest over the life of the loan!

By investing all (well, most) of the money that you save, you can turn that humming-bird's nest egg into an ostrich egg. If you contribute the $10,000 maximum to a 401(k) retirement plan and average a 10% return, you would have $1,082,000 at the end of 25 years. Increasing your investment return by just 2% increases that nest egg to $1,493,000. By saving money and investing wisely, you can have a ball before you retire and still retire comfortably.

On the other hand, leaving your finances to fend for themselves can lead to some nasty surprises. If you don't have a financial plan, how do you know whether you have enough life insurance? Your spouse and children could end up on welfare. Running up the balance on high-interest credit cards is so costly that it is difficult to ever pay them off. Without some up-front planning, you can't even guess how much money you really need to retire. And, if you fall short on your retirement savings, you'll miss out on the round-the-world cruise, or even worse, depend on your children for support.

So, what about all this online stuff? Do we really need it to take care of our finances? Nope. You can still get everything you need for your finances the old-fashioned way. But, your computer and the Internet can do more for you faster and with fewer hassles. They're tools. And the better you are with your tools, the more they do for you.

The cell phone is another gadget that went from toy to got-to-have. They have touch pads like most phones these days. But they aren't quite the same. Have you ever dialed a number and waited and waited for the call to go through? Then, you find out that you have to push Send! Or, you forget to push End to finish a call, and faint when your next bill comes in. Some people think that a cell phone can save them in case they get into trouble, only to discover that their cell phone service doesn't work in that out-of-the-way spot where the car broke down.

On the other hand, with cell phones we can tell everyone that the plans have changed and call the pizza shop exactly 20 minutes before we get there. We can give one phone number out that finds us no matter where we are. And soon, we will even be able to get information off the Internet on our phones.

The Internet is fast and convenient. It might take a while to browse through Web pages for the information that you want, but in the past, you would have to call each company during your lunch hour and request information. Then, you had to wait for days or even weeks until the packet arrived in the mail. Now, you can get information about the financial products you're interested in at your convenience—outside of office hours, without phone tag, and without listening to sales pitches or high-pressure sales tactics.

The Internet provides more and better services than you can get offline. The Web has millions of pages of information on every conceivable topic with more published every day. You can search all those pages for certain words or phrases in seconds. The Internet can deliver real-time quotes or news bulletins on stocks automatically as you work at your computer. You can look at stock performance charts, changing the time-frame to days, months, or years, or the performance criteria to price, earnings per share, sales, or just about anything else. You can download historical data directly into another program on your computer without entering any data.

The Internet can save you money, too! You get reduced brokerage commissions. You can comparison shop for things such as insurance, loans, or consumer products. And, you are more likely to get better rates because you can find the best rates so easily. Quite often, online store sites offer goods unavailable in a real store or even in a catalog. And you can order discounted goods knowing exactly what is in stock.

The Web also can be your teacher. If you're like me, you hate to talk to salespeople when you don't understand something. You're like putty in their hands! When you are just starting out, you can research any topic on personal finance and educate yourself before you talk to that salesperson or make decisions. You can learn about financial planning, techniques for saving money, how to get out of debt, mortgages, how to invest—whatever you want.

The Complete Idiot's Guide to Online Personal Finance is your introduction to online personal finance. It teaches you what you need to know to use your computer and the Web to make smart financial decisions. You will find online tools that help you choose the right financial products and sites that teach you even more about your finances. You will also learn about the potential problems with online finances and how to avoid them.

How to Use This Book

The *Complete Idiot's Guide* is organized to help you get started even if you are a beginner with computers, the Internet, and personal finance. However, if you have an urgent financial matter, you can also go straight to a particular topic.

Part 1, "The Idiot's Introduction to Online Personal Finance," introduces the full range of personal finance activities and explains why each part is important. It also describes how to use online resources to get your financial foundation in place: a financial plan and a budget (or spending plan). It has a chapter on getting out of debt, which is your first and most important step if you go wild with your credit cards. It also has hints for getting on the road to saving painlessly.

Part 2, "Using the Internet for Personal Finance," teaches you how to get an online bank account and use it. You learn how to find credit cards online that suit your needs, whether you want low rates, no fees, or easy credit qualifications. You learn about different types of loans and how to find the one you want using the Internet.

This section also offers some tips for finding houses and cars to buy online. You'll get a quick review on the insurance you need and find out how to shop for insurance online. Finally, you learn some of the things you can do with taxes online.

Money saved fuels the rest of your personal finances. Part 3, "Saving for Your Dreams," covers painless ways to save money and how to find new hints on saving on the Web. You also learn about tools for saving for a college education, retirement, or other big-ticket items.

Part 4, "Investing on the Internet," starts off with a brief introduction to the basics of investing. You find out that you won't get rich quick. But, there are a few key yet simple strategies for success in the stock market that will make you rich slowly. You learn some easy ways to build a portfolio that provides a good return while limiting your risk. Whether you want to invest in mutual finds, stocks, or both, you find out how to find and buy your investments online. Finally, you learn how to keep records and manage your portfolio to keep your investments successful and in tune with your needs.

In Part 5, "Don't Be an Idiot," you learn about the dangers of mixing finance and the Internet. You find out how to stay ahead of the con artists and protect your money and financial information. You also learn the best way to protect the information on your computer—even from yourself!

Part 6, "Appendixes," has two sections: Appendix A, "Getting Online," which takes you through the basics of getting online—what you need on your computer, what you need from your phone service, how to set up your computer and Internet browser, and how to get an account with an Internet service provider—and Appendix B, "Personal Finance Web Sites," which lists personal finance Web sites, including all the sites discussed in this book. The glossary includes definitions of Internet and finance terms used in this book.

Conventions

The information in this book is formatted to help you find what you need as rapidly as possible. A variety of visual elements are used to make you aware of potential hazards, financial terminology, software shortcuts, planning tips, and good ideas. At the beginning of each chapter you will find a listing of the major topics included to help you locate the information you want. The end of each chapter includes a summary of the concepts covered.

New terms are indicated in *italic* typeface. When entering data into your computer, a **bold** typeface is used to indicate text that you type. And, a `monospace` typeface indicates onscreen messages or text that appears on the screen.

In addition, *The Complete Idiot's Guide to Online Personal Finance* has all sorts of helpful hints about finance, your computer, and the Internet. These tips give you a leg up on success, point out good things to know, and highlight pitfalls to avoid. Look for the following elements:

Head of the Class!

There are some aspects of personal finance that are crucial to success. Use these tips to learn how to set up a financial plan destined for glory! You also learn some tricks to save more and make more money on your investments. Look closer if you're ready for some new techniques to make the most of your money.

Crash Alert

What do computers and the stock market have in common? They can both crash! Learn to avoid the pitfalls of personal finance whether on or off the Web.

Tool Tips

You can get by with the basics. But, you can sail through the Web if you know more about your computer, Web browser, and other programs. These tips help you use your computer and the Internet to whip your finances into shape.

Did You Know?

These sidebars explain some concepts you might not know. They also point out some Web sites you might not think to look for.

Part 1

The Idiot's Introduction to Online Personal Finance

Your personal finances are anything and everything that has to do with your money. Of course, no one cares about your money more than you do. A little planning up-front with some patience thrown in and your finances can turn that pumpkin into a royal carriage. But handle your finances badly and that prince can look like a toad. So, take a deep breath and learn to live within your means. Get out of debt, start saving, and your investments will be the fairy godmother you always wanted.

Chapter 1

What Is Personal Finance?

In This Chapter

➤ How your finances change with your phases of life

➤ Being a smart consumer to simplify your finances

➤ Knowing the easiest way to succeed

➤ Keeping track of where you stand

➤ Needing insurance to protect what you have when you're successful with your personal finances

Your personal finances include anything that has to do with *your* money. No one else—this is important—cares about your money as much as you do. The good news is that the choice is always yours. You can choose to do as much or as little with your finances as you want. You can also choose to use the Internet for as much of your finances as you want. And if you're reading this as the reality of a spouse and children dawns on you, remember you still don't have to change everything at once. A few insurance policies are critical, but you have the rest of your life to perfect the remainder.

First Comes Love, Then Comes Marriage

As you live your life, your circumstances change, along with your personal finance needs. What works when you're young and single isn't appropriate when you're married with children. Financial plans are effective tools because they keep you focused on your goals. But your financial plan isn't cast in concrete. With online financial plans, you can change your plan easily as your goals change with the stages of your life. The next few sections contain some general advice for these various stages.

Freedom's Just Another Word for Nothing Left to Lose

You're young. You're single. You don't depend on anyone and no one depends on you. You might say that you want to be carefree—you can't be bothered with all those pesky details of personal finance.

Well, when you're young and single, effective personal finance can be quite simple—particularly if you work online. Disability insurance, health insurance, and a good education are your best friends. The education ensures that you can support yourself. The insurance covers you if trouble arises. If you can't afford the insurance policies, see if your parents will help out a little while longer. Lord knows they'll probably pay the bills, if you get into trouble.

Golden Oldies

There's nothing wrong with the single life. As you grow older and stay single, remember that disability and health insurance are the key. You probably don't need life insurance. You do need retirement savings, the more the better. And you need an attorney, family member, or a trustworthy friend, who can take care of your finances if you are unable.

You can get your credit established with a low-cost credit card. And as you'll find out in Chapter 12, "Saving for Retirement," it's never to early to start saving for retirement—in fact, the earlier you start, the greater the rewards down the road… Figure 1.1 shows one example of a more aggressive model portfolio for those with a long timeframe.

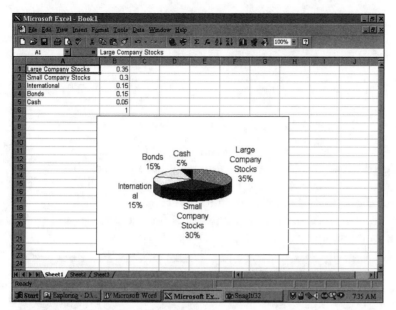

Figure 1.1

When you have lots of time for your portfolio to grow, focus on investments with higher returns.

Married with Children

Let's be honest. It's tough to be carefree when you have a spouse and children. Whether you are the main breadwinner or play more of a support role, your spouse needs some kind of help if you die. Your children need support as well.

Each spouse who works needs disability insurance. Everyone needs health insurance. If your income provides for your family, you need life insurance. With a family, it's particularly important to cover all the legal documents: a will so that your beneficiaries get what you want them to have, and a power of attorney, so that someone else can take care of things if you can't.

You also have a never-ending task of saving money. With children, you save for your retirement and the kids' college, not to mention braces and all the things that children can't do without. The portfolio in Figure 1.2 is one example of a starting allocation when you save for college early.

Did You Know?

The Brady Bunch

If both spouses say "I do," surrounded by the kids from their first marriages, you have to see if wills and insurance need changes for stepchildren. In addition, you might want trusts so that children from previous marriages get what you want them to have.

On My Own Again

If you end up unmarried with children to support, security is key. Make sure you have insurance in spades: disability, health, and life. You might have to re-establish credit. Saving money is tougher, but even more important. You need a will to designate a guardian for the kids. And most important, don't make any quick decisions. In this situation, you need to understand personal finance through and through. Bad decisions can cost you money you just can't afford to lose.

Figure 1.2

When you start saving early to pay for college, you make your job easier by investing some of your money in stocks.

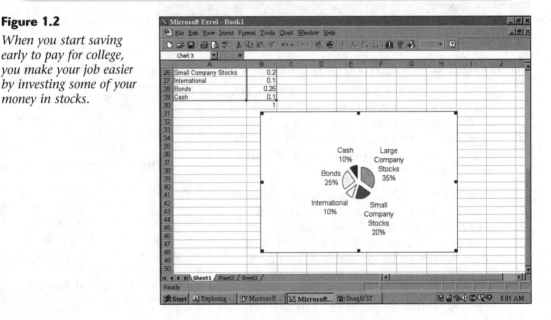

Doing What You Saved for All Those Years

The kids are gone. The house is paid for. You're retired. You still have your health. It's time to enjoy the money you saved and invested for decades. You don't need disability insurance. You don't need life insurance. You do need plenty of health insurance—at least a Medigap policy to cover what Medicare doesn't. In addition, after you turn 60, consider adding a long-term care policy to help pay for a long stay in a nursing home.

Your investments are more conservative. You look to bonds or dividend-paying stocks to provide you with steady income (see Figure 1.3). But you still have some growth-oriented investments, because retirement can last decades.

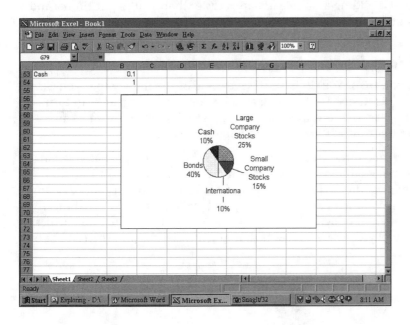

Figure 1.3

When you retire, you might want more of your money in bonds and dividend-paying stocks.

The real bottom line is to relax and enjoy yourself.

The Pieces of the Puzzle

The elements of personal finance fit together like pieces of a puzzle. The picture becomes clear when everything is in place. Fortunately, this is one of those puzzles with big pieces. And the picture is familiar—it's your life.

Expect the Worst, Hope for the Best

We'll delve into financial planning in detail in Chapter 2, "Planning." Regardless of where you stand, putting a plan together gets everything into perspective. You have to know what is important to you, so you can focus your life and your finances on achieving those goals.

Head of the Class

Field of Dreams

When you start planning, go for the gusto. Think about everything you want. You probably have a better chance of achieving your goals than you think.

With a financial plan, time, and discipline, you can get most of what you want. Be realistic. If you find that something is truly out of reach, you can put it out of your mind and look forward to everything else in your future. Fortunately, with your computer and the Internet, building a financial plan is easier than you might think. And you can play what-if to your heart's content to get just what you want.

A Penny Saved Is a Penny Earned

Money doesn't grow on trees. You do have to save some of the money that you earn to fund your dreams. Just the act of building a budget on your computer can turn your spending a little bit more toward saving. But personal finance software can make budgeting and tracking so easy, you barely mind the task.

The Internet holds so much information and provides so many tools, that you can become a smart consumer almost overnight. On the Web, you can make sure that you get the right financial products—banking services, credit cards, insurance, loans, mortgages—without spending a penny more than you have to. Learn everything you need to know about these products. Then, use the online tools to search for the best rates and fees. The money you save makes it that much easier to fund the rest of your financial plan.

Head of the Class

Going Once, Going Twice

You can find great deals on mortgages, loans, credit cards, and more on the Web. Lower interest rates on these financial products can save you oodles of money. But when it comes time to go shopping on the Web, make sure that the convenience of Internet shopping doesn't lure you into buying more than you planned. In particular, be careful with online auctions. Besides ending up with a stuffed warthog head that you thought you had to have, you could fall victim to fraud. Some sellers sell merchandise they don't have, or misrepresent its quality.

A Time to Grow

Some aspects of financial planning require a little patience. You might get everything you want—but no one said you'd get it right away. More powerful than saving money, investing means growing the money you save.

And time is one of the most powerful forces in finance. Just as inflation can eat your savings down to nothing over a couple of decades, investing can fertilize your savings from the proverbial acorn into a giant oak.

Analyzing stocks isn't difficult. A program of regular investing focused on long-term growth only requires a few hours each month. But if you're really short on time, or have an incurable doubt of your financial abilities, mutual funds handle your investments for you using professional money managers. Chapter 14, "Investing Made Easy," shows you how you can invest successfully without spending a great deal of time on your finances.

You Can Do It!

Volunteering for the National Association of Investors Corporation, I have had the pleasure of helping women and men in their 50s, 60s, and 70s, learn to research and buy stocks for successful portfolios.

No matter which approach you choose, you can learn more about investing and find the investments that make sense for you by using the Internet. You can learn, research, search, and buy without leaving your chair. And possibly the best aspect of the Web is that you can join online communities such as the ones at the Motley Fool (`www.fool.com`) or NAIC (`www.better-investing.org`). You meet and communicate in cyberspace with others who are learning to handle their finances. You aren't alone.

Doing It All Online

By now, chances are you're raring to go and get your financial house in order. But you might still have reservations about doing it on the computer. Don't worry—this book is designed specifically to help you do just that! If you're new to the Internet, turn to Appendix A, "Getting Online," for a quick primer on what the information superhighway is all about. Whether you're cybersavvy or a relative newbie, I'll show you exactly how to use your computer to gather information, organize your records, and make your financial planning less of a chore.

The Least You Need to Know

➤ Financial plans are an important part of achieving your goals. Your financial plan will change along with the circumstances in your life.

➤ You don't have to perfect your personal finances all at once. You have time to learn about being a smart consumer and investor.

➤ Your first step is to make sure that you have the disability, health, and life insurance that you need. If you're short on coverage, start with Chapter 8, "Protecting Your Money."

Planning

If you decided to attack your personal finances with your plan, you get a gold star! In his *Seven Habits of Highly Effective People*, Steven Covey gives us a good metaphor for planning. Without a plan, you'll be like the lost explorer hacking his way through the jungle, saying, "We're making great progress!" With your financial plan, you'll be standing in the canopy, saying, "I was in the wrong jungle. I want to be over there!"

Make Three Wishes!

You might think that planning your financial future is just one giant bore. But the first thing you get to do is make a list of everything you want. That's right! Even the fun stuff. Write down all the things you want: early retirement, a month in Tahiti, college education for your kids, a Mercedes sports car, owning your own home, the finest collection of black velvet Elvis paintings in the country, a building at your old school dedicated in your name. You have to know what it is you want, before you figure out how to get it.

Sometimes the goals we set in life can get in the way of those things we want to buy. Do you want to spend more time with your family, or become the president of your company? Maybe you want to paint or sing in a choir. If you really want to be a ski bum, it might be hard to buy a vacation house on the slopes in Aspen no matter how much you plan. So, add your goals in life to your wish list.

This list is your target. But, quite often, we want a lot of things, or we want to do things that limit the money we make. When you need to make trade-offs, all your bargaining chips are in one place—on your wish list. You can decide if the Mercedes is worth taking on a second job. Or you know you have to stay at your corporate job if you want the collection of black velvet paintings. Maybe the building in your name is plain out of the question.

One other thing you have to add to your wish list is when you want these things. Time affects how much money you can save as well as the types of investments you make. If you are saving for your kids' college education three years from now, you don't want a risky investment. You can't stop your kids from getting older just because you lost money with their college fund. But if your retirement is decades away, you can live through some short-term ups and downs in exchange for better investment returns.

To show you how planning works, let's follow a hypothetical family through their planning process. The Smith's both work and they are lucky enough to already own their own home. They have two kids, Kate and Jack.

Table 2.1 is the wish list that our hypothetical family, the Smiths, put together.

Table 2.1 The Smiths Start with Their Wishes

Wish	When
New car	2 years
College for Kate	5 years
College for Jack	8 years
South Pacific vacation for 20th anniversary	6 years
Buy a ski condo in Colorado	12 years
Retire at 60	21 years

You Can't Always Get What You Want

Unfortunately, you can't save all your money for the fun things. There are a few things that you should have in your plan whether you want them or not.

If your company provides health insurance, great! If not, get on the phone and get some. You might be the picture of health, but the cost of high-tech health care can make you sick.

Disability insurance is often overlooked. Just think about your plans if you were unable to work. You're still alive. You have expenses, but no income. If you're going to bother with a financial plan, plan to get disability insurance. And you need two kinds as well! Short-term disability insurance will support your lifestyle if you are sick for less than a year. Long-term disability insurance provides for you in case you are permanently disabled, although it won't completely replace your former income.

When we're young, we're invincible! Nothing bad can possibly happen to us! Ignore your optimism. Make sure you have enough life insurance. Your company might provide some, but it probably isn't enough. Your life insurance has to cover your family's living expenses: braces, college education, cars. If your spouse doesn't work, it has to cover everything. Chapter 8, "Protecting Your Money," covers the insurance you need and how to find it on the Web.

If you owe money on all your credit cards, start paying off your debt. What's the point of saving money in a money market fund paying 4% when you're paying 16% on your credit card? It is a lot easier to save money when you don't have to pay all that credit card interest. If you need help, Chapter 4, "Getting Out of Debt," is a chapter you shouldn't miss.

Regardless whether you want to retire early or work until you're 70, you need to plan for retirement. Social Security might be around, but you shouldn't depend on it. The earlier you start, the easier it is to save for your fabulous golden years. Table 2.2 shows the Smiths adding a safety net to their wish list.

Table 2.2   The Smiths Add Their Safety Net to the Wish List

Wish	When
New car	2 years
College for Kate	5 years
College for Jack	8 years
South Pacific vacation for 20th anniversary	6 years
Buy a ski condo in Colorado	12 years
Retire at 60 and travel	21 years
Disability insurance (need to add)	Immediately
Life insurance (adjust coverage?)	Immediately for both spouses
Pay off $3,000 of credit card debt	ASAP

Everything You Know About Your Finances and More

Building a financial plan online is especially easy because the programs ask you questions. All you have to do is answer them correctly! It will be a lot easier and faster if you have all your information collected before you start building the plan. So, what do you need?

The Things You Own

Start with your assets—the things you own. Although the planning programs might let you add your information in any order, organize your information by how fast you can get to the money. Start your list with a heading "Fast." You can add subheadings for the different types of fast assets. If you also add the name of each account and its account number to the list in addition to the dollar value of the account, you will have a great reference to your financial information when you are done.

The fastest assets are the things that you own that you can sell fairly quickly—within a week or two. These include

➤ Cash in checking, savings accounts, or money market accounts

➤ Money market mutual funds, other mutual funds, stocks, bonds, and other easy-to-sell investments

➤ Life insurance cash values

➤ Any money you are owed (for work you have performed or perhaps the poker hand you won)

➤ Other easy-to-sell personal property such as cars, jewelry, silver, or other precious metals (the black velvet painting collection doesn't count here)

An Organized File Drawer Is a Happy File Drawer!

If you haven't been very good about keeping and filing paperwork, look forward to a quiet afternoon (or weekend depending on how relaxed you have been) surrounded by your favorite folders and papers. You might as well organize them while you know where they are. It makes life that much easier next year.

Use a large folder or hanging file for each account or insurance policy you have. Add at least one folder for administrative information and one for statements. You can even put the large folders in order by speed of access: fast cash in front, not–so–fast, slow, and finally loans and insurance.

The next set of assets you want on your list are not as easy to get at. They might have penalties such as early-withdrawal penalties on certificates of deposit or the penalties the IRS adds if you withdraw funds from your tax-advantaged retirement accounts. You want to try to avoid using these assets because there is no point paying penalties unless you have to. You might call these assets "Not So Fast" on your list. These include

➤ Certificates of deposit with early-withdrawal penalties

➤ Retirement accounts, including IRAs, Roth IRAs, Keogh plans, and tax-deferred annuities

➤ Lump-sum value of a vested pension, if you have one

➤ Stock options, if you are lucky enough to have them

The last set of assets are those that can take months or even years to sell. You can label these "Sloooowww." These include

➤ Your home and any other real estate

➤ Art, including the black velvet paintings and antiques

➤ Other valuable personal property, such as collections, boats, RVs

➤ Investments that are not easy-to-sell for any reason

➤ Equity in a partnership or business

How Much Is That Doggie in the Window?

The Web can be a great help for figuring out how much things like houses, real estate, even boats, and some personal property are worth. Other items, such as collections and antiques, are harder to estimate. It pays to be conservative when you estimate the value of your beloved belongings. They might be priceless to you, but worthless to everyone else. It is always better to be surprised at how much more something is worth, than to realize that you are short of assets in your financial plan.

The Things You Owe to Others

Liabilities are what you owe to others. Your net worth is your assets minus your liabilities. Liabilities include

➤ Any current unpaid bills, such as rent, utilities, insurance premiums

➤ Balances on your credit card

➤ Auto or other installment loans

➤ Mortgages and home-equity loans on your house

➤ Any other mortgages or loans

➤ Any margin loans against investments

➤ Any income or property taxes that are due

➤ Taxes or penalties due on any investments that you sell

➤ Taxes or penalties due on any retirement accounts that you tap

Insurance, Taxes, and Expenses

Your assets and liabilities tell you where you are today. But to plan for the future, you also need to know about your security blanket: What insurance do you have, and what does it cover? To figure out how much you can save, you are going to need to know how much you spend. And as much as we try to avoid taxes, we have to pay them, so we need to know what percentage of income goes to the government. So, grab all your insurance policies and a year or two of tax returns. If you have any information on how much you spend each year, add it to the top of the pile. Table 2.3 shows the Smiths' finances.

Table 2.3   Here's the List of the Smiths' Finances

Item	Institution and Account Number	Value
Fast Assets		
Checking	First Union xxx-xxxx	$1,000
Savings	First Union xxx-xxxx	$3,000
Money market	Best Mutual xx-xx-xxxxx	$8,000
Mutual funds	Best Mutual xx-xx-xxxxx	$12,000
Stocks	VeryFine Discount Brokers xxx-xxxxx	$15,000
Property	Jewelry	$1,000
Property	Cars	$7,500
Not So Fast Assets		
CD	First Union xxx-xxxx	$1,000
Retirement 401(k)	Company plan xxx-xxxx	$65,000
Retirement 401(k)	Spouse's company plan xx-xxx-x	$80,000

Item	Institution and Account Number	Value
Sloowww Assets		
House		$200,000
Black velvet paintings		$2,500
Liabilities		
Current bills		$1,600
Credit card	First High Card xxxx-xxxx-xxxx-xxx	$3,000
Auto loan	First Union xx-xxxxx-x	$6,500
House mortgage	First Union xx-xxxxx-xx	$60,000
Property tax		$800
Taxes on investments		$3,500
Taxes and penalties on retirement account		$14,000
Insurance and Taxes		
Health insurance	Company sponsored	
Life insurance	Company sponsored	$35,000
Property insurance	Extra Careful Insurance Co.	$150,000
Last year's federal and state taxes		

Finding Places Online to Build Your Plan

After you've decided that a financial plan is something you can't live without, the good news is there are a lot of tools out there to help. On the Web or on your computer, the financial services industry wants you to plan. The more you know about your finances, the more likely you are to need something they sell.

Tools Right There on Your Computer

There are a lot of planning tools right on your computer for building your financial plan. A plan on your computer can be faster and more convenient because you don't even have to dial out. If you are concerned about security, your plan never leaves your home. Of course, if you delete it, you have to rebuild it. You also can add passwords to keep others out of the file.

Quicken Can Be Your Online Guide!

In addition to the tools that Quicken offers on your computer, Quicken 2000 has links to all sorts of financial planning sites on the Web. Look through the Quicken drop-down menus. You'll find links to find loan rates, credit checks, financial planners, home values, and tools for every other part of your personal finances.

Quicken 2000 has a planning center, shown in Figure 2.1, that offers planning tools for different financial decisions in your life. Quicken has planning tools for retirement, college, home purchase, debt reduction, savings, and special purchases. These planning tools help you figure out how to achieve your goals, and educate you at the same time.

Spreadsheets can do all the calculations you need to build a financial plan. But you have to be a financial expert to build a plan with a spreadsheet. Planning involves some pretty fancy calculations that consider compound growth rates on your money. You also would have to know what numbers are important, which assumptions to consider, and how to combine them all. If you could do all that, you wouldn't need this book, so let's move on to finding some existing tools.

Figure 2.1

The Quicken Planning Center is a one-stop shop for all your financial planning needs! Build a plan for college, a special purchase, or the rest of your life.

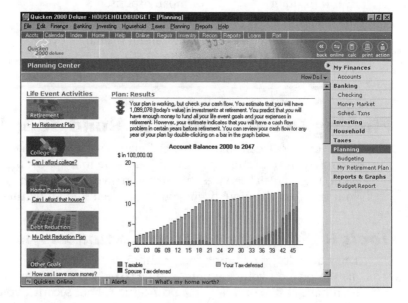

Online Sites with Overall Planning Tools

Much of the information on the Internet is used as bait. Companies post all sorts of useful information and provide helpful service as marketing gimmicks to sell you something. Financial planning tools are just about everywhere on the Web in the hope that you will use the broker, insurance company, or credit card when you start to implement your plan. My first search for "Online Financial Planning" brought back almost two million Web pages.

Finding a place to build your plan online is easy. Finding a useful planning tool could be tough. One convenient place to start looking is the Web site for your broker or mutual fund company. Look for "Planning" or "Financial Advice." It pays to look at the sites where you are a customer, because many of the planning tools only save your plan if you are a customer registered for their online services. A financial plan isn't much good, if you can't save it and change it as your life and goals change.

Another advantage is that the results of a plan are usually presented in terms of what the company has to offer. As a customer of that company, you will see what they can do to help you implement your plan.

Crash Alert

Be Careful Who You Tell

Because a financial plan needs so much information about you, pick sites of companies that you recognize and that you are comfortable with. A lot of new Web sites provide really handy applications. To use some sites, you have to allow them to use your personal information for marketing purposes when you register with the site. Check for that in the fine print during registration.

When you look for planning tools, you will find that many of them are broken up into several specialized tools: college, retirement, investment, estate, tax, and others. Right now, we want to find a tool that helps us build a comprehensive plan that includes all our goals.

The Vanguard Group Web site, www.vanguard.com, is one of my favorites. The Vanguard Group is one of the pioneers in low-cost mutual funds and index funds. Its site provides investment services, news, a lot of educational material, and a great planning tool, shown in Figure 2.2. You can build a comprehensive financial plan or you can pick different specialized tools. Vanguard lets registered clients save their data. You also can download its planning software if you do not want to build your plan online.

Figure 2.2

You can use the Vanguard planning tool online or download it to your computer.

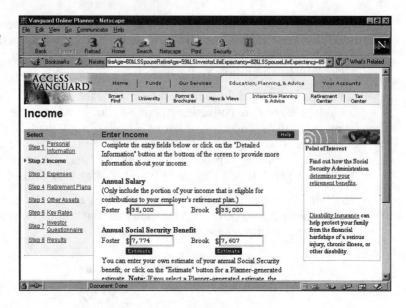

When You Only Need to Plan One Thing

Life rarely comes this simple. But sometimes you only want to plan one part of your finances. For example, you own your own home. You don't have kids. You charter your sailboat for a living, so your work is like a vacation to you. All you are really concerned about is retirement.

Crash Alert

Costs Are Skyrocketing!

The cost of a college education increases even faster than inflation. So, when you plan for college, you have to make sure that you estimate the actual cost of that education. Costs at some schools rise faster than at others. If you have a school in mind, see how much its costs have increased in recent years.

If you are planning to pay for a college education, the tool really only needs to know about things related to that education: when it starts, how long it lasts, how much it costs, how much you already have saved, and your desired investment return. Retirement is like the rest of your life except you don't have to go to work. So, a specialized retirement tool needs to know almost everything you would add to a comprehensive tool.

The Vanguard site has individual planning tools for retirement, college, investment, and estate planning. The American Express site, www. AmericanExpress.com, has tools for retirement, college, and insurance.

Even if you don't own Quicken, you can use the Quicken.com Web site to work out your financial plans. On the Retirement home page on www. Quicken.com, you'll find easy-to-use planning tools for retirement, financing college, and reducing debt.

Building a Plan Online

The planning features of Quicken 2000 are probably the easiest and most comprehensive of what's available. If you don't have Quicken, Quicken.com and Vanguard's online tools also are easy to use, although they don't have some of the handy fine-tuning adjustments of Quicken 2000.

Starting, Stopping, and Saving Your Plan

Using Quicken, you can start and stop anywhere you want. Quicken automatically saves your plan as you build it. Working on the Web isn't that simple. First off, if the site you are using doesn't let you save your plan, you have to finish the plan in one session. And you have to rebuild it if you want to see it later on.

If you can save your plan, you can look at it when you log on to the site later. When you work online, it is a good idea to save the plan frequently, just in case your telephone connection drops.

Tell Me a Little About Yourself

The first step to using any planning tool is to enter your assumptions, as shown in Figure 2.3. There are questions for just about everything about you except how much you weigh. In insurance planning, someone will probably want to know that, too! Here is where your list and those files come in handy.

Using Quicken, the About You section gets the basics: your name, date of birth, the age you plan to retire, how long you expect to live, and the names and ages of your children. You can even add children that haven't been born yet. Fortunately, Quicken only needs an approximate date of birth.

Go through your list of assets and liabilities and add the information into the appropriate section. Your assets will fall under Savings & Investments or Homes & Assets. Your liabilities go to Loans & Debt. There also are sections for Income and Expenses. If you make regular contributions to any savings or investment accounts, Quicken wants to know about it.

For your expenses, you can add a rough estimate if that is all you have so far. If you have been using Quicken to pay bills, it can prepare an estimate of your expenses from the transactions in your accounts. Because life rarely goes the way you think, you can change the estimates that Quicken provides to better reflect your expenses in the future.

Click **Edit** to change
your assumptions.

Figure 2.3

Just step through the planning assumptions to get your financial plan started.

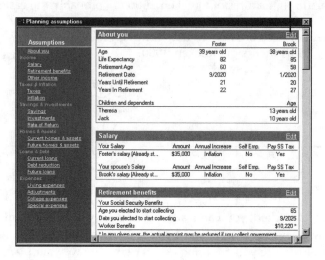

Rates, Rates, Rates

Along with all that information on assets and liabilities, Quicken wants a few other assumptions from you. The inflation rate eats into your savings and investments. As inflation increases the prices on the things you buy, your savings and investments buy less. And if your money buys less, you will need more of it. So, Quicken wants to know what inflation rate you think we will have in the future. By default, Quicken picks a rate close to the recent average.

Quicken also wants to know what rate of return you expect to achieve. Because common wisdom suggests that we invest more conservatively as we get older, Quicken wants a return for before retirement and one for after. Before we retire, when we still have an income and have time to ride through the gyrations of the stock market, we can invest a little more aggressively and try to earn a higher return. After we retire, we're living off our savings. Our timeframe is shorter. If our investments crashed we would be in trouble. So, we invest more of our money (not all) in safer investments with lower returns. We'll talk more about this risk versus return in Chapter 14, "Investing Made Easy."

You Can Take This Job And...

More and more of us dream of retiring early. Others just hope they can retire at all. A retirement planner helps you figure out what you have to do to achieve your dream—while you can still do something about it.

Most retirement planners calculate your Social Security benefits for you based on your salary and when you begin collecting. If you have a pension, you tell the planner about when the benefits start, the annual amount, any cost of living increases, and whether your spouse receives any of those benefits after you die.

Head of the Class

Planning for What Life Throws at You

All sorts of stuff can happen, as the bumper stickers warn us. Many of these so-called life events can impact our living expenses. Having a child and retirement are possibly the two most common expense-altering events. In Quicken, you can add events like these to your assumptions and specify how they will impact your expenses in dollars or by percentage.

401(k) plans just get more and more popular. In Quicken, you add 401(k) plans under Investments. Besides adding the current value of the plan, you can tell Quicken about your ongoing contributions to the plan. You can specify a percentage of your salary or an amount, when it starts and when it ends, if your employer matches a percentage or an amount of your contribution.

Whether you plan to climb Mount Everest or start whittling duck decoys when you retire, your living expenses will probably change. To get the best picture of your retirement plan, add an adjustment to your living expenses to reflect your new retired lifestyle. Checking in on the Smiths, they are adding $20,000 per year to their expenses when they retire, because they want to travel. Figure 2.4 shows the results for the Smiths' plan so far.

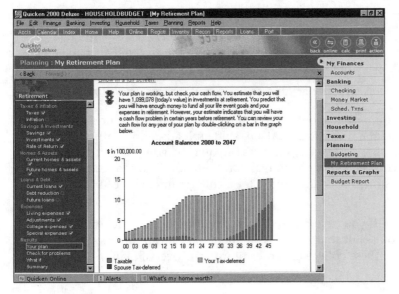

Figure 2.4

*By clicking **Your Results** in the **Retirement Planner**, the Smiths discover that they will have enough to retire, but they have some cash flow problems.*

I Want an Empty Nest, but Does It Have to Cost So Much?

The cost of a college education grows faster than inflation. So, it takes a lot of planning, discipline, and even creativity to get your kids through school. And that's just paying for it. Getting them to study is another story! And of course, you have to save for college expenses while you save for retirement.

In Quicken planning, you add college expenses to your plan by clicking **College Expenses** in the **Planning Assumptions** list. You tell Quicken what age your child will start school, and how long college will last. The next screen in the Quicken College Planner lets you see what tuition, room and board, and other costs have been by school. Even if you don't have a clue whether your child wants to stay near home or get away, be a doctor or a philosopher, you can use these numbers as a starting point.

Crash Alert

College Funding Is Tricky!

Getting the funds for college has more twists and turns than a good suspense novel. If you save money in the student's name, he might be denied financial aid because he has too much money. But you might have to apply for financial aid anyway, because you have to be denied the aid before you can get some school loans. You can look into scholarships, fellowships, and work-study.

When I went to graduate school, I checked into financial aid. I was surprised when I received a fellowship. With very few women in the Columbia Engineering School, I qualified for a full fellowship only available to women students.

You also can enter information about other sources of funding for your darlings' education besides the parental units: financial aid, student loans, and contributions that your child makes. Because college costs increase so quickly, you also can estimate how much faster college costs are growing compared to inflation. If you already have savings accounts or investment accounts set up for a college fund, you can add those to the planner.

The College Planner tells you how much money you have to save each month to buy that empty nest of yours. But that monthly figure doesn't mean much by itself. We really want to see how these college expenses fit into the overall plan.

I Want to Go to Pago Pago!

With retirement and college expenses defined, you might still have some other things you want. If you want a second home, a classic car, or maybe a boat, you can add that in Quicken under Future Homes & Assets. If you are looking at a big vacation, you can plan for that under Special Expenses.

When you add another house, you tell Quicken when you plan to buy it, how much the house will cost, and how fast you think it will increase in value. You can specify when you plan to sell it, such as when the first spouse dies or both retire, along with cost of improvements, Realtor's fees, and taxes. You also can add information on a loan for the house as well as income and expenses if you plan to rent it. You might have to guess on some of these numbers. Remember, it pays to be conservative, and to try to improve your estimates whenever you can.

For a special expense, you need to know when it will occur, whether it is a one-time cost or over multiple years, the amount, and whether you have saved any money toward it so far.

What Do You Mean I Can't Have It All!

When you add all your goals into your plan, you might think it looks pretty hopeless. So many things. So little money. Here is where the planning tools and some knowledge about the tricks and techniques of good personal finance come into play. In Quicken, you see the results in the planning center. If you are in the Retirement Planner, click **Your plan** under **Results**. Click **Check for Problems** to find out about issues and possible gotchas with your plan,.

Our hypothetical family, the Smiths, have run into trouble with their plan. Between college for the kids, the ski condo, and the South Pacific vacation, they run out of money right about when they retire. Let's use their problems to see how to make a plan work.

Okay, Maybe I Can Give Something Up

First, check all your assumptions. Can we afford the ski condo? Are all the sources of funding for college accounted for? What about a public college instead of a private college? Maybe we can live on less before we retire. Maybe we can live on less after we retire. What about getting better investment returns? How about a part-time job during retirement?

There are all sorts of things you can try. With most of your goals, you can decide to forego them or find another way to fund them. Retirement is hard to play with. So, make sure that your retirement plan on its own is working. In Quicken, you can go through your assumptions and exclude items from the plan. So, turn off the college expenses, the ski condo, and the fancy vacation. If your retirement plan is working too well—you die with millions in the bank—you could look at reducing your contributions. But only if you are really, really comfortable that your plan is foolproof.

Then take a look at college expenses. Turn the college expenses back on in the plan. Check the funding and the school expenses. Teach your kids about how hard it is to get the things you want. Make them take on summer jobs to earn money toward college. Make them take on student loans. With budding Einsteins or Jordans, look into scholarships and fellowships. Then, check the plan results again to see if your retirement survived college!

Now, look at those other wants of yours: the condo, the vacation. Add them back in. You can try moving purchase dates into the future, past those college expenses. You can try reducing your living expenses. (We look at that more closely in Chapter 10, "Saving Money.") Maybe you try increasing your income by taking on a second job, or a higher-paying job. If the ski condo blows your plan, no matter what, sigh heavily and turn it off. You might not want to delete it though. You might get an unexpected inheritance or win the lottery.

The Smiths' retirement plan is in good shape. It's non-retirement money and funding the other goals that they have to work on, as shown in Figure 2.5. So they decide to look at public colleges for their kids. They also add student loans and $500 per year contributions from their kids. The ski condo gets turned off in the plan. And they plan to postpone the South Pacific vacation until their 25th wedding anniversary.

Figure 2.5

The Smiths still need to look at ways to reduce their living expenses to make this plan work!

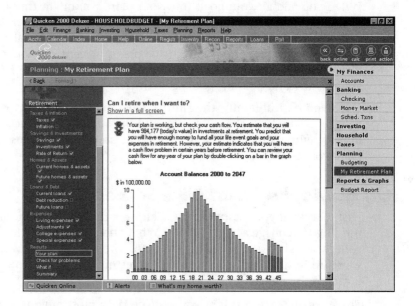

They still have an issue with cash flow—they don't have enough money to cover their expenses and savings goals in some of the years. In Chapter 10, we look at how they can reduce their expenses and make this plan work. We also check to see whether their security blanket has any holes. Do they have enough emergency funds? In Chapter 8, we check on their insurance coverage.

If I Knew Then, What I Know Now

You can see that a financial plan connects all your goals. Changes in one thing can affect something else. If you get a surprise raise, or you get laid off, your finances change. And as time passes, you can estimate those future plans better and better.

So, set aside a quiet weekend day once a year to review your plan. If college costs have increased more than you thought, change your assumption for how fast those costs grow. If your investment returns in your retirement accounts have not been as good as you expected, reduce your estimated investment rate of return. You have reduced your living expenses more than you thought you could. This checkup gives you a chance to correct your mistakes and gain inspiration from your success.

I Can't Do This by Myself

If all this planning and juggling and horse-trading makes you dizzy, you can always get someone to help. But golly, what's the difference between a financial planner, an accountant, and an investment advisor? Investment advisors can help pick the proper investments to achieve goals and plans. Accountants maintain your financial records and are a huge help in preparing your taxes with the ever-changing rules in the tax code. They also can help you plan to avoid big tax bites in the future.

Financial planners can provide advice on many topics including budgeting your money, saving, investing, your insurance coverage, and planning for all your life goals. Of course, they can also just help with one particular issue, if that is what you need.

Crash Alert

There Is No Free Lunch

If you decide that you are willing to spend some of your hard-earned money to get some help with your plan, make sure you know how your planner gets paid. If your planner is fee only, you pay him for his time. If the planner is on commission or is part fee and part commission, he gets a commission when you buy financial products from him. Be careful with a commissioned planner. He might want you to buy certain investments because of his commission—not because it is the best investment for you.

The best deal on planners might be at one of your financial institutions. Brokerage houses, credit card companies, banks, and other institutions might offer you financial planning at no charge. They get their reward when you invest in their products.

How Do I Get One of These Planners?

One way to find a financial planner online is to use the search engine on the Financial Planning Association Web site (www.fpanet.org). PlannerSearch (www.icfp.org/plannersearch/search.cfm) helps you find a certified financial planner by city, state, and zip code. Click **PlannerSearch**, and enter your email address. The search engine gives you a list of financial planners with their addresses and phone numbers, as shown in Figure 2.6. These planners are all certified by the Financial Planning Association.

Try the Yellow Pages!

You also can search for financial planners and other professionals using the online yellow pages. Online yellow pages, such as US West DEX, allow you to search for categories like accountants or financial planning consultants. You can specify a city and state. If you live near a large city, you can check the box for **Surrounding Area** to search the entire metropolitan area. The results show the company name, address, and phone number. You can click **See Map** to find out exactly where they are. In some cases, you can click **Email** or **Web Site** to send them email or go to their Web site. However, you will have to check their certification.

Check That Certification

We are talking about your money here. You want someone competent and ethical helping you with this stuff. Certification by the Financial Planning Association tells you that your planner has passed an examination given by the Association so he knows the material. He also must have several years of experience. You might as well let him learn on someone else. He ascribes to the Association's Code of Ethics. And he gets at least 30 hours of ongoing education every two years.

The FPA search engine gives you names of certified financial planners. If you find your planner in the yellow pages, make sure to ask him about his education, licenses, and certification. Ask about his experience. Find out if he specializes in certain aspects of planning. And, if possible, get examples of his work.

Reach Out and Talk to Your Planner

After you hire a financial planner, you should plan to continue the relationship. Your planner should help you review your plan and correct course as time passes.

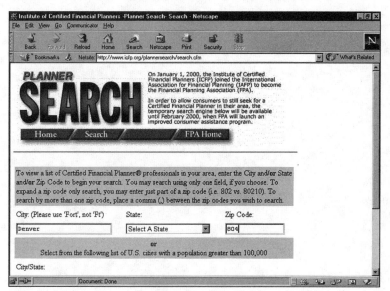

Figure 2.6

The FPA Planner Search can find certified financial planners by city, state, and three or more digits of your zip code.

Although a face-to-face meeting, is important at first, you can do a lot with your planner electronically. Email is a great way to send questions and get answers. Although you might want the interaction of the telephone if you are asking about something you aren't experienced with.

If you are using Quicken to handle your finances, you might even transfer files back and forth. For instance, maybe you added all your planning assumptions to Quicken, but couldn't figure out how to make it work. Your planner could do the juggling and send the file back to you.

The Least You Need to Know

➤ Your financial plan starts with a wish list of all the things you want, your personal goals, and when you want to achieve them.

➤ Make sure you have adequate health insurance and life insurance. Don't ignore disability insurance.

➤ Make a list of everything you own, along with its value. Financial institutions and account numbers make organizing your finances easier.

➤ Add everything you owe to the list.

➤ Organize your files if they aren't.

➤ Quicken 2000 has a great planning center. Quicken.com has good online planning tools with fewer bells and whistles.

➤ A certified financial planner can help you make your plan work.

Building a Budget

No matter how much money you make, chances are you will always want more than your money can buy. As our income rises, things that were luxuries begin to seem indispensable. So, you have to plan to save for the things you want—a house, an education, an enjoyable retirement, travel.

A household budget is not a pair of handcuffs on your spending. It is really a plan for how you will spend the money you make. When you spend less than you make, you are saving for your wish list.

What's in a Budget, Anyway?

Building a plan isn't so bad. Most people have a pretty good idea how they spend their money. You can probably rattle off all the bills you have to pay—the rent, utilities, telephone, gas, insurance, groceries—as well as half a dozen things you buy that you really don't need: the giant popcorn at the movies, the black velvet Elvis from the yard sale, the orange chocolate double-café latte each morning. The nice thing about a spending plan is that building it might be all you have to do. As soon as you see where your weaknesses are, you subconsciously start to scale back.

The first step is to estimate how much money you will make and how much you will spend. Don't forget to add in how much you want to save. Your first attempt might show you spending more than you make. Don't worry! With this first draft in hand you can start to fiddle with the numbers: cut down on movies, find cheaper insurance, plan a less-expensive vacation, decide to get a second job. We talk more about how to save money in Chapter 10, "Saving Money." When you are done, your budget should show your expenses plus your planned savings equal to your income:

Income =

Expenses

+ Savings

Building a Budget with Quicken

Quicken, Microsoft Money, and other personal finance software programs make building a budget easy. These programs include tools to build and manage your budget, and give you lots of advice on your personal finances, too.

In Quicken, a budget starts with a set of categories for your income and expenses. You figure out how much you think you will make or spend in each category. Then, you enter the income and expenses when they occur during the year. There's your budget! Let's look at how we get these categories set up and add the income and expenses.

Using Built-in Categories in Quicken

When you create a new Quicken file, Quicken adds a set of categories to that file for you. Quicken contains a group of standard categories that are useful for just about everyone. Quicken also has groups of categories useful for married people, people with children, and homeowners. For instance, for homeowners Quicken adds categories such as Housing, Home Repair, and Property Taxes.

To use these pre-defined groups when you create your Quicken file, select **New** from the **File** menu. In the Create Quicken File dialog box, click the **Categories** button. Click any check box that applies to your life, as shown in Figure 3.1, and then click **OK**. Quicken includes the categories associated with your selections in the category list.

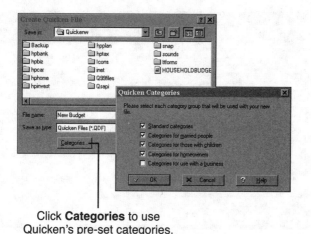

Figure 3.1

You can choose financial categories for Quicken to track for you.

Click **Categories** to use Quicken's pre-set categories.

To access these groups after your Quicken file exists, select **Category & Transfer List** from the **Finances** menu. Click the **Options** button, and select **Add Categories**. Select an entry from the **Available Categories** drop-down list. Mark any categories or subcategories you want to add and click the **Add** button. You can repeat these steps to add more categories from other Available Categories. Click **OK** when you are finished adding categories.

In Figure 3.2, we already added the categories from People with Children and are getting ready to select categories from the Married group.

Once you have selected the categories you want, click **Add** to add them to your list.

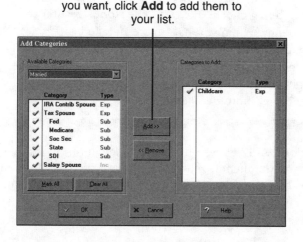

Figure 3.2

You also can choose or change financial categories from the Quicken Category & Transfer List options.

To see your current list of categories, select **Category & Transfer List** from the **Finances** menu. As shown in Figure 3.3, the Category & Transfer List window opens showing each category, its type, description, group, taxable status, and associated tax item.

Figure 3.3

The Quicken Category & Transfer List shows budget categories with their properties.

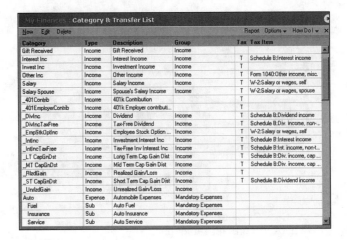

Category	Type	Description	Group	Tax	Tax Item
Gift Received	Income	Gift Received	Income		
Interest Inc	Income	Interest Income	Income	T	Schedule B:Interest income
Invest Inc	Income	Investment Income	Income	T	
Other Inc	Income	Other Income	Income	T	Form 1040:Other income, misc.
Salary	Income	Salary Income	Income	T	W-2:Salary or wages, self
Salary Spouse	Income	Spouse's Salary Income	Income	T	W-2:Salary or wages, spouse
_401Contrib	Income	401k Contribution		T	
_401EmployerContrib	Income	401k Employer contributi...		T	
_DivInc	Income	Dividend	Income	T	Schedule B:Dividend income
_DivIncTaxFree	Income	Tax-Free Dividend	Income	T	Schedule B:Div. income, non-...
_EmpStkOptInc	Income	Employee Stock Option ...	Income	T	W-2:Salary or wages, self
_IntInc	Income	Investment Interest Inc	Income	T	Schedule B:Interest income
_IntIncTaxFree	Income	Tax-Free Inv Interest Inc	Income	T	Schedule B:Int. income, non-t...
_LT CapGnDst	Income	Long Term Cap Gain Dist	Income	T	Schedule B:Div. income, cap ...
_MT CapGnDst	Income	Mid Term Cap Gain Dist	Income	T	Schedule B:Div. income, cap ...
_RlzdGain	Income	Realized Gain/Loss	Income	T	
_ST CapGnDst	Income	Short Term Cap Gain Dist	Income	T	Schedule B:Dividend income
_UnrlzdGain	Income	Unrealized Gain/Loss	Income		
Auto	Expense	Automobile Expenses	Mandatory Expenses		
Fuel	Sub	Auto Fuel	Mandatory Expenses		
Insurance	Sub	Auto Insurance	Mandatory Expenses		
Service	Sub	Auto Service	Mandatory Expenses		

If You Want More Detail...

Quicken provides a good start for a list of categories. But what if you're nervous about actually keeping track of what's already there? Or you want to follow your spending more carefully? Start out tracking at a level of detail you can handle. Don't try to change from not entering checks into your checkbook register to tracking your spending to the penny. When you have more detailed categories, you can always look at your budget with less detail. The downside of detail is that you do have to enter your spending or income in all those categories to get the benefit. Entering the data might sound like it would be easier with fewer categories, but you lose the ability to get more detailed reports.

Quicken memorizes transactions. After using Quicken for a few months, many people or businesses you pay will be on the memorized list along with their assigned category. You will rarely have to enter the category for a transaction. So you can get the benefit of the category detail without spending a lot of time.

Fitting Categories to Your Circumstances

After using Quicken's category list for a while, you might want to change things a bit. For example, you might want to add a category for pet expenses, so you can see just how many stray dogs you can afford to feed. You might delete Water and Sewer categories if you have a well and your own septic system. In Quicken, you can delete categories, which removes them from the category list completely. You also can keep the category, but turn it off in the budget window. You won't budget for sewer today, but at least you can turn it back on when the sewer comes through.

Add more detailed categories particularly in areas where you think you overspend. For instance, you might want to separate money you spend on lunch from dining out at dinner to see which one really is worse. Maybe you need a category for work clothes separate from casual clothes. You might be able to justify a new suit each year, but how did you end up with twenty turtlenecks?

You Can Use Categories to Help Make Important Financial Decisions

Categories also come in handy for deciding what makes more sense financially. If you have more than one car, you can add a subcategory or a class for each car to the Repair category. You can watch for when a car starts to cost a lot to keep running. You can even compare how much you spend on those car repairs against what you would spend on a car loan for a new (or newer) car.

You can make any changes you want to categories in the Category & Transfer List window. Use the **New**, **Edit**, and **Delete** buttons on the button bar in the **Category & Transfer List** window to create, change, or delete categories. When you create or edit a category, pay attention to a few of the settings. Use short but meaningful names: Bus Tickets, Fitness. You can always use the description field to explain short names. For Expense categories that are mandatory (like taxes), click the **Spending Is Not Discretionary** check box. For tax-related transactions, click the **Tax-related** check box and choose the tax form.

Use a Category to Keep Track of Business Travel Reimbursements

I used to travel a lot on business. I always had out-of-pocket expenses and expense reports wending their way through the system. Making sure that I had submitted my expenses and received my reimbursements was a never-ending job. So, I set up an income category for Expense Reimbursement. (An expense category would work as well because eventually it should all balance out.)

For example, you can add an expense to Quicken in a category called Expense Reimbursement. Check the transactions in Expense Reimbursement when you prepare an expense report so that you don't forget anything. When you deposit the expense check, use the Expense Reimbursement category. The balance will reflect all your unpaid expenses. That unpaid balance also can remind you about outstanding expense checks. And if all your expense checks are in and you still have a negative balance, you might have missed submitting some expense.

Creating a Budget Automatically

Now that you have a list of categories, the next step is to add amounts and timing. If you have been using Quicken for a while without a budget, Quicken can create a budget from your existing transactions. From the **Planning** menu, select **Budgets**. Click **Edit** on the button bar and then select **AutoCreate**. Figure 3.4 shows the AutoCreate Budget dialog box. You give start and end dates so that Quicken only uses the transactions between the dates to create the budget.

You can limit which categories to include in your budget by clicking the **Categories** button. You can click **Clear All** to clear all the categories, and then click **Categories** to add them back onto the list. You also can click selected categories to remove them from the list. Click **OK** when your category list is complete.

The Use Monthly Detail option builds the budget based on when your transactions occurred. It puts the income or expenses in the same month that it occurred in your transactions. The Use Average option averages the total amounts over the twelve months of the year. If you want Quicken to include all transactions even if they are small or infrequent, make sure to click the **Include All Nonzero Transaction Amounts** check box.

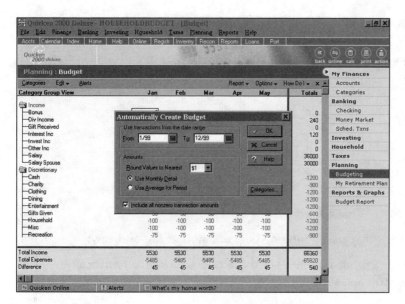

Figure 3.4

Quicken can build a budget based on existing transactions in your Quicken accounts.

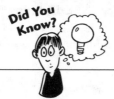

Did You Know?

Timing Income and Expenses Versus the Christmas Club Method

You can time your income and expenses two ways. You can add your income and expenses in the month that they occur by adding amounts into cells in the budget. This method can show you problem points when you have a lot of expenses in a month and your income doesn't cover them.

The Christmas club method divides your estimated annual amounts equally over the twelve months. This is easy to do when you create your budget. If you are disciplined enough to keep that extra money in your checking or savings account, the money will be there when your big bills are due.

Creating a Budget by Entering Amounts

You also can build a budget by entering amounts in the cells. The budget is really a grid where each cell relates to a category and a month during the year. To add an amount to a cell, just select the cell and type in the amount. For example, if your car insurance is due in February and August, click the cell for the February column and the Auto Insurance row and enter the amount for your insurance. Then, click the cell for the August column and Auto Insurance row and enter the amount.

If you plan to use the Christmas Club approach, enter the average monthly amount for each category in the first column of the budget. Then, click the **Edit** button and select **Fill Columns**. This copies your first month's numbers to each remaining month in the year.

Data Entry Shortcuts

There are a few shortcuts that make entering budget amounts fast and easy:

➤ For expenses, enter a positive number into the cell. Quicken automatically changes it to negative and shows it in red.

➤ To use the same number across a whole row, enter the number in the first column on the left. Then click the **Edit** button and select **Fill Row Right**. If your rent goes up in June, enter the new rent amount in June and select **Fill Row Right**. Quicken will fill the number in from July through December.

➤ If you receive a paycheck every two weeks, Quicken can calculate the monthly amounts and add them to the budget. Select the category to budget at two-week intervals. Click **Edit** and select **2-Week**. Enter the paycheck amount and then the first payday. Click **OK** and Quicken adds the amounts into the budget for you.

Category Groups and Subcategories: The Big Picture and Detail

Category groups, shown in Figure 3.5, are like big picture categories. You can use category groups to show really simplified reports of your finances, such as Income, Mandatory Expenses, and Discretionary Expenses. You can add, edit, and delete category groups. If you want to make the names more meaningful to you, you could change the name of Mandatory Expenses to Must Pay. You could add a group called Part-Mandatory for expenses that are necessary but can be cut down, such as groceries.

If you want to separate your savings from expenses, create a category group called Savings. Click **Options** in the button bar of the Category & Transfer List window and select **Category Groups**. Click the **New** button and enter the name of the category group. If you are going to move your savings to a savings account or money market account, you can assign those transfers to the Savings category group. Also, assign transfers OUT OF the savings or money market account to the Savings category group. If you take money back out of your savings, you reduce the amount that you saved. By assigning transfers out of the account to the Savings category group, your Budget versus Actual report will show your actual savings.

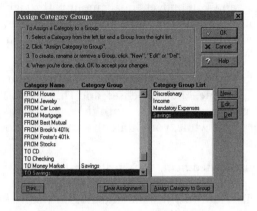

Figure 3.5

Category groups let you look at your budget at a higher level.

Subcategories are one way to get more detail. For example, you could create subcategories under Auto for Gas, Repair Escort, and Repair Ferrari. Subcategories show up in reports but are rolled up into the parent for graphs. Subcategories help to group similar expenses to make reports easier to read. In a category for insurance you could have subcategories for Life Insurance, Health Insurance, Disability Insurance, Property Insurance, and Car Insurance.

Check Out Classes

Quicken also has a feature called classes, which you can use instead of subcategories. You use classes along with categories. You can set up a class for different members of the family, different cars, different houses—whatever you need. You can keep track of the totals for a category using the budget. But you also can keep totals for all categories for a certain class. For example, you could have an Auto category with subcategories for gas, service, and insurance. If you create a class for your Ford Escort and a class for your Ferrari, you can assign any transactions to the category and the class. Then you can look at how much you pay for insurance or at how much the Ferrari costs overall.

Isn't Cash Flow Always Good?

Unfortunately, cash flow doesn't mean cash flowing into our pockets. Cash flow is the difference between money flowing in and money flowing out. Christmas Club budgeting is easy but it also hides when you have a lot of big bills due all at once. Let's say your car insurance ($400), life insurance ($200), and health club membership ($600) are all due in February and you budget equal amounts throughout the year. Your bank account would have only two month's worth of the money set aside ($200) for $1,200 worth of bills. If you don't have some cash set aside, you have a problem.

A budget in Quicken can show you these trouble spots. At the bottom of each column, there are numbers for Total Income, Total Expenses, and Difference. When the difference is negative, you don't make enough that month to cover your expenses. When you have used your budget for a while, you should have enough stored in your bank account to cover these bills.

But here it is February and you just started being responsible last month. What do you do? You can look at ways to postpone or reduce other expenses. Set up your large bills on a monthly installment plan. Monthly installments not only solve your cash flow problem, but simplify budgeting, too. As a last resort, you can always use some of your emergency funds to cover the difference—as long as you pay it back!

You can use the Quicken Cash Flow Forecast to find these problems for you. Under the **Planning** menu, select **Cash Flow Forecast**. Click the **Options** button and select **Update Forecast**. Set the date range to the next 12 months. Click the **Advanced** button. Select the **From Budget Data** option. Make sure to select all categories and to only select your checking account. When you click **OK**, the forecast report will show you your forecast checking account balance for the next twelve months. If the balance ever drops below zero, look at your budget for that month and the month before. Check to see if you can reduce your spending or postpone some expenses.

Using Savings Goals in Your Budget

One of the reasons we bother with budgets is so that we can plan to save money for the things we want. If we balanced our budget with just our income and expenses, there wouldn't be anything left to amass that collection of black velvet paintings.

If a handy online retirement calculator says that you have to save $500 each month to retire, you can add a category called Retirement Savings to your budget. Just enter **500** in each cell for Retirement Savings and make sure that your budget stays balanced.

But if you want to track your savings based on what you're saving for, Quicken has a feature called Savings Goals. You can define an amount of money that you want to save—say $15,000 for a down payment on a house—and a timeframe such as two years from now. Quicken will tell you how much you have to save each month to reach your goal. Quicken will even hide the money from your account balance so you won't be tempted to spend it. You can set up as many savings goals as you want, each with its own amount, start date, and end date.

In Figure 3.6, we're setting up a savings goal. Click the **Planning** menu and select **Savings Goal**. Click the **New** button on the button bar in the Savings Goal window. Enter a goal name like **House Down Payment**, **15,000** for the amount, and a date two years in the future.

When you click **OK**, Quicken will display the monthly amount at the bottom of the window. In this case, you need to save $600 per month to raise $15,000 over the next two years. You can add this savings goal to your budget.

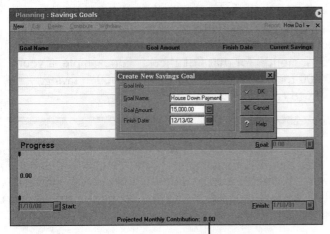

Figure 3.6

Setting up a savings goal in Quicken can help you save for a house down payment. Quicken will even hide the savings from your account balance.

Once you add your savings goal, Quicken shows you how much you have to save each month.

By adding the $600 per month to the House Down Payment category, you can make sure that your budget balances. Click **Categories** in the Budget window and turn on **From and To House Down Payment**. In the budget, enter **600** in the first column for the To House Down Payment category. Then, click the **Edit** button and select **Fill Row Right**. This adds the $600 per month to the budget. Of course, if this new savings goal throws your balance between income and expenses off, you will have to revisit your spending to see where you can cut costs.

Creating Your Next Year's Budget

Eureka! You survived one year of life with a budget. Now, you have to create next year's budget. To create another budget, click **Options** and select **Other Budgets**.

Enter a name for this budget. You can use AutoCreate to create next year's budget from this year's transactions. By selecting **Copy**, you can copy this year's budget. Remember that you can always make changes to the budget after it is created.

Head of the Class

Other Uses for Budgets

You can create other budgets to see what changes you can afford when you get a raise, your spouse stops working, or your lottery payments start. For example, can you afford to quit your job and start to consult? Build a budget based on only your mandatory expenses. Compare your savings to those mandatory expenses to see how long you can last before you collect your first consulting fee. (Unless you are really lucky, plan for 6 to 12 months for that first check!) For example, if your mandatory expenses are $20,000 for the year and you have $10,000 in savings, you can take almost six months to collect your first check.

You also can use a budget to figure out how much money you need in an emergency fund. If you want to have three months of emergency funds, divide the mandatory expenses for the year by twelve to get the average monthly mandatory expenses. Then, multiply the monthly expenses by three (or the number of months you want covered) to get your total emergency fund.

Building a Budget with a Spreadsheet

Budget calculations are mostly addition and subtraction—all possible with any spreadsheet product on the market today. We'll go through setting up a simple budget in Excel 2000 to show you how it's done.

Creating Categories with a Spreadsheet

For those of you who just can't bear to spend money on software, here are some tips on building a budget spreadsheet. We will start with the list of categories. The first worksheet is going to be our budget sheet. Click **Format**, select **Sheet**, and click **Rename**. Change the name of the sheet to **Budget**. Figure 3.7 shows the worksheet with the labels added.

1. Put the name of your budget in the first cell. This gives you space for column headings and identifies the budget at the same time.

2. Add the word **Income** just below the budget name.

3. Start adding income categories in the first column below the word Income. You can add them alphabetically or as you think of them. If you add them out of order, select all the cells for income categories when you are finished with your list. Click the **Data** menu and select **Sort**. If the setting shows sort alphabetically, click **OK**.

4. In the cell immediately below the last income category, add the words **Total Income**.

5. Skip one row, and then enter the word **Expenses**.

6. Add all the expense categories for the budget. Add them as you did your income. Sort them if you added them out of order.

7. Immediately below the last expense name, enter the words **Total Expenses**.

8. Add headings for the months across the top row.

Tool Tips

Consider the Cost of Your Time Before Building Your Own Tools

Sometimes it seems like someone is telling you that you need to buy more software every time you turn around. Wouldn't it be cheaper to use a spreadsheet or a database and just build your own budget? The answer is no! Quicken or any of the other personal finance packages offer oodles of great features for the cost of a couple of pizzas. You get planning, budgeting, tracking, financial advice, access to online banking, and much more. Meanwhile, you could spend the better part of a weekend putting your budget spreadsheet together and more time keeping it up to date. Don't waste your time building a budget spreadsheet. Save your money somewhere else.

Figure 3.7

Start your budget by adding labels for the budget categories down the side and for the months of the year across the top.

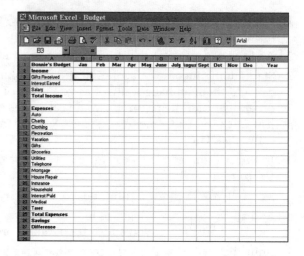

Selecting Cells in Excel

There are several ways to select cells in an Excel spreadsheet. No matter which selection method you use, a single selected cell has a thick boundary line around it. Multiple selected cells have a boundary line around the selection, and the cells are shaded.

➤ To select an area on a spreadsheet, press the left mouse button down in the first cell you want to select. Holding the mouse button down, move the cursor to the last cell you want to select. The area can be a part of a horizontal row, part of a vertical column, or a rectangular area covering several rows and several columns. After you have all the cells highlighted, release the mouse button.

➤ Another way to select an area is to click (and release) the mouse button in the first cell in the spreadsheet. Then click the mouse button while pressing the **Shift** key in the last cell to select.

➤ To select multiple isolated cells, click in the first cell you want to select. Then, click while holding down the **Ctrl** key. This will add each cell you click to the selected cells.

Creating and Summing Category Groups

Using subcategories or more than the basic category groups requires a lot more work in a spreadsheet, so we will stick with Income and Expenses as our category groups. Let's start with Income. In the cell of January's Total Income (cell B6 in this example), we are going to sum up all the income categories. Click cell B6. Double-click the sum sign in the Excel toolbar, shown in Figure 3.8. This places the formula =Sum() in cell B6. Select the cells for the January income and press **Enter**. Cell B6 should contain the formula =Sum(B3:B5).

Sum icon

Figure 3.8

This button automatically creates a Sum function.

To copy this formula to the rest of the months, make sure cell B6 is still selected. Click the **Edit** menu and select **Copy**, which selects cell B6 to copy. At this point, cell B6 has a vibrating dotted boundary line to show that it has been selected to copy. Select the cells for the Total Income for months February through December. Click the **Edit** menu and select **Paste**, which pastes the formula to months February through December. The pasted cells have a thick boundary line around them. Excel modifies the formula in each cell so that it sums up the income for the right month.

Totaling Expenses by Month

The next step is to sum up the expenses for each month. Click the cell for January Total Expenses (B25 in this example). Double-click the sum sign in the Excel toolbar. This places the formula =Sum() in cell B25. Select the cells for the January expenses and press **Enter**. Cell B25 should contain the formula =Sum(B9:B24). Copy this cell across for the total expenses for the remaining months of the year.

We have to create one more column to sum up the months to show the entire year. In the cell next to the heading "Dec," enter the word **Year**. Select the cell for the first income category (N3 in this example). Use the Sum function to add up all the cells for the category Gifts Received for each month of the year. Copy this formula down to the row for Difference. Figure 3.9 shows the formulas that sum up income, expenses, and the year-to-date totals. Columns D through M are hidden so you can see the year total column.

Figure 3.9

Use the Excel Sum function to total your budgeted income, expenses, and year-to-date totals.

The last step for our budget page is to add the formulas to see what the difference is between our income and expenses plus savings. Click the cell for January's difference (B27). Enter = and click in the cell for January Total Income. Enter - and click in the cell for January Total Expenses. Finally, enter - and click in the cell for January savings. You should have the formula =B6-B25-B26. Copy the January cell across for months February through December.

To enter budget amounts, just type numbers into cells. You can copy cells with numbers to fill in entire rows. For example, if you are going to use the Christmas Club method, enter the average monthly amounts into the January column. As shown in Figure 3.10, select the cells for January. Click the **Edit** menu and select **Copy**. Select the cells for the rest of the months. Click the **Edit** menu and select **Paste**.

Figure 3.10

Copy the cells for the January budget to the rest of the months.

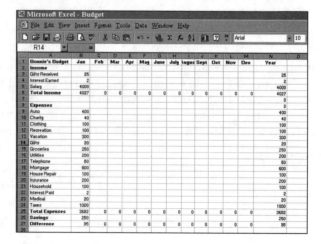

Building Worksheets for Actuals

A worksheet for your actual spending for a month is very similar to the budget worksheet. We need all the same categories. We will want to sum up the Total Income and Total Expense for the month. The main difference is that the columns will represent days of the month instead of months in the year.

Copying the Budget Worksheet as a Starting Point for Actuals

An easy way to get the worksheet for January Actuals is to copy the Budget worksheet. Click in the blank box between the heading A and 1. This selects the entire worksheet. Press **Ctrl+C**, which is the same as Copy on the Edit menu. Click the tab at the bottom of the Excel window that says Sheet2. Press **Ctrl+V**, which is the same as Paste on the Edit menu. Now we have a copy of the budget worksheet. We want to keep all the formulas, but we don't want the numbers. Select the cells for the income amounts (B3 through N13). Click the **Edit** menu, select **Clear**, and click **Contents**. This clears the numbers in the cells. Repeat this for the expense amounts (B9 through N24) and the Savings row.

There are already twelve columns for the actuals (one for each month). So, we want to add another nineteen columns so that we will have one column for each day of the month. Click the **C** heading at the top of the February column. This selects the entire column. Click the **Insert** menu and select **Column**. To repeat this Insert Column command, press **Ctrl+Y** another 18 times. Select the February column again by clicking in the heading **C**. Press **Ctrl+C** to copy. Select all the newly inserted columns. Press **Ctrl+V** to paste the February column in. Finally, change the headings in the first row of the worksheet to be the days of the month. Change Jan to **1** and so on. Figure 3.11 shows the completed January Actuals worksheet.

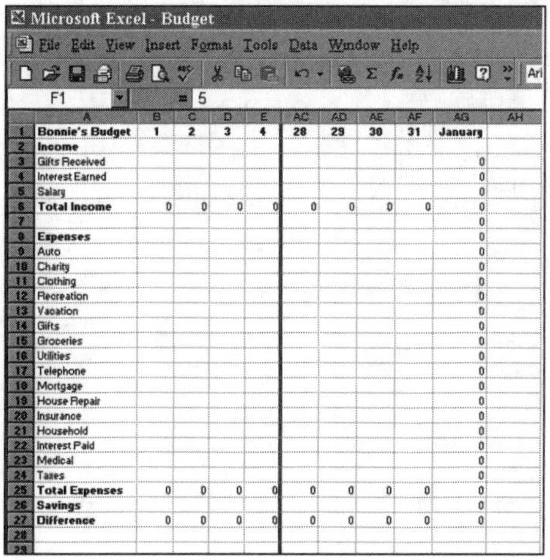

Figure 3.11

You can use the Budget spreadsheet to start the January Actuals worksheet.

To clean up this worksheet, click **Format**, select **Sheet**, and click **Rename**. Change the name of this worksheet to `Jan`. Also, click in the cell that says `Year` and change that label to **January**.

Creating Worksheets for Actuals for the Rest of the Year

Now, we want to create worksheets for February through December. Fun, isn't it? Click **Insert** and select **Worksheet**. This adds a new worksheet. Click **Format** and select **Rename**. Rename this worksheet to **February**. Click on the **January** tab to display the January worksheet. Click in the box between heading `A` and `1` to select the entire worksheet. Press **Ctrl+C** to copy. Click the **February** tab and press **Ctrl+V** to paste the January worksheet into February. Change the heading `January` to **February**. Repeat these steps for each month of the year.

With this spreadsheet, you can enter amounts by day and category. Just pick the cell for the day and category and enter a number.

Adding Up the Actuals

We want to summarize the actuals for the year. We are going to add another section on the Budget worksheet that adds up the monthly amounts on each of the Actuals worksheets, as in Figure 3.12. So, click the **Budgets** tab at the bottom left of the window. Select all the cells that we set up for the Budget (A1 through N27). Press **Ctrl+C** to copy. Now select an area of the same size just below the Budget area, such as A31 through N57. Press **Ctrl+V** to paste the budget cells. Change the label `Year` to **Year Actuals**.

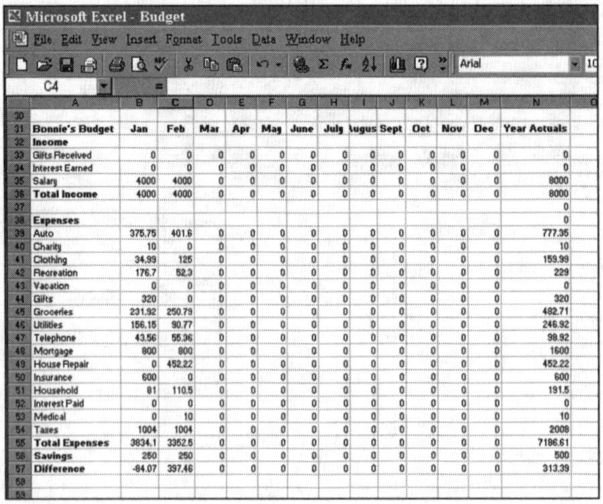

	A	B	C	D	E	F	G	H	I	J	K	L	M	N
30														
31	**Bonnie's Budget**	**Jan**	**Feb**	**Mar**	**Apr**	**May**	**June**	**July**	**Augus**	**Sept**	**Oct**	**Nov**	**Dec**	**Year Actuals**
32	**Income**													
33	Gifts Received	0	0	0	0	0	0	0	0	0	0	0	0	0
34	Interest Earned	0	0	0	0	0	0	0	0	0	0	0	0	0
35	Salary	4000	4000	0	0	0	0	0	0	0	0	0	0	8000
36	**Total Income**	4000	4000	0	0	0	0	0	0	0	0	0	0	8000
37														0
38	**Expenses**													0
39	Auto	375.75	401.6	0	0	0	0	0	0	0	0	0	0	777.35
40	Charity	10	0	0	0	0	0	0	0	0	0	0	0	10
41	Clothing	34.99	125	0	0	0	0	0	0	0	0	0	0	159.99
42	Recreation	176.7	52.3	0	0	0	0	0	0	0	0	0	0	229
43	Vacation	0	0	0	0	0	0	0	0	0	0	0	0	0
44	Gifts	320	0	0	0	0	0	0	0	0	0	0	0	320
45	Groceries	231.92	250.79	0	0	0	0	0	0	0	0	0	0	482.71
46	Utilities	156.15	90.77	0	0	0	0	0	0	0	0	0	0	246.92
47	Telephone	43.56	55.36	0	0	0	0	0	0	0	0	0	0	98.92
48	Mortgage	800	800	0	0	0	0	0	0	0	0	0	0	1600
49	House Repair	0	452.22	0	0	0	0	0	0	0	0	0	0	452.22
50	Insurance	600	0	0	0	0	0	0	0	0	0	0	0	600
51	Household	81	110.5	0	0	0	0	0	0	0	0	0	0	191.5
52	Interest Paid	0	0	0	0	0	0	0	0	0	0	0	0	0
53	Medical	0	10	0	0	0	0	0	0	0	0	0	0	10
54	Taxes	1004	1004	0	0	0	0	0	0	0	0	0	0	2008
55	**Total Expenses**	3834.1	3352.5	0	0	0	0	0	0	0	0	0	0	7186.61
56	**Savings**	250	250	0	0	0	0	0	0	0	0	0	0	500
57	**Difference**	-84.07	397.46	0	0	0	0	0	0	0	0	0	0	313.39
58														
59														

Figure 3.12

The Actuals summary worksheet references the totals on the worksheets for monthly actuals.

With this next step, do not press the Enter key until you are completely finished. Click in the cell for January Actuals Gifts Received (cell B3). Enter =, and then switch to the January sheet and click in the cell for January Gifts Received (AG) and press **Enter**. Click in the February Actuals Gifts Received (cell C3). Enter =, and then switch to the February sheet and click in the cell for February Gifts Received (AG3) and press **Enter**. Repeat this step for Gifts Received for each of the remaining months.

After you have the first row, we can copy these cells. Select the cells for Gifts Received Actuals for the Year (B33 through M33). We are going to copy these cells down into the other rows, but we don't want to overwrite the cells that add things up. Press **Ctrl+C**. Select the rest of the income category cells (C33 through M35) and press **Ctrl+V** to copy the formula. Copy the cell again into all the expense category cells (B39 to M54) and also into the savings cells (B56 to M56).

Crash Alert

Transferring Actual Data from Online Banking Doesn't Work Here!

One of the problems with an Excel budget is that you can't transfer your transactions from online banking or online credit cards. There isn't any way for Excel to know where to place the numbers in the spreadsheet. By using Quicken along with online banking, you can download your transactions complete with categories right into your Quicken check register.

Producing a Report with Your Spreadsheet Budget

Without going beyond what an idiot can do with Excel, we are going to produce a simple *Budget versus Actual* report. We are going to copy the budget area one more time to show the difference between the Budgeted amounts and the Actual amounts.

Select all the cells that we set up for the Budget (A1 through N27). Press **Ctrl+C** to copy. Now select an area of the same size just below the Budget area, such as A61 through N87. Press **Ctrl+V** to paste the budget cells. Change the label Year to **Budget vs. Actuals**.

To show the Budgeted versus Actuals, we want to subtract the actual amount from the budgeted amount. If the actual amount is more than the budgeted amount, the budgeted versus actual number will be negative. Click the Gifts Received cell in this new section. Type = and click in the Gifts Received cell up in the budgeted area (B3). Now, type - and click in the Gifts Received cell in the Actuals area (B33). Press **Enter** to end the formula.

Now, we have to copy this formula to the other cells in the budget versus actual area. Press **Ctrl+C** to copy this cell. Select the income cells (B63 through M65) and press **Ctrl+V** to paste the formula. Copy the formula to the expense cells (B69 through M84) and to the savings cells (B86 through M86).

Make the Over-Budget Amounts Stand Out

If you would like the negative numbers to stand out a little more, you can change how Excel displays them. To change negative number formats, first select the cells you want to change. Then click the **Format** menu and select **Cells**. Make sure the **Number** tab is selected. Click the **Number** category and then click the negative number format that you prefer.

Figure 3.13 shows the difference between the budgeted amount and the actual amount. The positive numbers show where the actual amount was less than the budgeted amount. Negative numbers show where the actual amount is more than the budgeted amount. In this example, the first month is under budget by $179.07, whereas the second month is over budget by $302.46. We will talk about what to look for in Budget versus Actuals reports in the next section.

New Feature in Excel 2000

Now you can cut or copy up to 12 separate pieces of information and paste them one at a time or all at once into another document. After you select cells and issue the Copy command, Excel adds the selected cells to the Clipboard. A small window appears with the Clipboard selections. You can select one of the entries in the Clipboard and select **Copy**, or select **Paste All** from the Clipboard toolbar.

Bonnie's Budget	Jan	Feb	Mar	Apr	May	June	July	August	Sept	Oct	Nov	Dec	Budget vs. Actuals
Income													
Gifts Received	25.00	0.00	0.00	0.00	0.00	0.00	0.00	0.00	0.00	0.00	0.00	0.00	0.00
Interest Earned	2.00	0.00	0.00	0.00	0.00	0.00	0.00	0.00	0.00	0.00	0.00	0.00	2.00
Salary	0.00	(4000.00)	0.00	0.00	0.00	0.00	0.00	0.00	0.00	0.00	0.00	0.00	(4000.00)
Total Income	27.00	(4000.00)	0.00	0.00	0.00	0.00	0.00	0.00	0.00	0.00	0.00	0.00	(3973.00)
													0.00
Expenses													0.00
Auto	24.25	(401.60)	0.00	0.00	0.00	0.00	0.00	0.00	0.00	0.00	0.00	0.00	(377.35)
Charity	30.00	0.00	0.00	0.00	0.00	0.00	0.00	0.00	0.00	0.00	0.00	0.00	30.00
Clothing	65.01	(125.00)	0.00	0.00	0.00	0.00	0.00	0.00	0.00	0.00	0.00	0.00	(59.99)
Recreation	(76.70)	(52.30)	0.00	0.00	0.00	0.00	0.00	0.00	0.00	0.00	0.00	0.00	(129.00)
Vacation	300.00	0.00	0.00	0.00	0.00	0.00	0.00	0.00	0.00	0.00	0.00	0.00	300.00
Gifts	(300.00)	0.00	0.00	0.00	0.00	0.00	0.00	0.00	0.00	0.00	0.00	0.00	(300.00)
Groceries	18.08	(250.79)	0.00	0.00	0.00	0.00	0.00	0.00	0.00	0.00	0.00	0.00	(232.71)
Utilities	43.85	(90.77)	0.00	0.00	0.00	0.00	0.00	0.00	0.00	0.00	0.00	0.00	(46.92)
Telephone	6.44	(55.36)	0.00	0.00	0.00	0.00	0.00	0.00	0.00	0.00	0.00	0.00	(48.92)
Mortgage	0.00	(600.00)	0.00	0.00	0.00	0.00	0.00	0.00	0.00	0.00	0.00	0.00	(600.00)
House Repair	100.00	(452.22)	0.00	0.00	0.00	0.00	0.00	0.00	0.00	0.00	0.00	0.00	(352.22)
Insurance	(400.00)	0.00	0.00	0.00	0.00	0.00	0.00	0.00	0.00	0.00	0.00	0.00	(400.00)
Household	19.00	(110.50)	0.00	0.00	0.00	0.00	0.00	0.00	0.00	0.00	0.00	0.00	(91.50)
Interest Paid	2.00	0.00	0.00	0.00	0.00	0.00	0.00	0.00	0.00	0.00	0.00	0.00	2.00
Medical	20.00	(10.00)	0.00	0.00	0.00	0.00	0.00	0.00	0.00	0.00	0.00	0.00	10.00
Taxes	(4.00)	(1004.00)	0.00	0.00	0.00	0.00	0.00	0.00	0.00	0.00	0.00	0.00	(1008.00)
Total Expenses	(152.07)	(3352.54)	0.00	0.00	0.00	0.00	0.00	0.00	0.00	0.00	0.00	0.00	(3504.61)
Savings	0.00	(250.00)	0.00	0.00	0.00	0.00	0.00	0.00	0.00	0.00	0.00	0.00	(250.00)
Difference	179.07	(397.46)	0.00	0.00	0.00	0.00	0.00	0.00	0.00	0.00	0.00	0.00	(218.39)

Figure 3.13

The spreadsheet shows the difference between the budgeted amount and the monthly actuals.

Tracking Your Progress

A budget is a plan for spending and saving your money. Checking up on how you are doing on your plan helps you stay on track, warns you when you start to stray, and points out where your estimates were unrealistic.

Producing a Budget Report or Graph in Quicken

Quicken makes it easy to produce a budget report for different time periods, accounts, categories, or settings. To produce the basic Budget report, click **Report** on the button bar in the Budget window and select **Budget Report**. This report shows the budgeted versus actual numbers for the year to date. To see the budget report by month, select **Budget Report by Month**. This report shows the budgeted versus actual numbers by month as well as the year-to-date numbers.

Click the **Customize** button on the button bar to make changes to the report. For example, if you want to change the report dates to the end of a particular month, click **Customize** and change the **From** date, the **To** date, or both. You can change the time period to half-month, quarter, or half-year by selecting from the **Column** box. Click the **Cents in Amount** check box to turn off the display of cents in the report. Click the **Accounts** tab if you want to limit the budget report to certain accounts. Click the **Include** tab to limit the budget report to certain categories.

When to Run Budget Reports

Your actual spending will never match your plan. Things happen. Timing changes. Even if you could build the perfect plan, it probably wouldn't be worth the effort. Over the course of a year your actual spending should be close to your budget— except for the unexpected taxes because you decided to convert to a Roth IRA, or the two new tires you didn't expect to buy. The shorter the length of time, the less accurate the budget will be.

It doesn't hurt to run the monthly budget report each month to check for any glaring errors or exuberant overruns. But you really can skip the monthly reports. The Budget versus Actual report gets better with time. At the end of each quarter, run the Budget report with the Column setting on Quarter. In July, you also can run the Budget report with the Column setting on Half Year. Wait until all your bills, bank statements, and credit card statements are in for a year before looking at your Budget versus Actual for the year. This gives you the most accurate picture of how you did for the year.

What to Look For

What should you look for when you run one of these reports? The Budget versus Actual report pulls you back when you start to spend too much. It also can show you where your estimates need some work. When you build your first budget, your estimates might not be very good. You thought you would spend $75 per month on gas, or $100 per month on recreation. The first thing to check in the report is for categories in red—where you overspent against your plan. If you are in the red on mandatory categories—auto gas, groceries, electric—you should go back in and change your budget. If the Budget versus Actual shows that you spend $150 a month on gas to get to work, there isn't much you can do about that. When you are keen to save money—to buy a house or pay for college—you can look into the bus or maybe a car with better gas mileage. Otherwise, you should go back into your budget and change your budgeted amount to $150.

Now, what about the $100 per month on recreation? If you are spending $200 per month, you have two choices. First, you can change your budgeted amount to $200. Unfortunately, if you do that with too many things, you won't have any money left for your savings. So, for discretionary spending, such as recreation, vacation, or clothing, take those numbers in red as a warning to cut back. Keep that red in the back of your mind so that the next time you think about going to the movies, you head for the video rental instead.

There is a positive side to this budgeting as well. What if you have a category that is consistently "in the black"—you are spending less than you thought? In a lot of cases, these categories help balance out the categories in the red. You can change the budget and move the money from the under-budget categories to the over budget. Let's be really optimistic. All your other categories are on target and you still have this extra cash. In this fortunate circumstance, buy yourself a nice dinner for being financially responsible and then move the rest of the money to savings. If you budgeted $100 per month on clothing, and discover that you only spend $50, reduce your budget to $50 per month on clothing and increase you savings transfer by $50 per month.

What If Categories with Regular Amounts Are Off-track?

You have a lot of categories that stay the same each month: rent, mortgage, cable TV, garbage. What does it mean if your actual spending doesn't match your budgeted amount? It might mean that you forgot to pay a bill, or that the check got lost in the mail. I once set up a monthly online payment that was supposed to be quarterly. After six months, the Budget versus Actual was way off. When I looked around, I caught my mistake.

Don't Spend That Found Money

One mistake that people often make when they start to use a budget is to spend the money they budgeted but didn't spend. When you run a budget report for a month, there is a good chance that you spent less than you budgeted. Many people mistake this extra cash as a windfall and splurge on a night out, a shopping spree, or some other luxury.

The first thing you should do when you see a lot of unspent income in a month is to check that you paid all your bills. You might have forgotten to pay your mortgage or your car insurance. If you use the Christmas club method of budgeting, you will usually have extra cash each month. That extra cash is your stockpile for when your big bills come due. If you spend it on luxuries, you will be in big trouble later on. If you have paid all your bills, and you aren't using the Christmas club method, put that extra cash in your savings account or an investment. If you need it later, you will have earned money on it until then.

The Least You Need to Know

➤ A budget is a plan for how you will spend the money you make.

➤ Quicken offers ready-made categories so you can build a budget quickly. If you have been using Quicken to track your transactions, Quicken can create a budget based on your past monthly detail.

➤ You can build a budget with a spreadsheet application, but it takes a while and doesn't offer all the features of a product like Quicken.

➤ After you create a budget, you should run a budget report once a quarter and after the year ends.

Chapter 4

Getting Out of Debt

In This Chapter

➤ How to tell if debt is a problem for you

➤ Using a debt reduction tool to find a way out

➤ Adding your debt reduction plan to your budget

➤ When you can't get out of debt by yourself

Very few people go through life without any debt. Debt lets us get things we want, like houses and cars, before we have enough money to pay for it. And interest is the cost of that privilege!

Debt can be a godsend! Debt lets us buy houses when we're still vigorous enough to climb the stairs to the front door. We pay a regular amount each month, and even get a tax break on the interest.

But instant gratification can get out of hand. If you end up buying things you don't even want, and then pay 18% interest on the credit card balance, your chances of saving for the things that really matter melt away.

If you're in trouble with debt, you're in trouble in your financial plan. Take the first step to controlling your credit card debt. Get online and find out how to stop paying and start saving!

Top 10 Signs That You're in Trouble

If not all debt is bad, how can you tell if you're in trouble? You can figure it out your-self, if you just stop buying long enough to pay attention. Or you can let the credit card companies decide for you.

1. You always pick the longest time to repay.

2. You never pay off your credit cards completely.

3. Your friends and associates don't know how you live so well.

4. You can afford to pay only the minimum on your credit cards each month. And sometimes you can't.

5. You take cash advances on one card to pay another.

6. You use cash advances for basics like food, rent, and utilities.

7. You ignore envelopes because you know they're bills.

8. You delay payments by mailing the wrong checks to your creditors.

9. You have a debt consolidation loan, and now you have balances on your credit cards again.

10. You get turned down for credit.

Credit card companies send out millions of offers for credit cards. And they don't really want customers who pay off their balances. They like people who run up their balances and pay those high interest rates.

But if their customers default, the credit card companies go from a fabulous profit to a complete loss. If you get turned down for credit, even the credit card companies think you're in trouble. They watch what you do with your account and rate your likelihood of defaulting. Here are a few of the warning signs:

➤ You pay only the minimum balance on your card.

➤ You pay late.

➤ You make partial payments.

➤ You take the maximum cash advance.

➤ Your balance always grows.

Tools for Reducing Your Debt

You might think that you have no choice. You need those things you're charging on the card. (If you've gotten to the point of charging groceries, you might be right!) But if you have an 18% credit card with a $3,000 balance (like our Smith family), it would take seven years to pay the balance off with the minimum monthly payment (about $60). In addition, you would pay $2,587 in interest—almost as much as you owed!

Try to think about your credit cards another way. Paying off credit card debt on an 18% card is like getting a guaranteed return of 18%. You can't get that guarantee anywhere in the stock market!

Kicking the Habit by Hand

Quitting using credit cards is like quitting smoking. No one will tell you that it is easy. But you can do it! And it is as simple as leaving your credit cards at home (and not using them over the phone, either). The first step to getting rid of credit card debt is to stop charging.

Studies have shown that people don't view credit cards as real money so they tend to spend more when they use them. Start writing checks or paying cash for your purchases. You'll probably buy less.

When you stop charging and start buying less, your debt disappears quickly because you aren't adding to your debt balance and you're paying off the balances you have. You might even save a little. If you use those savings to pay off the balance, you'll be out of debt in no time.

Head of the Class

Can I Live Without a Credit Card?

In most cases, you can get by without a card. Checks, traveler's checks, and bank checks will work. If you need a card because you purchase on the Internet or travel on business, think about getting a debit card from your bank or an American Express card that you have to pay off at the end of each month.

Getting Online to Get Out of Debt

What if "Just Say No" is too vague for you now that you've decided you want to be free of debt? A Debt Reduction Planner can add up everything you owe, and give you concrete steps to get you out of debt.

Most Web sites that offer a Debt Reduction Planner take you right to Quicken.com. So, start your journey to debt-free living with a trip to Quicken.com's Debt Reduction Planner, (www.Quicken.com/saving/debt). From the Quicken.com home page you can click the **Banking** tab and then click **Debt Reduction Planner** in the **Tools** list.

For each of your debts, enter the lender's name, the type of loan, the annual percentage rate, the current balance, your typical monthly payment, and the minimum monthly payment, as shown in Figure 4.1. When you have entered the data for a debt, click **Save**. Click **New** to add another debt. When you have all your debts on the list, click **Next** to see a summary of when you will be debt-free on your current payment schedule.

You Might as Well Get Your Paperwork Together!

You're going to need information about your debts, so go to your files and collect statements and other paperwork for each of your debts. Remember that this includes all your credit cards, any mortgages, home equity loans, second mortgages, auto loans, other installment loans, and any other debt you might have. You also need to know how much money you have in savings.

Figure 4.1

Enter all your debts into the Quicken.com Debt Reduction Planner and find out what steps to take to get out of debt.

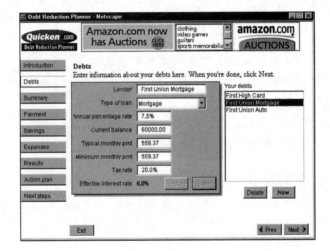

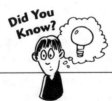

Pay Off Your Highest Interest Rate Debt First!

You can get out of debt the quickest and avoid paying a lot of interest if you're smart about your debt payments. Pay the most you can afford on the highest interest rate debt each month while paying the minimum on all other debt. After one debt is paid off, add the amount you were paying for that debt to the debt with the next highest rate. Your monthly payment toward your debt balances stays the same until all your debt is paid off.

If you have savings that you can use toward paying off your debt, click the **Savings** tab in the **Planner**. Enter the amount of savings that you want to apply today toward your debt. When you click **Save/Recalculate**, as in Figure 4.2, you see how much sooner you will be out of debt and how much interest you will save.

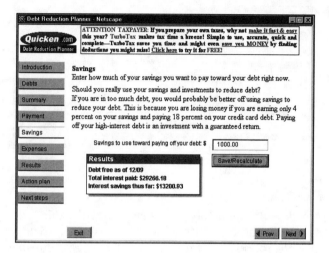

Figure 4.2

*You can apply some of your savings to paying off your debt. To see how much it helps your plan, click **Save/Recalculate**.*

On the **Expenses** tab you can enter an amount that you think you can pay each month toward your debt by reducing your expenses. **Save/Recalculate** shows your new debt-free timeframe and interest savings.

The **Results** tab shows you how much faster you are paying off your debt with your contribution from savings and expense reduction. If the graph inspires you to achieve more, you can enter a new savings or expense reduction amount. **Save/Recalculate** will show you your new improved debt reduction results.

Click the **Action Plan** tab to find out what steps to take to make your plan happen. Your Action Plan, shown in Figure 4.3, reminds you to stop charging. It even tells you how much to pay each month to each of your creditors to optimize your monthly debt payments.

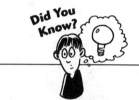

Did You Know?

Should I Use Savings to Pay Off My Debt?

If you have a lot of debt, you should consider paying off your debt with your savings. The difference between a 3% return on a savings account and 18% on a credit card is practically money in your pocket. After you get used to making a monthly debt payoff, you can turn that into a savings payment when you are out of debt.

Figure 4.3

The Action Plan gives you all the steps to eliminating debt in your life. Don't forget to click **Print** *to get a copy of your plan.*

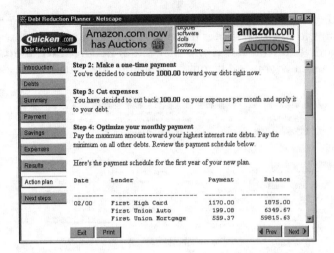

What Else Can I Do?

The Next Steps tab provides additional advice to help you with your debt. For instance, you can look for a credit card with a lower interest rate. If you are going to keep a balance on a credit card, find the card with the lowest rate possible. If you do get a lower rate card, find out if you can transfer balances from your old card to the new one.

Crash Alert

Don't Shortchange Your Emergency Funds!

Don't use all your savings to pay off debt. You should keep at least three months' worth of expenses in savings in case of emergency.

It pays to comparison shop on mortgage rates. Because of the amount that you borrow to buy a house, a small difference in the rate on a mortgage can add up to thousands of dollars in savings.

Adding Your Action Plan to Your Budget

If you have a budget, you want to add your monthly debt payment to your budget. This payment shows up as a transfer between the account you use to pay off your debt (probably your checking account) and the credit card or loan accounts.

In your Quicken budget, make sure that the category "To" your credit card account is included in your budget window. Then, you can add the payment amount from your debt reduction plan into the cell for January and click **Fill Row Right** on the **Budgeting** toolbar to copy it to the rest of the year. If the balance will be paid off before the end of the year, only add the payment amount to the number of months that you need.

Tool Tips

Debt Reduction in Quicken 2000

Quicken 2000 Deluxe contains the full version of the Debt Reduction Planner. If you use Quicken, build your debt reduction plan right on your computer. With the full version, you can specify categories where you plan to cut expenses to help pay off your debt. It also can automatically set up scheduled payments for you so you know when and how much to pay each creditor.

To make sure that you don't slide back into old habits, use scheduled transactions, as shown in Figure 4.4, so that Quicken reminds you to make those debt reduction payments. If you let Quicken set the scheduled transactions up for you, you don't have to do anything else!

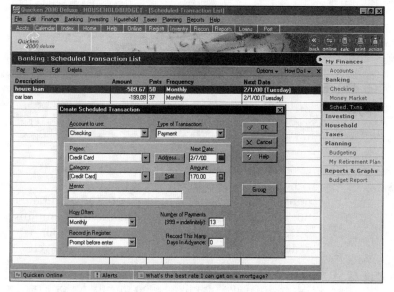

Figure 4.4

Scheduled transactions remind you to make your debt payment each month.

But if you want to set up a scheduled transaction yourself, select **Scheduled Transaction** from the **Banking** menu. Click **New** and fill in the account to pay from, who you are paying, the next payment date, the amount, and how often you want to pay. The category would be a transfer to your credit card account.

If You're Stuck in the Mire of Debt

If you've worked through the Debt Reduction Planner and you still can't imagine the action plan working, you might consider working with a professional. These people see your types of problems every day. They can help you get yourself organized to pay off your debt while working with your creditors to make it a little easier.

Debt Counselors of America is a not-for-profit organization that helps people with their credit and debt problems for small or no fee. Its Web site, www.dca.org, shown in Figure 4.5, is a gold mine of information and tools to get the gold back into your life. It has self-help publications online and available to download. But you can also get one-on-one support.

Figure 4.5

The Debt Counselors of America Web site provides education and tools to help you get out of debt.

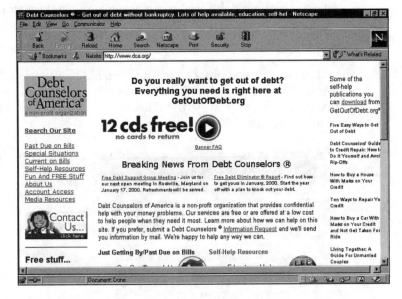

Debt Counseling Keeps You from Taking On More Debt!

One subtle advantage to working with a debt counselor is that you won't be able to rack up more debt. Many creditors won't lend you money until your debt reduction plan is well underway.

If you enroll in the One-Pay service, DCA works with your creditors to try to get you reduced monthly payments, and reduced or even eliminated interest and late fees. You pay one monthly amount to DCA and it distributes the money to all your creditors. You can check your account on its Web site and even track your expenses.

Using One-Pay you might even qualify for one of DCA's debt consolidation loans. If you maintain a good payment history with DCA, it will provide a good credit reference for you so that you can qualify for car loans or mortgages.

The Least You Need to Know

➤ Excessive debt, particularly with high-interest credit cards, terminally hinders any financial plan.

➤ If you are in debt, develop a plan to get out of debt and follow it. Switch your monthly debt payments into savings payments when you have paid off your debt.

➤ If you need more help, talk to a debt counseling organization. They can help you build a plan and even work with creditors to ease their terms.

Part 2
Using the Internet for Personal Finance

Graduate from playing Doom on your computer to playing the market with a winning strategy. Start using your computer and the Internet to turn your finances into a brick house that even a big bad wolf can't blow down. You can manage your bank accounts, find better rates for your loans, look into cheaper insurance, and even make paying taxes less painful.

Chapter 5

Online Banking

In This Chapter

➤ Using the Internet to find a bank with online access

➤ Learning the difference between types of online banking and whether any of them are right for you

➤ What to look for and what to avoid

➤ Getting an online bank account set up

➤ Learning the basic of online banking transactions

With automatic teller machines (ATMs), telephone access, and bank by mail, do you ever set foot in your bank these days? Why not go the extra step and do all your banking electronically? If you've thought about switching to online banking, this chapter will help you decide if online banking is for you. If it is, you'll find out how to get wired in to your bank.

Most people interested in online banking talk about instant account access from anywhere and online bill payments. But you can use telephone service systems for access to your account and, in some cases, bill payments. You can use personal finance software to pay bills, too. You might even discover that you think offline services are simpler and quicker.

If you follow your finances carefully and use your transactions in your personal finance software, an online banking Web site might leave you cold. If you have a lot of accounts at one bank and you transfer funds between them frequently, online banking might make sense. On the other hand, if you hit the ATM frequently, a local bank makes more sense just to avoid those pesky ATM fees. If your big complaint is paying bills and paperwork, check out an online bill payment service like the one available in Quicken.

Finding an Online Bank

Just because your bank has a Web site, doesn't mean it offers online banking. And even if your bank offers online banking, it might not be good. If you do switch to online banking, you'll want to make sure that your online bank is sound, its Web site easy to use, and its services and fees acceptable. Or you can compromise by finding a brick-and-mortar bank that offers online services that suit you.

Searching for Banks with Online Access

The Internet Banking link in the Finance/Banking area on the Yahoo! Web site (dir.yahoo.com/Business_and_Economy/Finance_and_Investment/Banking/) has only five links. But one is a gem. Click **Gomez Internet Banking Scorecard** to see Gomez Associates' rankings and reviews of 60 online banks. Gomez Associates ranks online banks by ease of use, customer confidence, on-site resources, relationship services, and overall cost. Click any of the criteria to see the banks ranked by that criteria, as shown in Figure 5.1. Or click **(review)** to see a review of the bank.

Gomez Associates also provides a ranking for different types of bank customers, including Internet Transactors, Savers, Borrowers, and One-Stop Shoppers. After you have narrowed down your search, you can use the comparison feature to compare two banks side by side.

Figure 5.1

Gomez Associates ranks online banks by ease of use. You can click on different criteria to find the online service that meets your needs.

Click a name to go to its Web site.

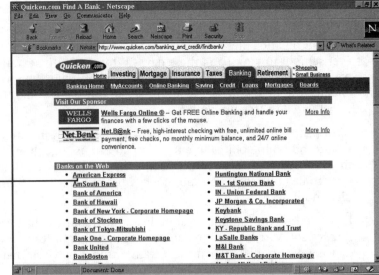

Another place to find a bank with online access is Quicken.com. In addition to a list of banks on the Web (`www.quicken.com/banking_and_credit/findbank/`), the Quicken.com banking section provides reviews of online bank Web sites (`www.quicken.com/banking_and_credit/online_banking/`). You can click any of the links in the list of banks to go to the bank's Web site to check out its services.

New online banks appear every day. If you don't find an online bank that you like today, check again in a month. But don't be too quick to move your money to a brand new bank. Give it time to settle in. See what others think before you entrust your daily finances to the new kid on the block.

What's in a Name?

Online banking can be called many things and can take several forms. Other names you might see include Internet banking, electronic banking, home banking, PC banking, and probably a few others.

PC Banking Started with Direct Connections to Your Bank

Online banking started with customers dialing into the bank's computers to perform their transactions. This form of PC banking, which is still available, usually requires special software on your computer. The quality of this software varies considerably. And it might be difficult to get your transaction information into your personal finance software.

The newer Internet-based banking enables customers to connect to the bank's computers via the Internet. Instead of using software on your computer, you perform transactions on the bank's Web site, so you can access Internet-based banking from anywhere you can access the Internet. You can bank 24 hours a day, just like with an ATM. But Internet-based banking cannot handle comprehensive financial planning software like Quicken or Microsoft Money.

Some banks offer banking through customized versions of personal finance software. You can set your transactions up offline and dial-in to transfer them. One advantage of this approach is that your transactions are available in your personal finance software, so you can easily bank online and manage your finances. Unfortunately, if you switch banks, you might have to switch software, and that could mean transferring data or even re-entering it.

What to Look for and What to Avoid

Start by looking for a review of the online banking site. Figure 5.2 shows a review on the Quicken.com site. These reviews can cut down the time it takes to narrow your search.

Figure 5.2

Read up on online banking sites with online reviews.

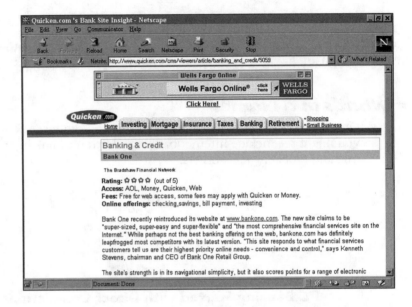

The first thing to look for is ease of use. If the bank's Web site is complicated to use, you'll find banking time-consuming and frustrating. Most of the banks offer demos that you can download.

Head of the Class

Check Out the Demo Before You Go Too Far

If you download a demo, run through it. And pay attention! By the time you've moved your funds and all your checks have cleared, it's too late to decide you don't like the user interface. When you sign up for your online banking, really put the site through its paces before you have too much time and data invested. If you change your mind, you might have to re-enter data at your new bank.

Also, check that the bank offers the features and services you want online. With most banks you can check balances, view account activity, transfer money between accounts, and perform some administrative tasks like changing your address. With more sophisticated sites you might be able to transfer your transactions to your personal finance software, apply for loans, or even look at images of your checks and deposit slips. Even with these more advanced features, make sure that the site is still easy to use.

We're talking about your money here, so security is important. All online banking uses the industry standard encryption techniques at a minimum. If you are particularly wary about someone getting to your dough, make sure that your online bank requires a browser with 128-bit encryption, such as Navigator 4.0 or Internet Explorer 4.0 or later. In addition, you need a username and password to get in and you should make sure to protect them.

Customer service should be next on your list. Make sure that you can call customer service if something goes wrong or you have a question. Many of the online banking services are free because you don't interact with a bank employee. So, you should check whether the bank charges for phone calls to customer service.

Check the fees that the bank charges. Internet account access might be free. Then again, you might have a certain number of sessions before the bank starts charging. Some banks offer free Internet account access for a while, but then start to charge monthly fees—quite often, higher than average. Access with personal finance software might have a monthly charge. And electronic bill-payment almost always has a monthly fee. In some cases, you can avoid fees if you keep enough money in your account. The moral of the story here is to read the fine print.

Find out if you need software on your computer. If you're new to online banking, the first thing to avoid is the older dial-in banking with specialized (proprietary) software. This will probably be replaced by Internet-based banking. If the bank uses personal finance software, find out if it is a special version or not.

And, finally, check that your online bank is financially sound, just as you would for a brick-and-mortar bank. BankRate.com provides an assessment of a bank's soundness with its Safe & Sound (SM) rating (`www.bankrate.com/brm/safesound/search.asp`). Select the type of financial institution you want to check and click **Go**. You can search by the first letter of the name of the institution, state zip code, asset size, or rating. After you select a particular

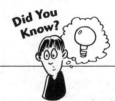

Did You Know?

Some Banks Have Deals Only Available on the Internet

BankRate.com has a link called Internet banking deals (`www.bankrate.com`) where you can find deals such as CDs with rates that you can only get by buying them online.

bank from the list, you can see the BankRate.com rating. You also can get a written report on your bank.

Comparing Online Services and Fees

Reading reviews of the different online banks might be the quickest way to narrow down your search. Most of the pertinent information about the online bank's service is all on one handy page. You can find out whether the user interface is decent or whether they offer the level of services you want, or the fees you wouldn't mind paying.

Then, when you are ready to look at some of the banks more closely, click the bank's name in the Quicken.com list. On the bank's Web site, you can find out about the bank's services, fees, security, software needs, and customer service. Figure 5.3 shows the online banking fees for Key Bank along with the tabs to find out everything else about its offering.

Figure 5.3

Go to a bank's Web site to find out everything about its online banking service.

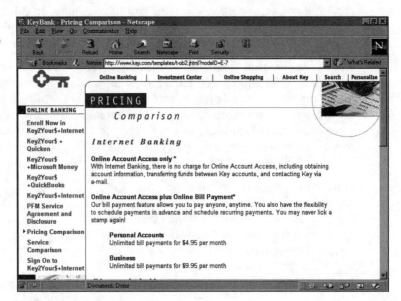

Getting an Online Bank Account

Online bank accounts take a little more work than paper ones. Although the online applications are more convenient, you have to do some setup on your computer to gain some of the benefits of online banking.

Applying

You can apply for your online banking with an online application. In addition, most banks also provide for mailing applications.

When you apply online, you provide most of the information on a paper application along with a few extras, as shown in Figure 5.4. The application requests items like your name, address, Social Security number, years at your current address, employer information, mortgage or landlord information, salary, closest relative not living with you, and what services you are applying for. In addition, an online application also will ask for your email address, and usually where you heard about the bank.

For applications by mail, you can fill the form out online, but print and complete the application. Then, you mail it to the bank. Or you can download the form in Adobe Acrobat PDF format. You print the PDF file, fill it in, and mail it.

Tool Tips

Don't Lose That Application

If you fill in an application online, check to see if you can save an unfinished application to complete at a later time. If not, make sure you complete and submit the application before ending your session. It's also a good idea to print the completed application before you submit it.

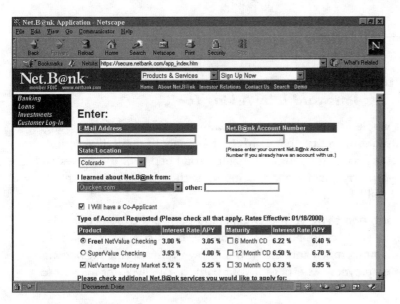

Figure 5.4
Online banking applications aren't very different from their paper counterparts.

Setting Up Your Computer

Of course, you will need Internet access and a browser on your computer. If your modem is fast enough for browsing on the Web, it will probably be fast enough for online banking. If the online services require software, get that software installed.

Make sure the browser that you use provides the level of security needed. The bank Web site will either specify a version of Internet Explorer or Netscape Navigator (usually 4.0 or later) or the security standard required.

If you are using online bill payments, you have to set up your payees. You have to enter information about the payee before you can pay one of their bills: address, phone number, account number, and perhaps a few other items.

Logging On

An application for online banking might ask for the username and password you want to use. In some cases, you might provide a username and receive the password in the mail or an email message. To log on, just enter the username and password at the logon page.

After you log on the first time, you might want to change your password. By resetting your password immediately, only you and the computer will know your password.

Crash Alert

Sometimes the Easiest Way People Steal Your Username and Password Is by Asking for It

You might have a whole list of usernames and passwords for the different things you do on the Internet. Don't use passwords that are easy to guess, like your birthday, your spouse's name, or your pet's name. And keep your usernames and passwords safe. If you carry them around, come up with some scheme so that a lost wallet doesn't tell all!

And, most important, don't give your username and password to someone who calls and says they need it to do maintenance on the bank computer. This practice is so common among miscreants that it has its own term—*social engineering*. Legitimate online employees—whether for your bank or ISP—will not ask you for that information.

What Can You Do with Online Banking?

With online banking you can do things like check balances, transfer funds, or look at past transactions. Offered in conjunction with banking, paying bills online usually comes with an additional charge.

Account Information

Online banking account information shows you your accounts, account numbers, and balances. In general, you can find out your account balance and your available balance as of a particular date. You might be able to view and change basic account information such as your address.

Transaction History

You can see the transaction history for your accounts. When you select a particular account, you can ask for more details like the example in Figure 5.5. You might have to enter a starting date and an ending date for the transactions that you want to see. The transaction history shows information much like your check register: the date, the payee, and the amount.

It also might show the status of the entries, such as pending or cleared. Some banks show your pending transactions in a separate list from the cleared transactions. In addition, some transaction lists might have icons that you can click to view an image of the check or to request a copy. Some banks might have an icon for stopping payment on the list of checks in your transaction history. Others might have a separate screen for selecting checks to stop payment on.

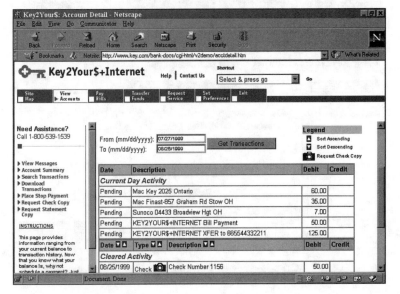

Figure 5.5

You can view your pending and cleared transactions when you request a transaction history. Some services provide icons so you can request a check copy or view an image of the check.

Transfer Funds

You can transfer funds between any of the accounts at your bank. Just select the account that you want to transfer from, the account to transfer to, and the amount that you want to transfer.

Bill Presentment Could Be the Next Big Thing

Unlike online bill payment, bill presentment means that you can view bills online and authorize the bank to make payments.

Pay Bills

Bill payment is one of the most helpful features of online banking. With online payment, you can enter a payment whenever you want but pay it right on time. You also can create repeating payments, so that your mortgage and other bills with regular amounts are paid automatically without you lifting a finger—or even having to remember. You also don't have to write out envelopes or pay for postage.

To gain all the convenience of online bill payments, you do have some up front work to do. Online bill payments have to have information about the company or person you are paying—name, address, phone number, and your account number.

But after your payees are set up, bill payments get a whole lot easier. To pay a bill, select the payee, and enter an amount and the date you want to pay them. Some banks, like KeyBank in Figure 5.6, display a list of your payees so you can just click the payee and enter the amount and date.

Figure 5.6

A list of your online payees makes paying bills simple.

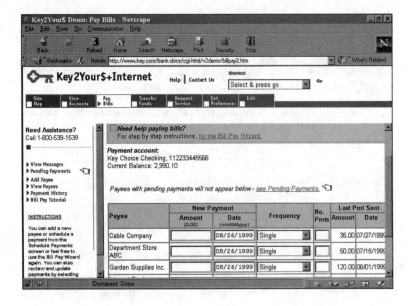

If you have payments, which you make at a regular interval and the amount doesn't vary, online bill payment makes your life a breeze. To set up a recurring payment, you still have to select or set up your payee. Then, you enter the frequency of the payment—monthly like your mortgage, quarterly perhaps like your garbage pickup, semi-annually like a lot of car insurance, or yearly for life insurance.

You also enter the total number of payments. If you have 240 payments left on your mortgage when you set up the recurring payment, enter 240 for the total number of payments. Finally, enter the date for the first payment. If you set up a monthly payment to start on the 15th, all the following payments will occur on the 15th. Figure 5.7 shows a typical recurring payment setup.

You might find that you need to edit your online payments. For a single payment, you can select a pending payment that the bank hasn't started to process and edit or even stop payment on it. Most online bill payment services can show you a list of your pending payments. In addition, you can view a payment history, as shown in Figure 5.8. You might be able to choose between a history of recent payments or a list of payments to a particular payee.

Master Merchants Make Online Bill Payments Even Easier

Master merchants are companies that have a payment arrangement in place with your bank. With master merchants, you only have to select the master merchant and enter your account number.

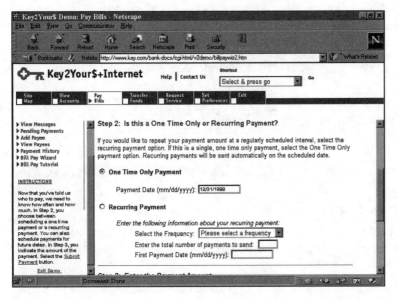

Figure 5.7

With recurring payments, you set one up and forget about it. The software takes care of the payment for as long as you want.

Electronic Payments Don't Happen at the Speed of Light

It's always a good idea to give your bank and your payee a little time to process your payment. Schedule your bill payments five days before they are due so that you avoid late charges on the occasional slow payment.

Figure 5.8

Online payment histories show you who you paid, how much, and when. With some banks, you might be able to view all your recent payments as well as all the payments for one payee.

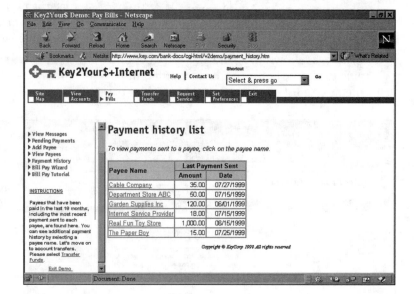

Downloading Transactions

If you are using Internet banking, you might be able to download your banking transactions to your computer. And, then again, maybe you won't. Check your online banking services before you sign up.

The most common formats for downloads are QIF and comma-delimited files. QIF stands for Quicken Interface Format. Personal finance software like Quicken and Microsoft Money read the transactions from these files into your personal finance software. Comma-delimited files include each transaction in one line in a file. A comma separates each piece of information for the transaction. Spreadsheet software, such as Microsoft Excel, knows how to bring comma-delimited information into a worksheet. But it is up to you to do something with it after that.

For online banking that uses Quicken or Microsoft Money on your computer, you build your transactions on your computer and send them to the bank. The things you will download from the bank are statuses on the transactions that you sent.

Crash Alert

Get Your Recurring Frequency Right

Don't forget to set the frequency of your recurring payments. Setting up a quarterly payment at a monthly frequency will drain your bank account for no reason. And your payee might not notify you that you are paying too much.

The Least You Need to Know

➤ Several sites provide lists of banks that offer online banking. Check site reviews to get a quick picture of whether the bank's online services are worth a closer look.

➤ If you don't transfer a lot between the accounts at your bank, but are tired of the paperwork of paying bills, look at an online bill payment service.

➤ If you frequent the ATM machine, a local bank might help you avoid a ton of ATM access fees.

➤ Internet-based banking provides 24-hour access but might have limited services.

➤ Use online banking integrated with a personal finance package if you want the convenience of online banking and the ability to track and plan your finances.

➤ Check a bank's online service for ease of use, the features you want, customer service, fees, and software needs. Check the bank's financial soundness just as you would a brick-and-mortar institution.

➤ All online banking services use a variety of measures to ensure that your online banking is secure.

Chapter 6

Your Credit

In This Chapter

➤ Picking the right features for a credit card

➤ Searching online for a credit card with the features that you want

➤ Online credit card transactions

➤ Keeping your credit card safe on the Internet

➤ Obtaining credit reports online

Credit cards at their best provide convenience, credit at little or no charge, and rewards for every dollar you charge on your card. At their worst, they lure their victims into debt with spending money that doesn't seem real.

This chapter tells you how to pick a card that's right for you. Then, it shows you how to find your card online.

Finding and Choosing the Credit Card for You

Credit cards aren't as simple as they used to be—annual fees, interest rates, grace periods, penalties, warranties, affinities, and other features. How do you decide which type of card makes sense for you? And, after you decide on features, how do you find a card with those features? Deciding on card features really hasn't changed much. The Web offers easy ways to find the card you want.

Matching Features to How You Pay

Picking credit card features still boils down to how you pay. If you pay your bill in full every month, start looking for a credit card with a low annual fee and a long grace period. The interest rate won't matter, because you don't pay it when you pay your bill on time and in full. The grace period is like a short-term, no-cost loan.

If you're still working off consumer debt, all you should care about is the lowest interest rate that a credit card company will offer you. The annual fee is peanuts compared to the interest you pay. And the grace period doesn't mean anything to someone who carries a balance.

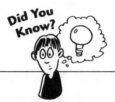

You Don't Need a Wallet Full of Credit Cards

A pile of credit cards limits your borrowing power when you go for a mortgage or other loans. Applying for all those cards can raise flags on your credit report, too. You need only one or two cards at the most, so drop all the department store cards. Their interest rates are among the highest, and they all accept major credit cards anyway.

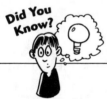

Many Cards Are Getting Rid of the Grace Period

People who pay their credit card in full don't make much money for the credit card companies. To entice these low-profit customers to leave, many cards are shortening or eliminating the grace period. With a card with no grace period, you pay interest from the moment you buy something until you pay your bill.

For those of us who are somewhere in the middle, usually paying the balance, but occasionally buying a big ticket item on credit, get one of each. Charge anything that you can pay off at the end of the month on the long grace period, higher-interest card. Charge items that you will pay off over time on the low-interest card.

If you manage your credit cards well, late fees and penalties might not matter. But you can use these terms to decide between two similar deals. Some cards charge late fees on top of interest if you pay late. And some cards charge fees if you exceed your credit limit. On top of that, they might jack up your interest rate if you are guilty of these offenses, even once!

Head of the Class

Watch the Terms on Your Cards

It pays to keep tabs on your credit card's terms. When a credit card company sells your account to another company, the new company can change the terms almost any way it wants. Many companies also are increasing fees and rates for existing customers.

So, get out your reading glasses or a magnifying glass and read the fine print that comes in your monthly statement. Your credit card company by law has to give only 15 days notice when it changes the rate. That change can apply to your existing balance in addition to your new purchases. Pay particular attention when you receive a notice that your account has changed hands. Your card's terms are bound to change.

Affinities, Warranties, and Other Things You Never Knew You Wanted

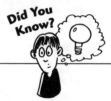

Did You Know?

Is Your Card Lenient?

Credit card companies used to give you from 5 to 15 days past your due date to pay your bill without hitting you with a late fee. Today, few companies allow even one day past the due date. You'll pay interest on your balance and you might have to pay a late fee, too!

The past decade or so has brought an explosion of cards made of precious metals with features we never knew we wanted. After deciding on annual fee and grace period versus interest rate, you might want to consider some of these other features.

Affinity cards are the result of an alliance between the credit card company and some other organization such as an airline, a charity, or a store. When you use the card, you build up points, dollars, or miles toward a reward. Many affinity cards carry an annual fee.

Gold and platinum cards offer higher credit limits along with other benefits. They also have higher annual fees. But some of the benefits, such as warranty services and car rental insurance, might more than offset the annual fee.

Head of the Class

Is Your Reward Worth the Price?

Consider how much you charge on your card to be sure the reward is greater than the annual fee. If your affinity airline miles are worth two cents each, you need to charge at least $3,250 a year to cover a $65 annual fee.

Warranty services can include purchase replacement if something breaks in the first 90 days, warranty registration, extended warranty protection, and extended service agreements. With warranty registration, the credit card company keeps track of all your product warranties so you have to make only one telephone call to arrange for repair. When you purchase with a gold card, the card company will offer warranty coverage beyond the manufacturer's warranty.

When you use a gold card to rent a car, the credit card provides secondary insurance coverage for collision and theft. Even if your regular auto insurance doesn't cover rentals, you won't have to pay the exorbitant rates that the car rental companies charge.

In addition, premium cards offer travel and emergency services that help when things go wrong when you are away from home.

Did You Know?

Credit Cards Offer Online Protection

You should check out a Web site for security and privacy policies before you fork over a credit card number. But credit cards offer more protection than other forms of payment. Usually, you are responsible for only the first $50 charged on a stolen card. In addition, you can dispute charges in case of fraud, damaged merchandise, or other problems. When you dispute charges, you don't have to pay the charge unless the dispute is settled. Even better, the credit card companies help you resolve the dispute.

Finding Cards with the Features You Want

The Internet has made it easy to find the card that's right for you. With BankRate.com's credit card page (http://www.bankrate.com/brm/rate/cc_home.asp), you can search for cards with different features. If you maintain a balance, you can search for the best overall credit rate. If you are trying to move your balance to a lower-rate card, search for cards with the lowest intro rates. Maybe you want the best credit card deal for frequent fliers, the lowest rates after the intro expires, the best gold card deals, or the best platinum card deals. You can search by all those features.

Don't Just Throw an Unused Card in a Drawer

If you decide to stop using a card, write to the credit card company and cancel the account. Unless you do that, the account stays open and visible on your credit report. The card number is still vulnerable to theft and the credit limit still affects your ability to get a loan or mortgage.

Just click the link for the feature you want and BankRate.com displays the main information for the credit cards with the best deal, as shown in Figure 6.1. You can see several factors at a glance:

➤ If the card has an intro rate and how long it lasts

➤ Whether you can transfer your existing balance or only make new purchases

➤ The rate after the intro and whether it is fixed or variable

➤ The index if the rate is variable

➤ The margin interest rate

➤ The annual fee

➤ Where the card is available

APR Lets You Compare Apples to Apples

APR stands for the *annual percentage rate*. The APR is a standard measure that you can use to compare interest rates from credit card to credit card.

In addition, BankRate.com shows the annual cost for the card assuming a $2,000 balance for the year.

If you want to find the lowest APR, the best cash-back card, the longest grace period, or the best deals on cards with no annual fees, go to Quicken.com (www.quicken .com/banking_and_credit/bankrates). Select the feature from the drop-down list and Quicken.com displays the APR, the annual fee, and the grace period, as shown in Figure 6.2. To see more information about the card, click the **Details** link.

Figure 6.1

Search BankRate.com's site for exactly the credit card you want.

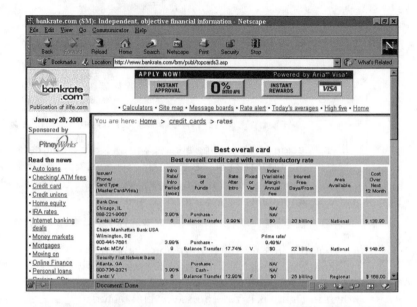

Figure 6.2

With Quicken.com, you also can find the best deals on cards including APR, grace period, no annual fees, and many other features.

Click **Details** to find out more about the card, including the bank that offers it.

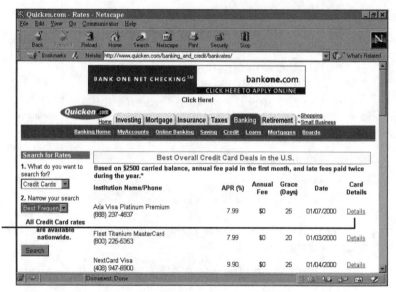

Online Credit Card Transactions

Credit cards vary greatly on what you can do online. Most credit card companies have a Web site where you can apply online, but some don't. Others let you see your transactions online. And a few let you download your transactions to your computer.

Applying Online

Online credit card applications aren't very different from online bank account applications. But you can apply online in a couple of different ways. After you find a card that you like, go to its Web site and see whether it has an online application. As an alternative, you can use an online financial services company such as LendingTree.com.

Unfortunately, neither BankRate.com nor Quicken.com provides links to the cards that appear in the list of best deals. If you want to try to apply for one of those cards online, find out which bank offers the card. On the Quicken.com list, clicking the **Details** link shows you more information about the card including the bank. Then, enter the name of the bank in your browser's search, as shown in Figure 6.3.

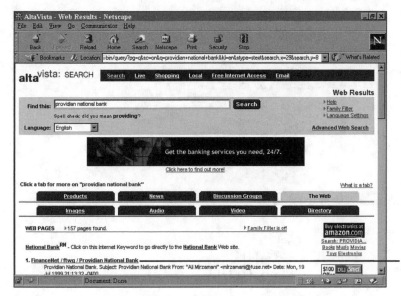

Figure 6.3

You can use a search engine to find the bank that offers the credit card that you want.

The first link might not be what you are looking for.

Tool Tips

Find the Right Link

Search engines on the Internet can bring back some links that seem like strange connections to your search words. Sometimes, you might have to scroll down to find the link you really want. Read the link descriptions to get an idea whether it's what you want.

Using the AltaVista search engine (www.altavista.com), the Providian National Web site doesn't appear until result number nine. But result ten actually takes you to Providian's credit cards. After you get to the bank's Web site, look for its online credit application. Providian National makes it easy to find. From its home page, just click the link **Apply for instant credit now**. Figure 6.4 shows one page of Providian National's online application. Fill out the application by entering your information or selecting from options.

Figure 6.4

Enter your information and select the options you want and you're on your way to getting a new credit card.

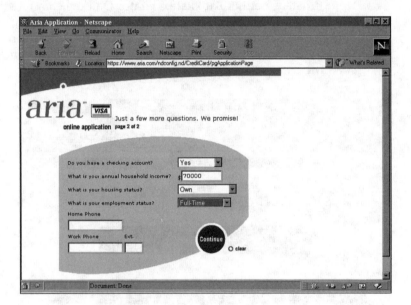

It's Not Over Until You Submit

When you fill out applications online, nothing really happens until you click **Submit** at the end. If you decide that you don't want to complete an application, just leave the Web page or end your Internet connection. But if you really want to apply, be sure to click **Submit** before you go on to something else. It's always a good idea to print your application before you submit it.

Although you apply online, many cards still process your application the old-fashioned way—sending a paper copy of your application to someone to review and decline or approve. A few cards offer instant credit approval, which means that the lender processes your application electronically.

Lending Brokers Can Get You Multiple Offers with One Application

Another way to apply for a credit card is with an institution such as LendingTree (www.lenderstree.com). When you apply with a broker such as LendingTree, your application goes to multiple lenders around the country. Then, you receive offers from those lenders and can choose which one you want.

Other Transactions

Some cards are more "online" than others. Although the list grows daily, the most wired credit cards come from Bank of America, Discover, American Express, NextCard, and ATT Universal.

With these cards, you can do a lot more than apply online. Depending on the card, you can get instant credit approval, view your account, pay bills online, check your rewards, receive online discounts or promotions, and even download your transactions into your personal finance software. Several online credit cards also offer online guarantees, protecting you from any fraud that might occur when you shop online.

Crash Alert

Don't Be Fooled by Bogus Online Credit Card Offers

There are bogus credit card offers online. Don't respond to offers that require a fee up front and request that you send your financial information to them via email.

The NextCard might be the best example of online services. You can check your account balance as shown in Figure 6.5, sort your transactions, design customized reports, and pay your bill online. You can set up email alerts to notify you when there is activity on your card. To start saving immediately when you get a lower-rate card, you can transfer balances online. NextCard offers shopping discounts when you shop on the Web. When you receive your online statement, you get discounts based on your buying trends. Plus, you can redeem your rewards online. You can categorize your purchases for tax reporting. And you can download your transactions into Quicken or Microsoft Money.

Figure 6.5

Online cards enable you to get your account balance, check transactions, pay your bill, and perform other tasks online. In addition, you can get discounts and rewards for using your card to purchase online.

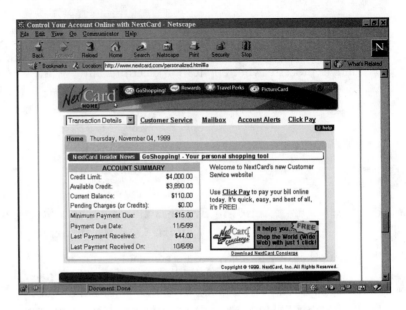

Credit Reports Online

Credit reports include information about you and your credit history that might indicate your level of credit risk: date of birth, address, jobs you have held, outstanding loans, open credit card accounts, credit limits, and payment history.

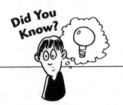

Did You Know?

Keep Tabs on Your Credit Report with All Three Major Credit Reporting Bureaus

Equifax, Experian, and Trans Union are the three major credit reporting bureaus. Your credit report might not be the same for each. From time to time, check your report with each bureau to make sure they are accurate.

A Good Credit Report Goes a Long Way

Lenders and other institutions might check your credit report before offering you a loan, a credit card, a lease on an apartment, a life insurance policy, and even a job offer. So, it pays to keep your report healthy and accurate.

Healthy credit reports are those showing a steady job and address along with reasonably good payment histories. Sickly credit reports include bankruptcies, liens on your property, being sued for money owed, a lot of credit cards, high credit limits, or a lot of recent applications for credit.

Checking In on Your Credit

The federal Fair Credit Reporting Act helps keep your credit report accurate and private. You can request a credit report at no charge if you have been denied credit, insurance, or other items within the past 60 days because of something on your report. The company that turns you down must tell you which bureau furnished the report.

You also can get one free report each year if you are unemployed and seeking employment, on welfare, or your report is inaccurate because of fraud. Otherwise, the credit bureau can charge up to $8 for a copy of your report. You can get a free copy of your credit report if you live in Colorado, Georgia, Maryland, Massachusetts, New Jersey, and Vermont—but only if you order by telephone or mail.

You can write or call any of the credit bureaus to receive a copy of your credit report. But you

Your Credit History Might Look Better Than You Thought

Negative information can remain on your report for only seven years. But bankruptcies stay on for 10 years. Many smaller companies don't report your little mistakes to the bureaus.

also can go to their Web sites. You enter the information they request and submit your request, as in Figure 6.6. The credit bureau verifies your request, mails you a copy of your report, and charges your credit card for the fee if applicable.

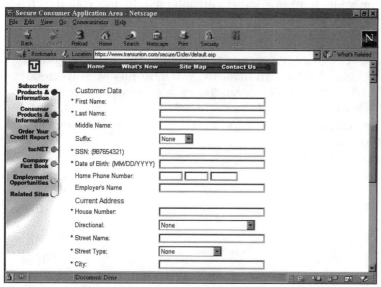

Figure 6.6

Fill out a form online to request a copy of your credit report.

Some Web sites have links offering free credit reports. The credit reports are free, but beware! You might end up subscribed to a credit monitoring service or some other service you don't want. The first few months of the service are free, but then the charges show up on your credit card.

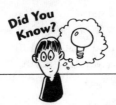

> **Did You Know?**
>
> ## Credit Bureaus Might Be the Cause of All Those Credit Offers in Your Mailbox
>
> The credit bureaus sell your name to creditors and insurers who then send you offers for credit or insurance. By calling the 800 number included on those offers, you can get off the list for two years. To get off the list forever, you must request a form for that purpose from the credit bureau and return it to them completed.

Fixing Your Credit Report When It's Wrong

Because negative information stays on your report for seven years, you do want to correct mistakes on your credit report. Correcting your report is a paper process and can range from simple to your worst nightmare. It's best to keep copies of all correspondence from the beginning just in case.

When you find errors on your report, mark them up and mail the report to the credit bureau. Federal law gives the credit bureau and the creditor 30 days to resolve any issues and they must remove any information that they cannot confirm.

Unfortunately, sometimes the credit bureau and the creditor insist that the information is correct and you think it's wrong. In that case, you must fill out a dispute form. After your report is correct, ask the credit bureau to send a copy of the corrected report to anyone who has requested information in the last six months, potential employers who have inquired in the last two years, and any smaller credit bureaus that they sell information to.

The Least You Need to Know

➤ Pick a card with no annual fee and a long grace period if you pay your balance each month. Pick the lowest interest rate if you maintain a balance.

➤ Keep no more than two credit cards—one for convenience that you pay off each month and one with a low interest rate for purchases you pay for over time. Lots of credit cards look bad on your credit report and might be stolen.

➤ Check the small print on your credit card disclosures when they arrive to make sure that the features you want are still there.

➤ You can search for a credit card on the Web based on the feature you want the most.

➤ A few online credit cards offer online account maintenance and discounts for using your card to purchase on the Web.

➤ You can request a copy of your credit report online. Even if there is a charge for the report, it is good to check your report for accuracy from time to time.

Chapter 7

Using Other People's Money

In This Chapter

➤ Learning the pros and cons of the different mortgage options today

➤ Using online mortgage calculators to find out your monthly payment or total interest

➤ Using the Web to get information on loans and applying online

➤ Searching online for the best mortgage rate

➤ Finding loans with terms you can live with

➤ Using the Internet to shop for houses and cars

Unlike credit card balances, mortgages and loans can be a smart financial move. Using other people's money (or a bank's), you can purchase a house today and pay for it over 30 years. You can even deduct on your tax return the interest you pay. The value of your home usually increases substantially. And you pay the bank off with dollars that gradually lose their value.

But because of the amount that you borrow, a small difference in an interest rate can mean a lot in interest payments. Between an 8% and 7.75% interest rate, the difference in interest paid over the life of a $160,000 mortgage is just less than $10,000. So, shop carefully for your house and your mortgage.

You can find information and tools on the Web to help you with your purchase from start to finish. You can learn more about the area you want to live in, or the car you want to drive. You can search for the exact car you want to buy and get quotes online. Or search for houses that meet your criteria. Whether you want a great rate or a lender willing to overlook some issues in your credit history, this chapter can be your online guide.

Choosing the Right Loan

The 30-year mortgage used to be your only choice. Now, there is a host of different features to choose from with a dizzying number of different interest rates and fees. These additional choices can be to your advantage if you choose wisely. Check out these loan types to see which features might be right for you.

Fixed-rate Mortgages

Fixed-rate mortgages have a set interest rate for the life of the loan, no matter what inflation or other interest rates do. You can count on your mortgage payment staying the same until your house is paid off. If interest rates drop, you can always refinance at a lower rate. Fixed-rate mortgages are a good deal when their rates are close to the regular rate for adjustable-rate mortgages (not an introductory teaser rate, which is explained later).

Fixed-rate mortgages make the most sense for people whose income won't increase, such as retirees, or when interest rates are particularly low. If you don't like the idea of your mortgage payment changing, or you couldn't afford a higher payment, then a fixed-rate mortgage is for you.

Adjustable-rate Mortgages

With *adjustable-rate mortgages (ARMs)*, the interest rate and your monthly payment change along with interest rates overall. Because some of the risk from interest rates rising falls on you, the interest rates on adjustable-rate mortgages are lower than fixed-rate mortgages—sometimes two or three percentage points lower. As long as you feel comfortable that inflation will stay controlled, ARMs are cheaper than fixed-rate mortgages.

Did You Know?

Skip the Multilist Books; Search for the Right House on the Web

Using sites on the Web, you can look for houses in the area you want. These real estate sites can search for a house by price, square footage, and number of bedrooms, bathrooms, or car spaces. You can limit your search to a county, city, or even a street. Searching the database retrieves the houses that meet your criteria. Clicking the link for the house displays more detailed information as well as pictures and maps if they are available. For a more complete discussion of online real estate, see Matthew O'Brien's *The Complete Idiot's Guide to Online Buying and Selling a Home.*

ARMs are good for folks who need a lower payment initially or for those who plan to own their house for only a few years. However, make sure that you can afford the higher payment if interest rates do go up, even if only for a year or two. Adjustable-rate mortgages have a lot of features to compare:

➤ Index

➤ Teaser rates

➤ Per-adjustment cap

➤ Lifetime cap

➤ Rate adjustment period

➤ Payment adjustment period

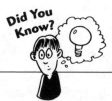

Hold onto Your Hat! Rates Have Been Going Up

The Federal Reserve Board has bumped up interest rates several times in the recent past. And Alan Greenspan has implied that more rate hikes are in store. As interest rates go up, the rates on all new mortgages go up. But with ARMs, your payment on an existing mortgage goes up, too! Even though your payment might increase over the next year or two, you might still choose an ARM if you think these rate increases won't last too long.

The adjustable-rate changes when the index it is linked to changes. The interest rate on an ARM will be the rate on its linked index, plus some additional amount called the *margin*. For example, if your ARM is linked to the six-month T-bill with a margin of 2.5%, and the six-month T-bill rate is 5.1%, your ARM rate is 7.6%.

Many ARMs offer an introductory rate discounted from the loan's normal rate. Sometimes these discounts can be as much as 3% less. Before you take the plunge with a great *teaser* rate, make sure you can afford the monthly payment when the ARM reverts to its normal rate.

ARMs might have a cap at each adjustment—a maximum change in the interest rate at any one time. For instance, if an ARM has a per-adjustment cap of 1%, then the rate can increase only 1% at a time if rates are going up quickly. But it can go down only 1% at a time, if rates drop quickly.

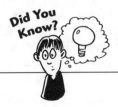

ARMs with an Index That Changes Frequently Might Cost the Least

Treasury bill rates change frequently, so rates on ARMs linked to Treasury bills will change frequently as well. Over a cycle of interest rates rising and falling, you are better off with an ARM that follows interest rate changes quickly.

In addition, ARMs can have a lifetime cap—the maximum increase or decrease in the interest rate over the life of the loan. If your ARM starts at 6% and has a lifetime cap of 4%, the rate can go no higher than 10% or drop below 2% no matter what the linked index does.

The *rate adjustment period* is the length of time between adjustments. The shorter the rate adjustment period, the lower your initial interest rate (and the margin over the index) will be. Be sure that the payment adjusts whenever the rate adjusts. You don't want to keep a high payment after your rate adjusts downward!

Hybrid ARMs Offer a Combination of Fixed-rate and Adjustable-rate Benefits

Hybrid ARMs, also called *delayed-first-adjustment ARMs*, include a period in which the interest rate is fixed, typically three, five, seven, or ten years. For the remainder of the loan, the hybrid ARM reverts to a one-year adjustable rate.

Balloon Mortgages

Balloon mortgages offer a low fixed interest rate for a period of time, such as three, five, seven, or ten years. When the time is up, the entire loan comes due. Commercial lenders might refinance your loan if interest rates haven't risen drastically, and you've paid on time.

Balloons make sense for people who are certain that they will relocate or buy another house before the loan comes due. You can make the balloon payment with the proceeds from selling your house. However, there's an element of risk involved here; if your home decreases in value, you might not be able to meet the balloon payment with the proceeds, or you could have less left over than you'd planned.

Be Sure You Can Afford an ARM When Rates Go Up

Check what the monthly payment would be if the ARM hit its lifetime maximum. If you don't think you could pay that monthly payment at the earliest point that the ARM reached its cap, look for an ARM with a lower lifetime cap or with longer adjustment periods. For example, a one-year ARM that starts at 6% with a 2% per-adjustment cap and a 6% lifetime cap could reach 12% as quickly as three years out. The monthly payment on a $150,000 mortgage would go from $899.33 to $1,542.92.

Other Important Mortgage Features

The lender charges you *points* up front for the privilege of paying a ton in interest. One point is 1% of the loan amount. The more points you pay up front, the lower your interest rate. So, if you plan to stay in your house for at least five years, pay the points up front and save on interest down the road. Less than five years, you are better off with a higher rate and fewer up-front fees. Lenders might offer to roll the points into your mortgage amount. Although doing so reduces your out-of-pocket costs when you buy, you pay a lot in interest on that money down the road.

Lock-ins guarantee the rate and points offered when you apply. If rates are falling, you are better off letting your commitment float. If rates are rising, pay the extra fee to lock in the initial rate. Some lenders offer lock-ins that protect you from higher rates, while passing on lower rates to you.

Low-documentation Loans Don't Check You Out as Much

Lenders might offer low-documentation loans, which close quickly with very little review of your finances—employment, income, and debt. You pay a higher interest rate and must have a good-looking credit history. Low-documentation loans make sense for people with variable income, the self-employed, or those with a high debt load. But the down payment can be as much as 30%.

With prequalification, a lender quickly reviews your finances and sets an amount that you can borrow. Prequalification protects you from paying an application fee only to find out that you can't afford the house. Prequalified borrowers might have an advantage bidding for a house because the seller knows that the borrowers can get the loan. In any case, prequalification makes a lot of sense because you know exactly what you can afford, and the seller knows you can close the deal faster.

Avoid any mortgage with a prepayment penalty. Things happen. You want to be able to pay off your mortgage early without having to pay a penalty. Indeed, as pointed out elsewhere, paying down your loan early is a huge advantage—you save in interest and accrue equity faster.

Payment Calculators

Lenders have guidelines that they use to determine how much money they will loan you. However, you might not want the monthly payment that their loan limit gives you. In addition, you should check how the monthly payment would change if you are considering an adjustable-rate mortgage.

Payment calculators can give you an idea of how much you will pay each month as well as what you will pay over the life of the loan. HSH Associates' payment calculator (`http://www.hsh.com/calc-amort.html`), shown in Figure 7.1, is a classic. It not only calculates your monthly payment, but also can show you the effects of prepaying your mortgage. You enter the amount of your loan, the interest rate, the length of the loan in years, and the starting month and year. The calculator shows you the monthly payment, the total interest over the life of the loan, and the interest for the next two years. If you ask to see the full amortization table, the calculator will show you how much interest and principal you will pay each month of the loan.

Figure 7.1

HSH Associates provides a payment calculator that can show you the monthly payment, total interest, the effects of prepayment, and much more.

If you enter prepayment information, you can see how much you would save.

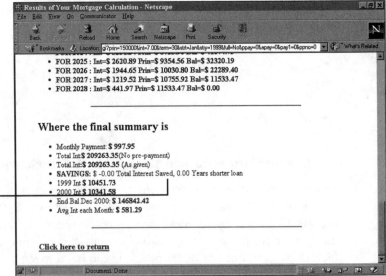

The HSH calculator also can help if you are considering prepaying your mortgage. For instance, let's say that you want the mortgage paid off when you retire. You can enter a monthly prepayment amount, an annual prepayment amount, or a one-time prepayment. The calculator results include your total interest without prepayment, total interest with prepayment, your total interest saved, and how much shorter the loan would be.

Finding Great Rates

Interest rates, terms, and fees can vary widely from lender to lender. In the past, people used to get their loans from their local bank because it was just too hard to find better deals. The Web makes it easy to find a great deal on a mortgage. And, in some cases, you can even apply online!

HSH Associates (www.hsh.com) and the Quicken.com Loan Center (www.quickenloans.quicken.com) are two sites that are tough to beat. HSH Associates is a publisher of mortgage and consumer loan information. The HSH site includes a lot of educational material, information on rates, statistics on indexes, and links to lenders by area. When you're ready to pick a mortgage, HSH sells a homebuyer's kit with complete data on loans in your area. Because HSH doesn't sell your name or banner ads, the site is fast, your name is protected, and data is comprehensive.

The Quicken.com Mortgage Center can show you mortgages from its participating lenders. You can see mortgages based on your zip code, the value of the house, the loan amount, the type of mortgage, and the points you are willing to pay, as Figure 7.2 shows.

If you really like to shop, check out the loans available from several sites. Other Web sites that link you to lenders include

➤ BestRate—www.bestrate.com

➤ RateNet—www.rate.net

➤ OnMortgage—www.onmortgage.com

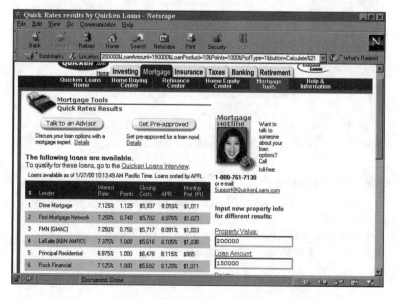

Figure 7.2

At Quicken.com, you can find rates, prequalify, and apply for mortgages from participating lenders.

Searching for the Right Mortgage

On Quicken.com, you can answer questions in a more complete loan interview to search for and prequalify for a loan. The interview includes questions about the house: the value, location, and use. You provide information on your income, debts, and credit history. Quicken.com suggests the type of mortgage that you might want to start with, but you can specify a fixed-rate, adjustable-rate, or balloon mortgage. You finish the interview by specifying a loan term, the points you are willing to pay, and whether the lowest rate or lowest monthly payment is important.

If you are concerned about the privacy of your financial information—and you should be—you can read all about Quicken.com's security and privacy policies at `quickenloans.quicken.com/Help/security.asp`. When you complete an online interview, Quicken.com sends your data to the lender of your choice only when you ask them to. The lenders use your information only as you specify. Intuit does not sell, share, or provide your name and personal information to third parties.

Quicken.com displays the loan that best fits your criteria. However, you can view the list of all loans that you are prequalified for, as shown in Figure 7.3. You can sort the list by interest rate, points, Effective Rate, APR, or monthly payment. You also can sort by loan type, closing costs including points, and average days to close.

Figure 7.3

By filling out a loan interview, Quicken.com can prequalify you for the loans that best meet your needs.

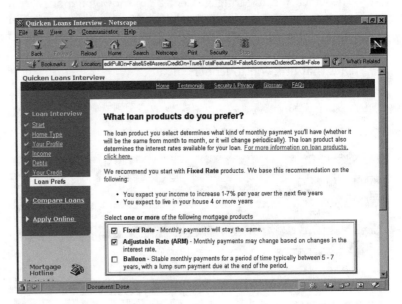

Checking the Other Features

When you compare different mortgages, look at the *annual percentage rate (APR)* instead of the interest rate. The APR takes into account the amount you are borrowing, the length of the loan, and the points. The APR shows the cost of the mortgage as a rate per year so that you can compare loans with different interest rates, points, and terms.

Quicken.com's Effective Rate Might Be a Better Measure Than the APR

Quicken.com also provides the Effective Rate for each mortgage. The *Effective Rate* is similar to the APR, but it also considers how long you expect to keep your mortgage. For example, a loan with a low interest rate and high up-front points will have a much higher Effective Rate if you plan to stay in the house for only two years.

After you find a loan that looks good, you can look at complete information about the loan, including a breakdown of all the fees that make up the closing costs. When you have settled on a loan, just click the link **Apply Online** to apply for the loan. You have to add only a bit more information to what you provided for the online prequalification.

An Online Application Commits You to Fees Just Like a Paper Application

When you apply online, you will still have to pay the application fee—unless you cancel your online application within 24 hours.

Auto Loans on the Web

Auto loans and other personal loans are a lot simpler than mortgages. Your only choice is how many years you want to take to pay off your car. Auto loan terms are usually three, four, or five years.

BankRate.com (www.bankrate.com/brm/rate/auto_ratehome.asp) can show you the rates for auto loans in your area. Its list includes any fees that the lender charges, or discounts if you use automatic debit. You can click the lender names that display as a hyperlink to go to their Web sites.

Get Online to Find Your New Car, as Well as How Much Your Old One Is Worth

Whether you're researching a new or used car to purchase, or trying to find out what you can sell your current car for, CarPoint (`carpoint.msn.com/home/New.asp`) can give you the lowdown. You can find the latest trade-in values, car reviews, invoice prices, rebates, recall history, and repair costs. If you research a new car on CarPoint, you can enter exactly the features you want, and get quotes from dealers near you.

Finding a Loan When Your Credit History Is Bad

Getting a mortgage or auto loan with a bad credit history isn't impossible—it's just different. You can get an idea of your credit rating with an online credit calculator. HSH Associates has a credit grade calculator (`www.hsh.com/credscorecalc.html`), shown in Figure 7.4, that asks a few questions and gives you a score. You tell the calculator how many late payments you have had and how late they were, plus some other indicators such as personal bankruptcy, foreclosures, and creditor judgments. As you pick options in the calculator, it displays your credit grade.

Figure 7.4

Use HSH Associates' credit grade calculator to find out whether you need to look at loans for those with impaired credit.

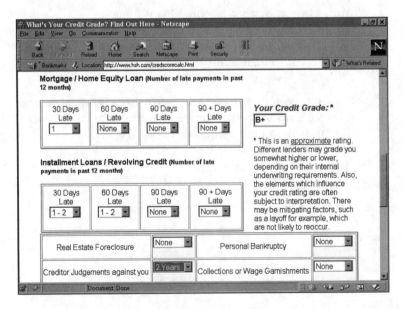

If you find that your credit grade is B, C, or D, you can go to HSH's Impaired Credit Showcase to see lenders that work with borrowers with lousy credit histories. In general, you will have to call the lenders for quotes on these mortgages, because the rates will depend on your individual circumstances. The Impaired Credit Showcase is a much safer solution to finding a loan when your credit history is lacking. You might see ads online that promise to loan money to those with bad—or no—credit. That might be true, but the high rates that they charge probably won't help you improve your credit history.

The Least You Need to Know

➤ Fixed-rate mortgages provide the security of a fixed monthly payment for the life of the loan. They are best when rates are low.

➤ Adjustable-rate mortgages offer lower initial rates, because you carry some of the risk if rates go up. Look at ARMs with a lifetime rate cap that you can live with.

➤ Paying points up-front lowers the interest rate you pay on the loan. If you plan to keep the mortgage for only a few years, you are better off with fewer points and a higher interest rate.

➤ Payment calculators can tell you how much your monthly payment will be, how much interest you will pay, and how prepayments will affect your loan.

➤ Mortgage Web sites can show you mortgages that are available for your criteria, compare mortgages by different features, prequalify you for a loan, and provide access to online applications from lenders.

➤ Use an online credit grade calculator to find out whether you have to get an impaired credit mortgage.

Chapter 8

Protecting Your Money

In This Chapter

➤ Finding sites on the Web where you can learn everything you need to know about insurance

➤ Using online insurance calculators to figure out how much insurance you need

➤ Comparing insurance quotes online

➤ Searching for brokers, agents, and insurance companies online

With insurance of all types, you pay a premium up-front so that the insurance company foots the bill in case something bad happens later. Sometimes it seems silly to pay those premiums year after year, when everything is fine and you keep finding four-leaf clovers. But get caught without insurance coverage when disaster does strike, and all the hard work on your finances could literally go up in smoke.

When you buy insurance, get only as much coverage as you need. And pay as little as possible for that coverage. Insurance agents, particularly independent agents, can help you figure out what coverage you need and get quotes. But the Internet is the place to go to do your homework. The more you know about insurance, the better your coverage and the lower your premiums.

What Insurance Do You Need?

Insurance has gotten complicated over the years—but good coverage doesn't have to be. The basics of your insurance needs are quite simple.

Learning More About Insurance

If you want to start at the beginning, Quicken Insurance (www.insuremarket.com/tools/tools.htm) includes a series of Web pages that explain the basics about almost every kind of insurance there is: auto, home, life, disability, long-term care, and health. Quicken Insurance also explains other types of insurance including annuities, business continuation, and umbrella liability.

For a site that provides links to everything about insurance, click **Personal Finance** on the InvestorGuide home page (www.investorguide.com) and then click **Insurance** to go to Investor Guide's Insurance section, shown in Figure 8.1. Another link, www.investorguide.com/Insurance.htm#allpurpose, takes you to a list of links for insurance information. The easy-to-navigate Investor Guide's Insurance site points you to several good overall insurance sites, online quotes, online purchases, company ratings, insurance calculators, and more. The Consumer Insurance Guide (www.insure.com) site provides news and a ton of hints on being a smart insurance consumer.

Figure 8.1

Investor Guide's Insurance section can take you to sites to learn about insurance, calculate your coverage needs, compare prices, ratings, and even buy insurance online.

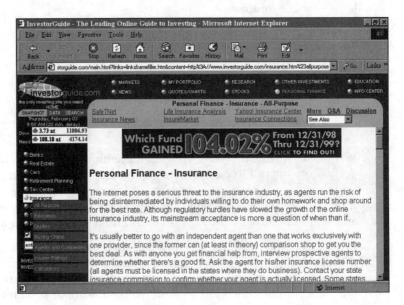

Life Insurance: A Gift from You to Your Loved Ones

Life insurance is all about providing for others after you're gone. If you don't have a spouse or kids who need your financial support, don't buy life insurance. Period. You're better off using the money for disability insurance.

Singles with dependents might need life insurance if their ex doesn't provide for the kids. Spouses who don't work might need life insurance, if only to cover the cost of childcare. The working spouse of a one-income couple without children should probably have life insurance. Double-income couples with no kids need only enough coverage to keep the surviving spouse out of financial trouble—say, to pay off a big house mortgage. Married folks with kids need insurance, and a lot of it.

If you do need life insurance, nine times out of ten, term life insurance is the way to go. Term life insurance is nothing but a payoff when you die. The premiums go completely toward your insurance coverage, so they are pretty reasonable. The cost increases as you get older, but, for most, you won't need life insurance after you hit 60 or so.

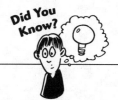

Do You Need Life Insurance at All?

If you have no dependents, you really don't need life insurance. That includes kids, college students, young singles without kids, and older folks whose kids are out on their own.

What About Cash-value Insurance Such as Whole Life or Universal Life?

Cash-value life insurance provides life insurance coverage along with some form of savings or investment option. The premiums are high, but tend to stay the same as you get older. The money beyond what's needed for the insurance premium, and the agent's commission, goes into tax-deferred savings or investments. As the savings build up, they might eventually pay for your annual premium, so you can easily keep a cash-value policy into your old age—if you need to! Most people are better off with the cheaper, simpler term coverage.

With a term life insurance policy, the insurance company has to do only one thing—pay out to your beneficiaries when you die. You want an insurance company with a good rating, because they have to stay in business long enough to pay off on your policy. Otherwise, get the absolute cheapest premium you can find.

Head of the Class

Don't Take Risks with Insurance Companies

You buy insurance to protect yourself from risks. Don't let an insurance company with a low rating for financial health add to your risks. Insurance companies can and do go bankrupt when hit with lots of claims, as happened when Hurricane Andrew blew through Florida in 1992. A good rating means that the company has sufficient financial resources to cover unexpectedly high claims—although insurance benefits are not guaranteed. A.M. Best and Standard & Poor's are two of the services that rate insurance companies. A.M. Best ratings go from a low of F to an A++ for highest. A rating of B or lower is considered vulnerable.

The annual premium for a term policy that starts at $200 could be several thousand when you hit 60. You can buy a term policy with premiums that don't change for a period of time, such as 10 or 20 years. Of course, the premium is higher than you would pay for vanilla term insurance the first couple of years, but over the life of the policy, you actually pay less.

Don't Get Sick Over Your Medical Bills

Whether you get health insurance through work, or pay for yourself, the cost of medical care—and health insurance—keeps going up. Unlike life insurance, health insurance is a must. Without it, your finances—and your life—are at risk. These days, the choices in health care amount to HMOs, preferred provider organizations (PPOs), and the almost extinct full-service plan.

HMOs take care of your every health need, often covering wellness and preventive medicine. With low premiums and very little paperwork, HMOs might seem like a dream come true. But, in HMOs, doctors get incentives to save money, which might not be in your best interest. In an HMO, you might have to be more persistent to get the tests and treatment you need. In addition, you're usually limited to seeing doctors within the HMO. When you see doctors outside the HMO, you might have to pay a much larger portion of the bill, if not all of it.

Crash Alert

Don't Go Without!

Health care is almost nonexistent for those without some form of insurance. If you can't afford coverage on your own, start by checking with organizations that you belong to for group insurance. Group insurance premiums often cost less. Take as large a deductible as you can afford to decrease your premium. Or see whether you can afford coverage in a health maintenance organization (HMO) plan. If you still can't make ends meet, consider getting coverage at least for major illnesses.

Head of the Class

Key Features for Your Health Insurance

If your policy covers 80% of costs, look for a policy with a cost ceiling. Otherwise, you could end up responsible for $200,000 on a million-dollar procedure. Also, look for policy maximums of $500,000 or $1,000,000. Service benefits are preferable to indemnity benefits. Whereas a service benefit covers a percentage of the cost, indemnity benefits pay a fixed dollar amount. And, with the way health-care costs are increasing, a fixed dollar amount might not go very far.

Preferred provider plans also can be cost effective. In these plans, you can see health-care providers in the preferred pool for a copayment or a small percentage of the cost. You also have the flexibility to see providers outside the plan. But you will pay perhaps 20% or 30% of the cost of the services.

Disability Insurance

Disability insurance protects your ability to earn a living. Before you say that you can't afford disability insurance, just imagine what your life would be like if you weren't able to work.

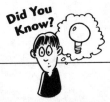

Did You Know?

More People Need Disability Insurance Than Need Life Insurance

Although many people have life insurance to protect their families in case they die, a lot of folks skip disability insurance. And yet, for people under 60, you stand a lot higher chance of becoming disabled than you do of dying.

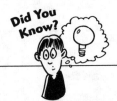

Did You Know?

Disability Insurance Doesn't Replace Your Income

Disability policies usually cover 60% to 70% of your income. If they covered 100%, the insurance companies fear that no one would want to go back to work.

Different policies define disability in different ways. The more expensive policies protect you if you cannot perform your occupation—a concert pianist who can no longer play the piano. Less expensive policies pay only if you can't work at all—if the fingers that can't tickle the ivories can hand out burgers at a fast-food joint, you aren't disabled! Check into *income replacement* coverage. It is less expensive than *own-occupation* coverage, but still replaces the same amount of income.

In addition, the riskier your job, the higher the disability premiums. Different insurance companies classify job risk differently, so you should find the insurer that rates your occupation the least risky.

Disability insurance also comes in two forms: short-term and long-term. *Short-term disability* kicks in quickly, but covers you only for a period of time, such as three or six months. *Long-term disability* doesn't start right away, but it will replace part of your income if you are disabled for a long time or permanently.

Be sure that you have the right to renew your policy every year, and that you would get benefits until you turn 65.

Auto Insurance

Auto insurance can include a lot of features. To keep your auto insurance affordable, it's important to get the features you need, and skip the ones you don't.

Bodily injury liability coverage pays medical costs, loss of earnings, and pain and suffering, if your car injures someone. This coverage is essential, because lawsuits are common, and the award dollars can be high. In fact, liability coverage is mandatory in most states. You should buy as much coverage as you can afford. First, you should be able to pay for the damage you cause. Second, if an uninsured driver hurts you, your liability coverage pays for your expenses.

Skip Short–term Disability Coverage If You've Got Solid Emergency Funds

If you've stashed three to six months' worth of emergency funds away, you don't really need short–term disability coverage. That is exactly what emergency funds are for!

Property damage liability coverage pays for damage to property, which is usually the other car. You should have enough to cover the cost of an average car.

Medical payments coverage pays medical bills or funeral expenses for anyone injured in your car. In general, health insurance pays most medical bills, so you can cut auto insurance expenses by purchasing only enough medical payments coverage to meet your health insurance deductible.

Personal-injury protection covers your own medical bills, funeral expenses, some lost wages, and replacement services. It's required coverage in no-fault states. But if you can use your health and disability insurance as your primary coverage for your own medical bills, you can reduce the amount of personal-injury protection.

Umbrella Liability Provides Even More Protection

If you have a lot of money, you might want to add *umbrella liability coverage*. Umbrella liability can either extend the dollar amount to a million dollars or more, or cover items not covered in a basic liability such as invasion of privacy or defamation of character.

If your car is new or is worth enough that replacing it would cramp your style, collision and comprehensive coverage is essential. Collision covers the cost of repairs to your car, whereas comprehensive covers miscellaneous damage to your car such as hail, fire, or vandalism. For example, you probably want collision coverage on a five-year-old, expensive car. The more expensive the car, usually the more expensive it is to repair. On the other hand, if your 1987 Toyota Tercel is worth only $500, there is little point paying for collision coverage. You can probably afford to pay for damages less than the deductible. If the damages are more than $500, you're better off buying another car.

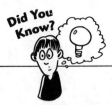

Protect Yourself from Others with Little or No Coverage

Some people skimp on or even forego liability coverage. Uninsured/underinsured motorist coverage protects you in these cases. Usually, the limits for your bodily injury liability and uninsured motorist coverage will be the same.

Home Insurance

Insurance on your home pays to replace your home and belongings when disaster strikes. Home insurance also pays for injury or damage to others that occurs on your premises.

You should insure your home for 100% of its replacement cost—what it would take to rebuild your house, not its current market value. Houses are rarely destroyed completely. But, with coverage for only 80% of the replacement cost, you're at risk for tens of thousands of dollars.

Coverage for other structures on your property, such as a doghouse for the in-laws, usually has a limit of about 10% of the replacement cost of your house. If you added an exercise room, complete with ballet bar and hardwood floors, to your detached garage, be sure to increase the coverage on your other structures.

Head of the Class

Document Your Belongings While You Have the Chance

To get reimbursed from your insurance company quickly and fully, documentation is key. A videotape or photographs of everything you own, with sales receipts for the pricier stuff, ensures that you remember what you had and shows what it's all worth. Keep the videotape, photos, and receipts in a safe deposit box, so your records aren't destroyed with the goods.

Personal property is a tough one. First, almost everyone puts off building an inventory of his or her stuff. So, you won't know what you have, and you have no idea how much it's worth. In general, the insurance company figures your personal property at about half the replacement cost of your home.

Coverage for valuables such as jewelry, silver, boats, guns, business property, and other items has limits on a standard policy. If your valuables exceed those limits, get separate coverage.

Get the Right Coverage for Your Stuff

Even if you don't have a great collection of black velvet paintings, get replacement-cost coverage for your belongings, if you can afford it. Regular coverage reimburses for only the current value of your things: clothes, furniture, whatever. The difference between the current value and what you will pay at the department store will overwhelm you.

Life Insurance Calculators

According to InvestorGuide, you should use more than one life insurance calculator to get an idea of how much life insurance you need. Some calculators make assumptions that don't apply to you, and others are built to sell you insurance.

The QuickenInsurance Family Needs Planner (`http://www.insuremarket.com/basics/life/Intro.fnp?SOURCE=SMART_FACT&FORM=INTRO`) steps you through questions about what your life insurance has to cover. You enter estimates for immediate expenses such as your funeral, the first few months of household bills, estate taxes, legal fees, and others. You also estimate items such as the mortgage, and your kids' college expenses. Then, to figure in ongoing expenses, the Planner asks about additional items based on your phase of life. For instance, if you are in the child-rearing phase, you estimate how much money your family needs each month after you're gone.

In the last step, you tell the Planner how much emergency cash and life insurance you have as well any retirement funds your family could use. When you're done, the Planner shows you the estimates you provided and an estimated amount of insurance, as shown in Figure 8.2. You can change any of your assumptions and recalculate your insurance needs.

Disability Calculators

To figure out how much disability insurance you need, go to the Life and Health Insurance Foundation for Education site. Try Life-line.org's disability calculator (`www.life-line.org/disability/index.html`), which asks for your current annual gross earned income, annual investment income, and how much of your income goes to pay expenses. Click **Analysis** to find out how much disability coverage you need.

Figure 8.2

QuickenInsurance Family Needs Planner steps you through calculating how much life insurance you really need based on your phase of life.

This shows that your session is secure.

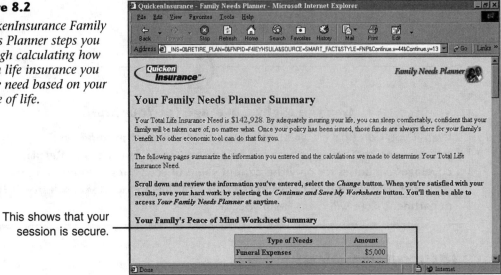

Finding Insurance on the Web

When it's time to buy insurance, the Internet can really help. You can get quotes, check company ratings, and in some places purchase a policy online.

Getting Quotes

In the past, getting quotes from different companies took a lot of time, and exposed you to the sales pitches of any number of insurance agents. With the Web, you have a lot more options.

Some sites provide links to numerous insurance-quote Web sites. You can answer one set of standard questions, and get quotes from a number of different insurance companies. Some sites provide quotes by mail; with some, an agent calls you in a few hours; and others provide instant quotes online. Even a few insurance companies, such as Progressive (www.progressive.com), offer online quotes along with quotes from some of its competitors.

By answering a half-dozen questions, Quotesmith (www.quotesmith.com) can provide life insurance quotes from more than 300 companies. The quotes also show you the companies' financial ratings, provide links to view the policy details, and enable you to request an application, as Figure 8.3 demonstrates.

It's always a good idea to read the details of the policies before making your final decision. For example, life insurance quotes shown on the Web might be the lowest, but available to those who meet the most stringent health criteria. If your cholesterol or blood pressure is high, or you have heart disease in your immediate family, the rates you get could look a lot different.

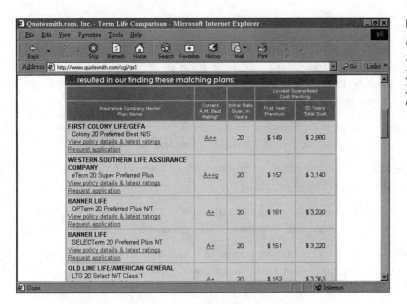

Figure 8.3

Quotesmith can provide instant quotes for most of your insurance needs after you answer a handful of questions.

Finding Insurance Companies on the Web

After you've found some good-looking quotes, you can check out the companies' financial ratings at the Consumer Insurance Guide site (`www.insure.com/ratings/index.html`). You can see ratings from Standard & Poor's or Duff and Phelps, and can specify what rating level you want to see. You can sort the companies by size or rating.

If you're looking for a particular insurance company, use the directories at the Insurance Industry Internet Network (`www.iiin.com`). You can find insurance companies on the Web, insurance brokers and agents, insurance-related resources, and even a job with an insurance company.

Buying Insurance Online

Legal issues currently limit our ability to buy insurance online. eHealthInsurance (`www.ehealthinsurance.com`) is beginning to sell health insurance throughout the United States. When you go to its site, enter your zip code to see whether it has made it to your state yet. Several companies sell auto insurance online, but it is available only in some states. Click the link **Buying Online** at InvestorGuide Insurance (`www.investorguide.com/Insurance.htm#buying`) to see who sells online.

The Least You Need to Know

➤ Buy life insurance only if someone else depends on your income, or would have to pay someone else for the things that you do. Term life insurance is simple, inexpensive, and effective.

➤ Health insurance is a must if you want treatment for your illnesses. If you can't afford even an HMO policy, at least get coverage for major illnesses.

➤ If you or your family couldn't make ends meet if you weren't working, you need disability insurance. No arguments!

➤ Liability coverage is the must-have of auto insurance. In addition, if your car has value, you want collision and comprehensive coverage.

➤ If you can afford it, replacement-cost coverage is the way to go with home insurance. The better your documentation of your house and belongings, the easier it will be to collect from the insurance company.

➤ Online insurance calculators can help you figure out what coverage you need as well as the amount. Try several calculators to be sure that you get just the right amount.

➤ You can get quotes, comparison shop, check company ratings, and find brokers, agents, and insurance companies on the Web. But online purchase is on the way slowly—as states and insurance companies work out the legal issues.

Chapter 9

Taxes

In This Chapter

➤ Finding out where on the Web you can learn more about taxes and the tax forms you need

➤ Downloading the tax forms you need

➤ Learning about different ways to file your taxes

➤ Reading up on antitax activities

The only thing worse than having to fork over your hard-earned cash to the government is filling out your tax return in the first place. The tax code is complicated. There are thousands of forms to choose from. And then, you still have to figure out what numbers to put where!

The Internet can provide some relief to the chore of doing your taxes. And you might even find some ways to save money on your taxes while you're at it. Check out some of the sites with tax information such as Excite's tax section (www.excite.com/money/taxes/) to learn more about your taxes and get free advice.

Quicken and TurboTax both provide a lot of educational information on taxes, if you are brave enough to do your taxes yourself.

Certified Public Accountants and other tax professionals can fill out your tax return, find deductions you might have missed, and file your return for you. Their work is only as fast and as good as the information you give them, so it pays to keep your paperwork organized. They do charge for their services, but you might discover that the deductions they find more than make up for the fee they charge.

Getting Tax Forms on the Web

Tired of going to the library or post office to get tax forms? You drive there only to find out they don't have the form you need—or you stand there and stare because you have no idea whether you need that form or not. You break down and grab one of each.

The Web at least solves these problems. You can find out what forms you need and then download them right to your computer.

Learning More About the Forms You Need

The IRS Web site doesn't tell you much about which forms you need. However, you can browse through the IRS publications online (www.irs.gov/forms_pubs/pubs/index.htm). Publication titles describe the tax situation that they discuss, such as "Moving Expense" or "Medical and Dental Expenses." Browse online or download these publications to learn about handling these situations on your tax return and which forms to use.

SaveWealth offers an educational site which is provided by The Preservation Group. It identifies the uses of different IRS forms, as shown in Figure 9.1. SaveWealth provides some other tips, such as which 1040 form you should use, 1999 tax changes, tax professionals and Certified Public Accountants in your area, and books on taxes.

Figure 9.1

SaveWealth tells you what you use each IRS form for, and provides advice and links to other sites about taxes.

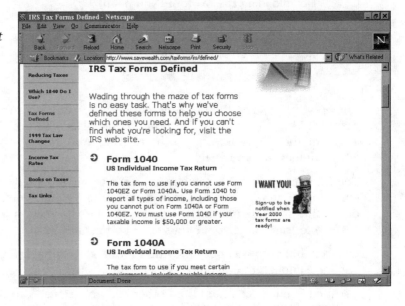

TurboTax from Intuit is a software package that helps you fill out your tax forms. Just as Quicken includes lots of financial advice, TurboTax explains taxes and tax forms to you. Some online brokerages offer TurboTax free to its customers, or, like E*Trade, offer a free copy if you open an IRA account with them.

Finding Forms

You can find your Federal income tax forms at the IRS's site, `www.irs.gov/forms_pubs/index.html`. For convenient one-stop shopping of both Federal and state forms, the State University of West Georgia hosts a site (`www.westga.edu/~library/depts/govdoc/tax.shtml`) with links for the IRS and state

> **Tool Tips**
>
> ### Use Quicken Categories to Figure Out Your Tax Forms
>
> Quicken attaches tax items to its ready-made categories. By looking at your Category & Transfer list in Quicken, you can see which forms you need when you use different categories.

Departments of Revenue. Its links include the pages where you can read about and download the IRS or state tax forms and instructions, as shown in Figure 9.2.

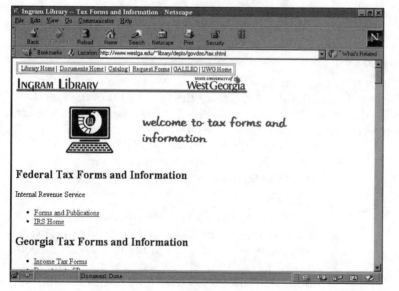

Figure 9.2

The State University of West Georgia provides links to the IRS and each state's Web site for tax forms.

Clicking **Internal Revenue Service Forms and Publications** takes you to an IRS page, shown in Figure 9.3, where you can download all the IRS forms and publications (in this case, `www.irs.ustreas.gov/prod/forms_pubs/`). Click **Forms and Instructions** to see the list of documents that you can download. If you have Adobe

Acrobat Reader on your computer (and you should, if you download files on the Web), select PDF as your file format. PCL and PostScript are printer formats that you use with third-party software.

Figure 9.3

The IRS provides down-loadable versions of all its tax forms, instructions, and publications on its Web site.

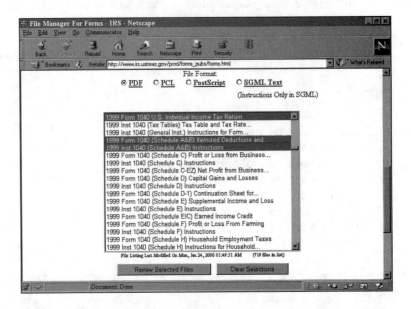

Downloading Forms

On the IRS site, click each form that you want to download. When you have all the forms that you want selected, click **Review Selected Files** to see a list of the files that you selected. To download a file, click the title. For a PDF file, the form displays in your browser. You can select **Save As** from the browser File menu to save the PDF file to your computer. In the Save As dialog box, be sure that the folder in which you want to save your tax forms displays in the Save In text box. Click **Save** to save the file.

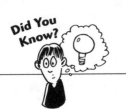

Save a Tree—Read Publications Online

Sometimes, you have to print out instructions and forms. But you can save a lot of paper (and money) by reading publications and instructions online and printing only what you need.

As a testament to the complexity of our tax code, there are more than 700 forms that you can download. Even with the forms in numeric and alphabetical order, it can sometimes take a while to find the form you want. If you need only one or two forms, it might be easier to use the search function on the IRS site. Click **Search for a Form or Publication** on the IRS Forms and Publication page (www.irs.ustreas.gov/prod/forms_pubs/). Then, enter the keyword or form number in the search text box and click **Search**. You can view and download the form you want by clicking its title in the list.

The Adobe Acrobat Reader Enables Everyone to Read Documents

PDF stands for the *Adobe Portable Document Format*. With this format, you see documents exactly as they were originally composed whether you download them from the Web or receive them via email or other sources. PDF files have built-in compression, so they are much smaller than the originals. The files work on most operating systems and are compatible with just about every printer. Using the Adobe Acrobat Reader you can view, print, and search PDF documents. Most sites that provide PDF documents for download also provide a link to download the Acrobat Reader, which is free. Or you can get it yourself from www.adobe.com.

Filing Taxes Electronically

The IRS offers several options for filing your taxes these days. Filing electronically has a lot of advantages. IRS e-file is available 24 hours a day, 7 days a week. The IRS e-file program gets you your refund in about half the time because the IRS processes electronic returns before paper ones.

Some People Don't Like the IRS

Not everyone quietly fills our their forms and pays the IRS. The Libertarian Party (www.lp.org) hosts a Tax Protest Day each year. Audit-proofing strategies on Uncle Fed's Tax Board (www.unclefed.com/Audit-Proofing/index.html) discusses different ways that people use to protest their taxes—as well as how effective they are. Meanwhile, search the news for **Tax Protest** or **Tax Reform** to follow the current demands for abolition or reform of the tax code as we know it—in this election year, you're sure to hear a lot.

In addition, when you file electronically, the IRS can catch errors on your forms when you submit your return, making sure your return is correct the first time and your refund gets to you as fast as possible. Electronic filing gives you proof within 48 hours that the IRS has accepted your return—no more penalties or interest because your paper return was lost in the mail.

Filing Using a Personal Computer

If you want to prepare and file your taxes online, the IRS provides a partial list of online filing companies (www.irs.gov/elec_svs/company.html). To use your personal computer to file your taxes, you need tax software on your computer. The IRS list provides phone numbers for the companies offering software for online filing. If you can obtain the software online, the list shows the Web site.

TurboTax is one of the most popular tax software packages. You can buy TurboTax and load it on your computer if you want to prepare your tax return offline, and file electronically. In addition, you can now use TurboTax for the Web to prepare your return online. You can import data from Quicken 2000 to your online session. With your username and password, you can log on as many times as you need to complete your return.

You also can pay your taxes electronically by credit card or direct debit from your checking or savings account. If you use direct deposit in conjunction with electronic filing, your refund arrives even faster.

You Can File Your Federal and State Returns Electronically, at the Same Time

Federal/state e-file will submit your federal and state returns at the same time. Available in all states through authorized e-file providers, taxpayers in some states can use Federal/state e-file when filing through their computers.

Filing by Telephone

The IRS TeleFile program is available to certain taxpayers who file fairly simple returns. People who receive a TeleFile booklet in the mail fill out the booklet and call a toll-free number to file. Using the touch-tone keypad, these taxpayers enter their tax information and file their return. With TeleFile, there are no forms to mail and no fees. You can find out whether you qualify by reading the TeleFile page on the IRS Web site (www.irs.gov/elec_svs/telefile.html).

Tax Professionals Can File Electronically for You

Whether you prepare your own return or have someone prepare it for you, authorized IRS e-file providers can electronically transmit your return for you.

130

The Least You Need to Know

➤ You can learn about the tax code and tax forms on the Internet.

➤ You can download tax forms, instructions, and publications for the IRS and every state.

➤ You can file your tax return electronically through an authorized provider, using software on your computer, or, in some cases, your telephone.

➤ Filing electronically is available 24 hours a day, 7 days a week; speeds up your refund; reduces mistakes; and gives you a confirmation that the IRS received your return within 48 hours.

Part 3
Saving for Your Dreams

Money doesn't grow on trees. You do have to save money to achieve your goals. Price-shopping on the Internet, online savings calculators, and Web sites with savings tricks or guides to college financial aid help you save the money that feeds the goose and keeps those golden eggs coming.

Saving Money

Saving money is the fuel that makes your financial plan go. To put money into savings or investments, you have to save money first! There's little point in getting 5% or 6% interest on savings if you are paying the 18% on that credit card balance.

Some of the money you save goes to emergency savings—easy to access and safe. Money saved for other goals goes into investments so that your money works with you. But first, you have to figure out how to save some of the money you make.

Nifty Tricks for Saving Money

You can save money in a lot of different ways. Some ways can save you a lot; some save just a little. And some of them are pretty painless! But, whether you save a lot or a little, each dollar you save gets you closer to your goals.

Payroll Deductions Make Saving Easy!

Use your company's payroll deductions to set aside the money before it even gets to your checking account. In addition to deductions for a 401(k) plan, look at setting up your paycheck so that part of your check goes into savings.

Painless Strategies for Saving a Lot

Saving money can be painfully simple and painlessly effective! You've heard it before. Pay yourself first! Transfer a fixed amount out of each paycheck (a fixed percentage if your income isn't steady) into your savings. You can set your budget up to work with the money left over after savings. But, truth be told, what you don't see in your checking account, you won't spend.

If your discipline is lacking when it comes time to write that check over to savings, try using automatic transfers. Your bank can set up regular transfers from your checking account into any account you use for your savings: your bank savings account, a money market fund, or even the cash account at your brokerage. Even better, many mutual funds bypass or reduce the initial deposit amount if you commit to a monthly purchase.

Saving Steadily Even When You're Income Isn't

When your paychecks vary in amount or in frequency, create your budget based on the lowest monthly amount you expect to make. In your flush months, you have that much extra to save. Plan to save a set percentage of each check instead of a fixed dollar amount. And set aside emergency funds for at least six months of expenses to cover more thin months than you anticipated.

Reinvesting all your dividends and interest hides that source of income from your spending temptation. Dividend reinvestment is one of the most dependable and financially rewarding techniques around. For example, if you could have invested $1,000 in the Standard & Poor's 500 index in 1926 and reinvested all your dividends through 1998, you would have $2,350,890. If you had spent your dividends, you would only have $963,600.

Guaranteed Big Saving Techniques

The bottom line on saving money is spending less than you make. It's as simple as living within your means. Even if you have solid-gold taste and a paper-thin income, you can still save money by eliminating the waste in your life.

When your wish list calls for big savings, you might as well start with the savings tactics with the biggest payoff. In case you weren't listening before, pay off your credit card debt.

Another potential savings jackpot is refinancing all your high-rate loans. Reducing your mortgage rate from 10% to 8% on a $160,000 mortgage would drop your monthly payment by almost $250! You would decrease the interest you paid over the life of a 30-year loan from $324,326 to $242,751.

If your car loan has a high rate, refinance it or consider using monthly savings to pay it off early. Keep the cars you buy for 10 years instead of selling when they're paid off. You can save hundreds of thousands of dollars over your lifetime on this alone. (Of course, you have to maintain your cars better while you own them if you want them to last.) You also can buy less expensive cars and forego any bells and whistles you don't need. You pay less on the car, less on insurance, and less on repairs because there isn't as much to break.

Insurance premiums add up. Price-shop every insurance policy you own. Increase your emergency funds and take higher deductibles. You can save hundreds of dollars each year.

If you like to vacation in places that have a high season and low season, like ski areas or the Caribbean, schedule your holiday right after the prices drop. A house on St. John in the Virgin Islands might cost $3,500 for a week between November 1 and April 15. But on April 16 you can rent that house for a week for $1,600. Participate in airline traveler programs. Free airfare can reduce the cost of a vacation by 50% or more.

Did You Know?

Include an Extra Principal Payment Each Month and Watch Your Mortgage Melt Away

You can save on interest, shorten the life of your mortgage, and build up equity in your house faster, just by sending an additional payment of principal with each mortgage payment. For example, if you pay an additional $50 in principal on a 30-year mortgage of $160,000 at 8%, you pay the mortgage off in 25 years instead of 30, and save $44,750 in interest.

Head of the Class

If You Smoke, Quit

Quitting smoking saves you money and trouble all the way around. You won't spend your money on cigarettes. You'll save money on insurance, doctors' bills, mouthwash, and tooth whitening. And you'll get to enjoy a longer, healthier retirement.

The Little Savings Add Up

You can always find ways to save a little more money. If you don't think the pennies count, just remember you need $100 in a good money market fund to earn $5 in interest each year. A good habit to get into is to always stop to ask yourself if you really need something before you buy it.

Here are some ideas for finding more cash for your dreams:

➤ Cook at home more often, and bring lunch to work. You'll save money and probably eat better.

➤ Join a discount club like Sam's or Costco. Buy what you need in bulk. Just make sure that you really need 40 pounds of pasta! On the other hand, don't buy a lot of something you don't use often just because it seems like a bargain.

➤ Shop at outlets. Always shop for clothes out-of-season: bathing suits in the fall, ski clothes in June.

➤ Try out the generic or store brands at your supermarket.

➤ Always buy from your shopping list unless you can use something that is on sale big time.

➤ Rent things you use occasionally, such as a chain saw or snow blower, instead of buying.

➤ Use your library instead of buying books (except this one, of course—I'm sure it'll pay for itself).

➤ Rent movies or borrow them from the library. You'll save on tickets and snacks.

Pennypinchers Online

After you learn to love the money you save, you'll be tempted to become a confirmed tightwad. You can join a discussion group on frugal living or subscribe to an online magazine to keep a flow of money-saving ideas flowing into your household.

Try searching the Web for **Frugal Living**. Webcrawler returned almost 100,000 pages on frugal living on the Web.

Check out Excite's Frugal Living section (quicken.excite.com/saving/frugal/), shown in Figure 10.1. You'll find tools and articles for getting the most from your money. In addition, it has financial forums where you can chat with others about saving money. The Savvy Savings forum has all sorts of tips and tricks submitted by other folks like you.

The Cheapskate Monthly (www.cheapskatemonthly.com) is an award-winning Web site hosted by Mary Hunt (see Figure 10.2). You do have to give up a small amount of your hard-earned savings for an online subscription. But the members section includes a monthly newsletter, scads of tools for saving monthly, discussion boards, searchable back issues, and lots of other great bits. Even non-members can use some of the tools on the site like the Money Quiz. And you can browse through all the money-saving tips that people submit to the site. You can take a look at the preview issue of the newsletter to see if you want to subscribe.

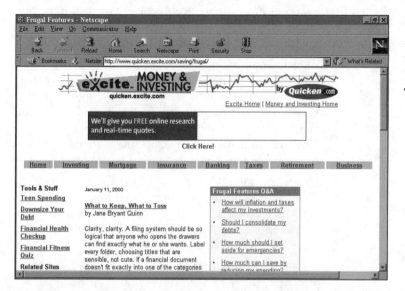

Figure 10.1

Excite has tools and discussion forums where you can learn more about frugal living.

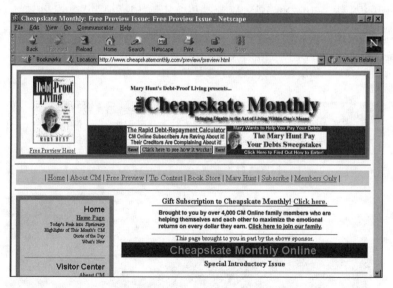

Figure 10.2

The Cheapskate Monthly Web site has a host of great features for subscribers. But you can browse the preview issue and subscriber-submitted tips for free!

Shop the Web to Save Money

With the explosion of the Web, we now have another option for shopping. Without leaving your home, you can buy just about anything you need.

Using the Web to Price Shop

If you've been on the Web, you know about Amazon.com. What started with books has grown to music, gifts, clothing, fancy teapots, and everything else. Small, specialized businesses can now sell their wares around the world. And we, as consumers, can find multiple vendors, read up on their offerings, compare their prices, and buy!

Crash Alert

Buy What You Need, Not What You See!

Remember your budget! Make sure that the abundance of goods and the ease of purchase doesn't turn you into a maniac buyer.

An important aspect of Web shopping is convenience. You can shop in your pajamas at any time of day. Instead of spending your time and gasoline driving around finding what you want at a good price, you can click through some Web sites and have your purchase shipped right to your door. You also can clear out your mailbox by canceling catalogs. Who needs paper when you can see products online?

One of my favorite features of Web shopping is being able to find unusual products and doing my research on which product I like best before the company ever knows who I am. Even if you call a company to get information, you're on its mailing list.

Shopping catalog sites has a big advantage over shopping from paper catalogs. Have you ever tried to order something from the catalog clearance section, only to find that it is already sold out? Or you have to enter second-choice colors on your order slip? When you use a catalog's online clearance section, such as Land's End's, shown in Figure 10.3, the Web pages are hooked into inventory, so you can only choose what is still available. In addition, many catalog sites offer items online that aren't even listed in the paper catalog.

Figure 10.3

Land's End enables you to shop and gamble at the same time. Hold out for larger savings, but risk the item selling out!

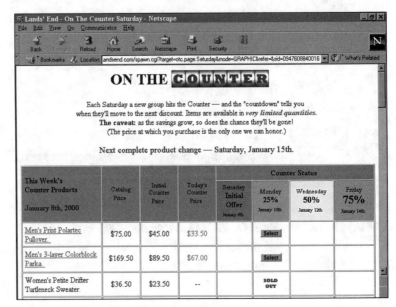

This Week's Counter Products January 8th, 2000	Catalog Price	Initial Counter Price	Today's Counter Price	Counter Status			
				Saturday Initial Offer January 8th	Monday 25% January 10th	Wednesday 50% January 12th	Friday 75% January 14th
Men's Print Polartec Pullover.	$75.00	$45.00	$33.50	Select			
Men's 3-layer Colorblock Parka.	$169.50	$89.50	$67.00	Select			
Women's Petite Drifter Turtleneck Sweater.	$36.50	$23.50	--	SOLD OUT			

Wrestling Down the Best Price Online

When you're looking for something that you can buy in several places—books, CDs, computer software—you can compare prices on the Web.

If you have certain online vendors that you like to use—say Amazon.com, BarnesandNoble.com, and Fatbrain.com for books—you can open up three browser windows, one for each Web site. Position them side by side and search each one for the items you want. Include all the items you want and set up the order so that you can see the total cost at each site. Then, order from the site that is cheapest overall. Figure 10.4 shows a cheaper price at Egghead.com, but don't forget to check shipping costs.

Factor in Shipping Costs When You Price-Shop

Shipping and handling fees can vary widely from site to site. When you price-shop on the Web, make sure to check shipping fees before you buy. Be careful that the Web site doesn't select next-day air as the default shipping. Unless it is the day before Christmas, consider the U.S. postal service or regular UPS shipping—it's cheap and fairly fast. If a Web site doesn't post shipping fees, be wary.

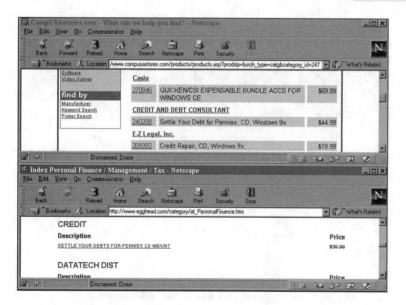

Figure 10.4

Display browser windows side by side and compare prices on the items you want to buy.

Your Own Personal Concierge

A newer development in e-commerce is the appearance of sites that compare prices for you. StreetPrices.com searches more than 250 different online stores and finds the best deals for the product you want. You can search by categories or for specific

Take Advantage of Offers on Newer Web Sites

There are new e-commerce sites every day and many of them offer discounts or dollars off your first order.

products. For example, in Figure 10.5, I chose the **Flowers** category and the **Anniversary** option. StreetPrices.com found nine flower arrangements priced from $29.95 to $74.95.

You also can find great deals using one of the newer auction-style Web sites. At Priceline.com (www.priceline.com) you can bid for airline tickets, hotel rooms, cars, home financing, and even groceries! You set your price and the parameters, such as the maximum number of layovers, that you want. If a seller accepts your offer, the purchase goes on your credit card, and the deal is done.

Figure 10.5

StreetPrices.com can search hundreds of online stores to find you the best deal.

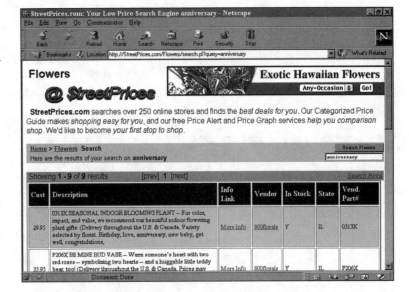

How Comparison Shopping Sites Make Money

Most Web sites make money by selling advertisements (in addition to a product or two). The sites that search other sites make money by selling ads, but they also might get paid just by getting you to an online store. And they might get a commission on any sales.

Finding the Best Interest Rates on Your Savings

Although you will probably invest most of the money you save for those future goals, you will always have some money in that haven of security—savings. Because savings are meant to be safe and secure, the return you get is usually low. But it doesn't have to be pitiful!

Where to Cache Your Cash

When it comes to savings, timeframe is important. Keep the money that you need almost immediately to a minimum because it earns the lowest return. The money earmarked for use between six months to a couple of years out can go into savings with higher rates. There is no free lunch. When you get higher rates, you might have higher risk or restrictions on withdrawals.

Put your ready cash—your emergency savings and money for purchases in the next month or so—into a money market mutual fund. Passbook savings and even the money market accounts at banks rarely pay an interest rate high enough to keep up with inflation.

Head of the Class

How to Select a Money Market Fund

Before you choose a money market fund, check its features:

➤ Make sure that the minimum balance and minimum check amount is in line with your plans.

➤ Look for low expenses and fees (under 1/2% total expense ratio).

➤ Look for a fund offered by a major mutual fund company. They're safer and often perform better than those offered by small companies.

➤ Make sure that they invest in top-grade securities.

For longer-term savings look at certificates of deposit. CDs come in all sorts of maturities, so you can buy CDs to match when you will need the money. The longer the maturity, usually the higher the rate. If it turns out that you need the money sooner, you can always end the CD, although you might have to pay a penalty.

If you live in a state or city with high tax rates, you might consider U.S. Treasury bills or notes. You have to jump through more hoops than when you buy a CD (it is the

Crash Alert

Bonds and Bond Mutual Funds Are Different!

When you buy a bond or Treasury security, the interest rate stays the same for the life of the bond. Bond mutual funds have to keep buying bonds as more money comes into the fund or holdings mature. When bond rates drop, so will the return on your fund.

government after all), but you won't pay state or city taxes on the interest. You also can buy these securities through a broker, but the fee might eat up any tax advantage.

You can invest in U.S. Treasuries and other types of bonds through mutual funds. Mutual funds have the advantage that you can access the money any time you want—even by writing a check if you have check-writing privileges. Bond mutual funds also might have different tax implications from bonds.

Searching for Savings Rates on the Web

With the Bank Rate Monitor Web site, you can search for rates on just about any financial product. Select **Money Market** and specify the state you live in, a nearby city, and the criteria you want to search by. Bank Rate Monitor lists the funds for you along with the rate they offer and the minimum balance. Figure 10.6 shows a search for money market accounts sorted by yield.

Figure 10.6

The Bank Rate Monitor site can show you money market funds ranked by yield.

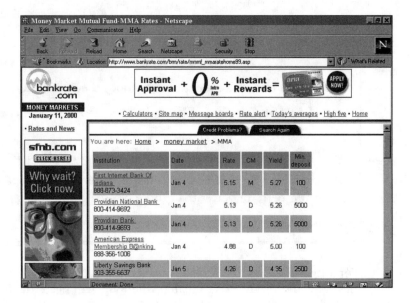

To search for CD rates, select **Savings|CD** from the menu. Pick a state, a nearby city, and the CD maturity that you want. When the list of CDs displays, you can click the top of each column to sort by institution, date, rate, yield, or minimum deposit, as Figure 10.7 illustrates.

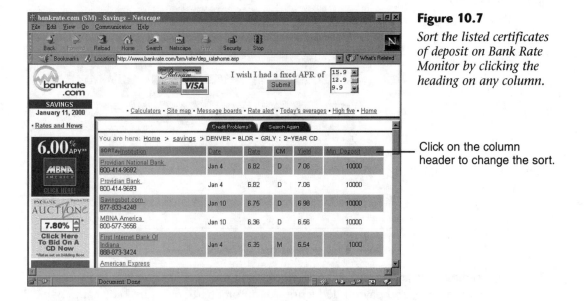

Figure 10.7

Sort the listed certificates of deposit on Bank Rate Monitor by clicking the heading on any column.

Click on the column header to change the sort.

Comparing Bond Mutual Funds Online

Finding the right bond or U.S. Treasury fund takes a little more work than buying CDs or even U.S. Treasuries. Quicken.com's Fund Finder (www.quicken.com/investments/mutualfunds/finder) can help you sort through the thousands of mutual funds available. With the Fund Finder you can use ready-made searches for the most popular request or use a step-by-step wizard to set a few criteria like return and fees. Or you can use their full search that enables you to set 20 different attributes.

By default, the Fund Finder shows the Basic display, which shows you the recent return, Morningstar rating, manager tenure, and expense ratio. Select the performance display, as shown in Figure 10.8, to see how the funds have performed over the last 1-, 3-, 5-, and 10-year periods.

In Chapter 17, "Investing in Mutual Funds," I look more closely at the entire universe of mutual funds.

Figure 10.8

The Quicken.com Fund Finder can show you all the bond mutual funds that meet your criteria.

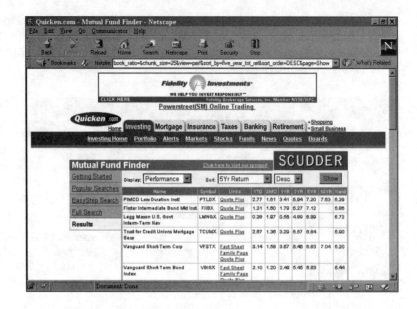

The Least You Need to Know

➤ Hiding your savings before you can think to spend it is a painless way to save your money, and payroll deductions or automatic transfers make it happen automatically.

➤ Reinvesting dividends and interest not only helps you save but increases your investment return.

➤ Refinancing high-rate loans is a guaranteed big savings.

➤ Online sites about frugal living keep you informed on ways to keep pinching the pennies out of your spending.

➤ With online shopping you can hunt for bargains without leaving the house.

➤ Pick the type of account for your savings based on how long until you need the money. Then search the Web to find the best rate.

Saving Money for College

Whether you plan to spoil your kids by paying for their college education or teach them the value of independence by making them pay for it themselves, a college education is one of the big investments of a lifetime. For top-flight private schools, it can be a huge sum of money. High-quality and reasonably priced schools abound. Either way, a college education these days is a practical necessity.

To quote College Board President Gaston Caperton, "The cost of not going to college is much higher than the cost of going to college."

Planning Ahead for the Cost of College

College costs skyrocketed in the past—increasing 10% a year. The good news is that the increase in college costs is the lowest it has been in several years—an increase of less than 5% for all categories of educational institutions. The bad news is that these increases are still higher than inflation, so you have to plan ahead to make saving for college as painless as possible.

Make Sure Out-of-State Fees Don't Hike the Price of a Public School

Students who attend an out-of-state public school have to pay additional fees, which increases the annual costs. Although the average additional cost was about $5,200, it can jump as high as $13,000 more than tuition for in-state students.

For 1999, the average annual tuition for a four-year private school was $15,380, whereas a four-year public school tuition averages $3,356. Meanwhile, a two-year public institution charges $1,627.

By starting to save early, you have the time to invest your college funds in higher-risk, higher-return investments. With higher returns, your monthly savings can be lower, and easier to fit into your budget.

Planning isn't just about finances. As your kids get closer to college age, you have to consider location, types of schools, admission tests, the major your child is interested in (as if they will even know after they graduate!), sports, and more. The College Board Web site (www.collegeboard.com), shown in Figure 11.1, is a great place to start with a college search tool, financial aid tools, test registrations, and even online college applications.

Figure 11.1

The College Board Web site offers college search, financial aid planning and search, online applications, and admission test registration.

Click here to find out about college costs and how to save for them.

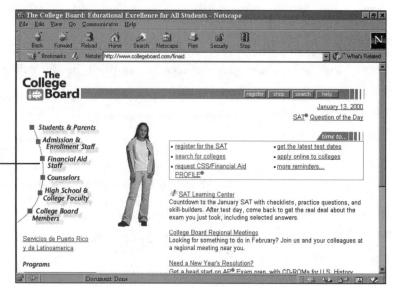

Finding College Costs Online

The College Board Web site includes a link to the Chronicle of Higher Education site, which shows tuition and fees for schools by state. From the Financial Aid page, click **1999-00 College Costs**. Then, click **State-by-State Tuition and Fees** at the end of the page (http://chronicle.com/free/v46/i08/stats/). Finally, select a state from the drop-down list. Figure 11.2 shows the results for Colorado.

Click the topics on the left of the Chronicle of Higher Education's site to learn even more about higher education. For instance, if you are interested in attending a school via the Internet, click **Distance Education**.

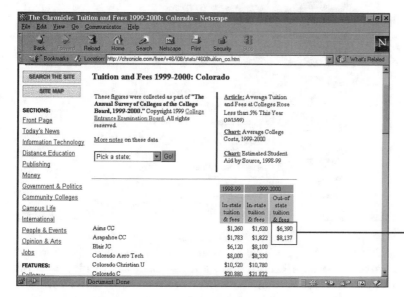

Figure 11.2

Find out how much in-state and out-of-state tuition and fees are for schools in each state.

Out-of-state tuition can be much higher than in-state.

If you needed a trip to the emergency room when you saw how much a Harvard Law degree costs, U.S. News Online (`http://usnews.com/usnews/edu/careers/dollars`) provides a ranking to the best values in schools. From the U.S. News Education page, click **Best Values**. The value ranking considers the schools academic quality in relation to the costs for a student who receives the average amount of financial aid. Click the link for the category of school such as **National**. Figure 11.3 shows the rankings, including the percent of students who receive grants based on need, the annual cost after receiving grants, and the percent discount.

Head of the Class

Planning Doesn't Stop on the First Day of School!

The U.S. News Education section has a college planning calendar that shows the steps your student should take through all four years of reading, writing, and 'rithmetic.

Using Quicken 2000 to Find College Costs

The Quicken 2000 College Planner has a complete and very easy-to-use college cost section. Click **Planning** on the **Quicken** menu bar and select **College Plans** from the drop-down menu. The Planner discusses the costs that make up a college education, including tuition and fees, room and board, books and supplies, and other personal expenses.

Figure 11.3

Find out which schools offer the best value for a quality education at the Education section of U.S. News Online.

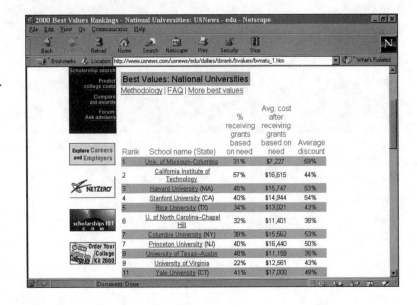

Click **Edit** to find out about college costs. Select a state in the drop-down list. You can select **Public**, **Private**, or **Specialized** schools and Quicken will display a list of schools that match your criteria. Check each check box for the expenses that you expect to pay for your child. When you click a school, the typical expenses from the 1998–1999 school year display, as shown in Figure 11.4.

Figure 11.4

The Quicken College Planner shows the 1998–1999 school year's costs for tuition and fees, out-of-state costs, room and board, books and supplies, and other costs.

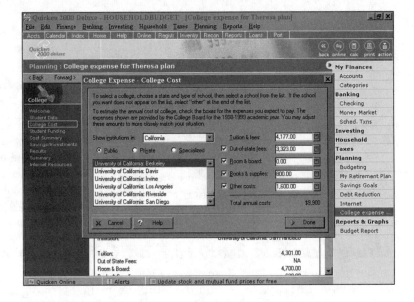

Building a College Savings Plan Online

Now that you know whether you're climbing Mt. Everest or the stairs to the second floor, you still have to figure out how to pay for the privilege! A college calculator helps you figure out how much you need to save for that sheepskin.

Online College Calculators

College calculators all need about the same information, although they might ask for the data in a different order. If you have ready the information in this example, you can use any college calculator on the Internet.

If you're convinced that student loans are in your child's future, start at the Student Loan Marketing Association (SLMA or Sallie Mae) Web site (www.salliemae.com). Its series of calculators walk you through forecasting college costs, determining how much to save, and estimating how much to borrow. If you do need a student loan, it also has calculators for how much you will pay in interest, the impact of the loan on your monthly budget, and the effect of different repayment plans.

Start with the Forecasting College Costs calculator. Enter your estimate for college expenses including tuition and fees, room and board, books and supplies, and personal expenses. The Sallie Mae cost calculator also provides for transportation and special needs expenses.

Click **Next** to go to the following page. Enter the annual inflation rate for college costs and the number of years until your child starts school.

The Sallie Mae site offers two calculators for savings. In the first, you enter how much you save each month to see how your current plan holds up against your goal. The second calculator determines how much you need to save each month to meet your college goal. Figure 11.5 shows the projected monthly savings to pay for one year of school.

College Cost Increases Have Slowed Down

For the 1998–1999 school year, tuition and room and board costs rose just under 5% on average for all categories of institutions.

Don't Overestimate Your Investment Return

If you start saving for college 8–10 years ahead of time, an investment return of 6–8% is realistic. But, if you start saving later, you need to use more conservative investments and should limit your estimated return to no more than 6%.

You can continue with the Expected Family Contribution calculator if you want to see how your family's finances will affect the chance for financial aid. Estimate both your net assets and your child's. You also have to enter information on income and taxes, how many children are in college, and the size of your family. Click **Calculate** to see your expected contribution.

Figure 11.5

The Sallie Mae Savings Calculator can calculate the regular savings needed to meet your college expenses or determine how far your current savings plan reached toward your goal.

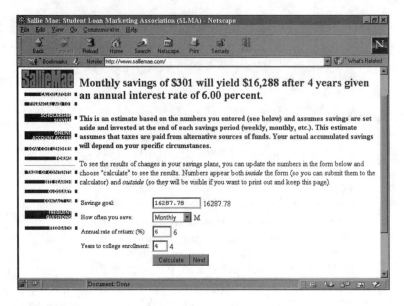

The Quicken College Planner

The Quicken 2000 College Planner walks you through the steps for planning for a college education. The Planner also includes explanations of the makeup of college costs, pros and cons of funding sources, financial aid, and the financial vehicles suitable for college funds. Best of all, Quicken can create a scheduled transaction for the monthly savings so you won't forget. And you can add your monthly savings for college to your budget as well.

In the Student Data section, enter the name of your child, the number of years until they start college, and the number of years that they will attend college. Clicking **College Costs**, you can learn about typical amounts for different expenses and find the 1998–1999 costs for any school.

The Student Funding section discusses the different sources of funding besides the parent and child. You can include an annual contribution from your child and any annual gifts. If you have an estimate for financial aid or student loans, enter them as well.

The Cost Summary shows the annual college expense after deducting other funding sources. In the Savings/Investment section, click **Edit** to add your estimate for the college cost inflation rate. You also can include any existing funds saved toward college. The Planner displays the monthly savings target needed until your child graduates from college, as shown in Figure 11.6. Click the **Schedule** hyperlink to add a scheduled transaction for your college fund contribution.

The Quicken College Planner Uses Your Pre-retirement Rate of Return

The Planner uses the estimated rate of return that you entered in your overall assumptions. Because this rate is probably higher than you should use for college savings, change the rate of return to 6% or 8% before editing the Savings/Investments. After you have a monthly saving target, change the rate of return assumption back to your original value.

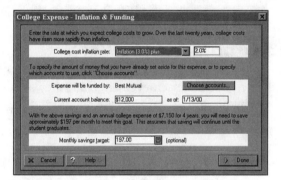

Figure 11.6

The Quicken College Planner steps you through every aspect of paying for a college education.

Getting Money from Others to Pay for College

If the monthly savings target looks bleak, and you didn't consider financial aid, you are in for a surprise. Financial aid is on the upswing. Plus, the College Board's annual report, Trends in Student Aid 1999, cites that more than $64 billion in total aid was available to students in 1998–1999 to help cover college costs.

It pays to go back and find out just how financial aid can help. Then, you can edit your college funding assumptions to see how much you really have to save.

The Mapping Your Future Web site includes a great guide to financial aid called Ten Steps to Paying for School (www.mapping-your-future.org/paying). This guided tour, shown in Figure 11.7, identifies the steps you should take and when. Click any of the hyperlinks to learn more about the different options for financial aid.

Figure 11.7

The Mapping Your Future Web site educates you on all the options for paying for school and tells you when to do what to get some college money.

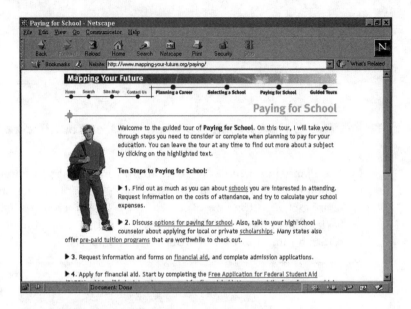

Scholarships and Grants Are the Best!

Scholarships and grants are monies that you do not have to pay back. You can receive a scholarship for academic or athletic achievements. But they also are available based on an ethnic group or religious affiliation. The Federal and state governments give grants to students deemed to have financial need.

Head of the Class

Think Twice Before Saving for College in Your Child's Name

Financial aid formulas weigh your child's assets more heavily than yours. If you save in your child's name, your child might not qualify for as much financial aid. However, you should consider transferring college funds to your child's name if you're a member of one of the higher tax brackets.

The Scholarship Search program, ExPAN, on the College Board site (www.collegeboard.org/fundfinder/html/ssrchtop.html) helps you find scholarships, internships, loans, and other types of financial aid based on your level of education, talents, and background. Also, check out FastWeb's site (www.fastweb.com) to search one of the largest databases of scholarships and grants.

A good education before college can be a great investment. Give your child the best education you can find, from kindergarten through high school. Investment of time at this stage is at least as important as your financial outlay, if any, for your child's education. Good grades and good test scores could snag your child an academic scholarship.

Work-Study Programs

The Federal government provides jobs to students with financial need to help them pay for school expenses. With a work-study program you can get paid for work in your field of study—the cash is nice, but the work experience pays huge dividends later on! Work-study wages start with minimum wage, but can go higher depending on the work you do.

After college begins, it doesn't hurt to watch for work-study opportunities in your field of study. Professors always need help with their research. Somewhere in those hallowed halls is a bulletin board with some interesting assignments—even for freshmen!

Borrowing Money for School

As a last resort, consider student loans. Although repaying a student loan might teach your child more about the reality of life, a job during college or their first house mortgage will do that soon enough. Fortunately, if you must borrow, the government subsidizes student loans. You get a low interest rate and lenient repayment plans—but that doesn't mean you can skip payments!

Both FinAid.com and SallieMae.com are great sites to start your search for educational loans. FinAid.com provides a good overview of all the loans you can use for an education. SallieMae.com talks about what to look for in a lender and has a Lender Locator to help you find a loan. After you have a student loan, you can check your balance, interest payments, and other loan information with online account access.

Crash Alert

Don't Get Duped with Financial Aid Scams!

Go to the FinAid Web site (www.finaid.com/scholarships/) and click the **Common Scholarships Scams** hyperlink to find out how to avoid losing money in a scholarship scam. FinAid's advice is simple, "If you have to pay money to get money, it is probably a scam."

Did You Know?

Don't Count on Sports Scholarships

Sports scholarships are hard to come by. You're better off studying for an academic scholarship.

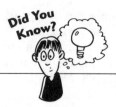

What to Look for in a Lender

For student loans, check out these features:

➤ Find out how the rate is determined and how often it changes.

➤ See if the lender offers rate reductions for prompt payment and electronic payment.

➤ What kind of repayment plans do they offer? You might like graduated or income-based repayment plans.

➤ Can you prepay your loan without paying penalties?

➤ Look for service features like electronic processing and payment, online account access, and good customer service hours.

Places to Stash College Fund Cash

You've dug up all the financial aid you can and it's still not enough. You have to save some money for college. Because education is important, there are a lot of options for college savings.

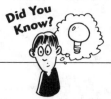

Prepaid Tuition Plans Limit Your Child's Choice of Schools

Prepaid tuition plans are usually restricted to public schools in the state, although some might pay for selected private schools. If your child decides to go elsewhere, you only get your original contribution back.

Prepaid Tuition

With a prepaid tuition plan, parents buy units of education (shares worth one year's tuition, for example) at current tuition rates. When junior goes to college, those units cover the tuition, no matter how much tuition has increased.

The return is often higher than what you would receive from a bank or CD, and might be exempt from state and local taxes. In addition, other family members or friends also can buy units to help contribute to your child's education.

Mutual Funds for an Early Start

If you start to save money early, say when your child is under 10 years old, invest your regular monthly college savings into good-quality growth-oriented mutual funds and reinvest all earnings and dividends. Index funds that invest in the S&P 500, a mid-cap growth index, or a small-cap index are easy and usually are low-expense alternatives. These are taxable accounts. But, with a couple of decades to grow, the return on these mutual funds will make the chore of saving much easier.

After your child hits teenage years (when they are surly and know everything), start to move the savings in these mutual fund accounts into more secure savings discussed in the next section.

Saving Toward the Countdown

When you are looking at five or six years before school starts, you should put your savings into safer investments. Growth mutual funds provide a great return over the long run, but a drop in the market right before school starts could devastate your child's college plans.

Zero-coupon bonds are one option for the safer part of your college fund. You buy zero-coupon bonds at a discount and receive a fixed value when they mature. You can buy zero-coupon bonds so that they mature when your child starts school. However, the imputed interest on zero-coupon bonds is taxable each year.

For safe savings at least five years before school starts, U.S. Series EE Savings Bonds are also good. In 1999, married taxpayers with a modified adjusted gross income (MAGI) under $79,650 don't have to pay taxes on the Savings Bond interest. The exclusion phases out and goes away at $109,650.

Longer-term certificates of deposit are another option. Buy the CDs so that they mature when your child will need the money.

Crash Alert

Safe Investments Barely Keep Up with the Increase in College Costs

Don't use zero-coupon bonds and CDs until you only have five or six years left. At 5% or 6%, their returns are barely higher than the increase in college costs.

Education IRAs

Congress created the Education IRA in 1997. You don't have to pay taxes on your earnings—ever, if the money is used for education! Sounds like the answer to your savings problems. Well, almost.

First, eligibility begins to phase out for married taxpayers whose MAGI is more than $150,000. Contributions are not tax deductible. And you will pay a 10% penalty and regular income taxes if the distributions are not used for education.

Second, you can contribute up to $500 per year for each child under 18. If you invest $500 each year for 18 years and manage an annual return of 10%, your Education IRA would be worth about $23,000. In the meantime, if college costs increase by 5% a year for those 18 years, expenses of $9,000 per year will result in a four-year college bill of almost $100,000.

It's All a Matter of Timing

Starting when your kid hits 12, move some money (15% to 20%) from your growth investments into safer ones. By the time he is 15, half your college fund should be safe. When he starts school, all your college funds should be safe.

Each year when you move your funds, buy zero-coupon bonds or CDs so that they mature at the beginning of a school year. As soon as you have enough funds that mature at the freshman year, start buying for the sophomore year.

A Web Site Dedicated to the Education IRA

Strong Funds host a Web site dedicated to Education IRAs. Check out www.educationira.com to learn more.

College Savings Plans

Some states offer college savings plans, where you can save money for school and get tax advantages along with a return on your money. However, these plans don't lock in the cost of tuition like the pre-paid tuition plan.

To find out what types of plans your state offers, go to the College Savings Plans Network Web site (www.collegesavings.org). An affiliate of the National Association of State Treasurers, the site is a clearinghouse of information on state programs. You can click your state in the map of the United States to go to the Web site for your state's program or to send them email.

You Can Use a Roth IRA for Education

One provision of the Roth IRA enables you to withdraw earnings from the account to pay for higher-education expenses. You don't have to pay a penalty for early withdrawal, but you will have to pay taxes on the earnings.

If your retirement savings are going great guns, you might want to think about your Roth as a college fund. Don't shortchange your retirement for college savings!

You Still Have to Save to Cover All College Costs

Prepaid tuition plans only cover tuition, so you still have to save money for room, board, and other expenses. College savings plans might cover those other expenses, but they don't guarantee that you'll have enough money to cover the costs. So, make sure that you are saving enough for all the costs associated with college.

The Least You Need to Know

➤ College is no longer a luxury. Plan to send your kids to school.

➤ College costs are growing at about 5% a year, so it pays to start early and invest your money.

➤ Whether public, private, four-year, or two-year, there is a college you can afford.

➤ Online calculators can tell you how much school will cost, how much financial aid your child could get, how much you have to save, and much more.

➤ Never assume that you earn too much to qualify for financial aid.

➤ Start investing your college fund early in growth investments. As your child becomes a teenager, start moving funds to safer investments like CDs and zero-coupon bonds.

➤ Education IRAs have a lot of advantages, but they won't cover all your costs.

Chapter 12

Saving for Retirement

In This Chapter

➤ Online calculators that tell you how much to save

➤ Tax-advantaged places to keep your retirement money

➤ Investments for retirement

➤ Other sources of retirement funds

Chances are that you have to save for your retirement. Although company-sponsored, company-funded pensions reigned in the past; employee-funded and employee-directed 401(k) plans rule today. With luck, your employer might match part of your contribution. And, of course, there's Social Security. But even this hallowed institution has had its ability to provide for everyone questioned.

Planning for Your Glorious Golden Years

We are all living longer. That means we get to enjoy more years in retirement—a couple of decades or even more. For those of us who want to retire early, we could be retired for as many years as we worked! Of course, to enjoy that retirement, we need enough money to last all those years. And we can't save that overnight. It takes planning, good investments, and time.

The Early Bird Catches the Worm Every Time

For building an ostrich-sized nest egg, there's nothing like time on your side. When we're young, it seems like there's no way to save for retirement. But consider the example of the early bird and you might try to find a way.

The early bird starts at age 21, saving $2,000 a year for retirement. After 10 years, the early bird stops contributing. If the early bird's investments return 10% a year for 45 years, the early bird retires at 66 with $565,559, having contributed only $20,000. On the other hand, the late saver doesn't start saving until he's 31. He contributes $2,000 a year and makes the same 10% return. When he retires at 66, he has $596,254, but he contributed $70,000 over 35 years. If the early bird kept contributing his $2,000 each year until he retired, he would have contributed $90,000, but would have a nest egg almost double the late saver's—$1,161,813. Even though an early start is a tremendous advantage, don't despair if you're getting on the train a bit late—there's still plenty of time if you get serious about saving now.

Online Retirement Planners

Whether you want to work online or on your computer, Quicken offers the best retirement planners around. If you don't own Quicken 2000, use Quicken.com's online planner (www.quicken.com/retirement/planner). It doesn't have all the features of the planner in Quicken 2000, but it will tell you how successful your current retirement savings will be, and what else you need to do with about 20 minutes of your time. Click **Explain** to find out more about what the planner is asking for.

Start with personal information for you and your spouse, as shown in Figure 12.1: your age, retirement age, and life expectancy. Then enter your salaries on the **Salary** page. The Economic Assumptions section can estimate your pre- and post-retirement tax rates as well as inflation.

Figure 12.1

Fill out a few easy forms in the Quicken.com Retirement Planner to find out if you're on track for retirement.

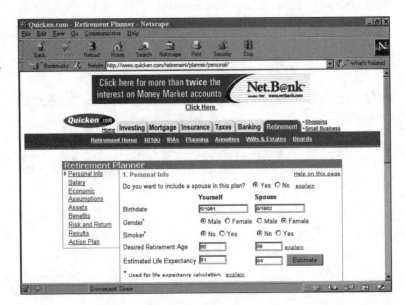

Add all the information about you retirement assets including your 401(k) plans, deductible IRAs, and Roth IRAs. When entering your employer's 401(k) match, you have to calculate the dollar maximum even if their limit is a percentage of your contribution. Social Security and pensions go in the Benefits section.

Moving Around in the Quicken.com Retirement Planner

When you finish adding data on a page, you can click **Next** to continue with the next page, or **Previous** to return to the last page. You can also click the tabs (**Personal Info, Salary, Economic Assumptions, Assets, Benefits, Risk and Return, Results,** and **Action Plan**) to go directly to a page.

In the **Risk and Return** section, you can select investment returns for before and after retirement. The Planner suggests an investment allocation that historically produced that return with the lowest risk. Chapter 14, "Investing Made Easy," talks about using asset allocation in your investments.

Finally, you can see whether your plan works or not by clicking **Results**, as in Figure 12.2. To see what step you should take, go to **Action Plan**. Unlike the Quicken 2000 Planner, the Quicken.com online planner does not take into account selling your home at some point in retirement.

The Quicken Retirement Planner

The Quicken 2000 Planning Center considers your retirement plan along with the rest of your financial plan. After you answer all the questions about your finances, the Planner not only tells you whether your retirement plan works or not, but also whether the plan holds water before retirement, too.

It's Better to Make Conservative Estimates

To be safe, use an investment return of 10% (a bit lower than the long-term average return in the stock market) for your pre-retirement savings. If you estimate higher and can't produce those results, your plan will be in jeopardy. For after-retirement return, drop to 8% to reflect an investment mix with lower risk.

Figure 12.2

*If your plan isn't working, go to **Action Plan** to find out what you can do.*

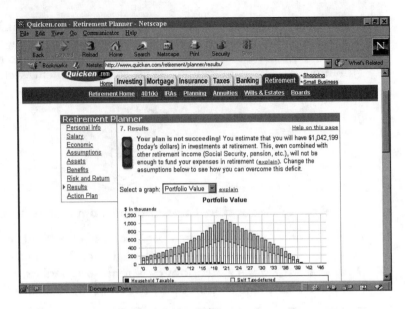

You Can Add Salary Adjustments for the Most Accurate Picture of Your Finances

For each salary in the Quicken Planner, you can add salary adjustments for changing jobs, promotions, bonuses, or more or fewer hours. You can specify when this adjustment starts and set the salary as an amount or a percentage change.

Let's do a quick review in case you skipped planning in Chapter 2, "Planning." To see if your retirement plan works, Quicken needs to know about you. The About You section finds out your current age, the age you plan to retire, and your life expectancy. Your current age and your retirement age tell Quicken how much longer you have to save and grow your investments for retirement. Your life expectancy tells Quicken how many years your retirement funds must last.

In the **Salary** section, you enter your salary, how much you expect your salary to increase each year, when the salary starts, and when it ends. You also check whether you pay Social Security taxes on your salary.

In Quicken 2000, retirement benefits are those retirement sources that you do not have to fund—Social Security and pensions. In the **Retirement** section, you pick the age you plan to collect Social Security and Quicken can estimate your benefits for you. If you do have a pension, add that in this section. You enter the age that the pension starts, the yearly amount in today's dollars, the cost-of-living increase, and whether your spouse will receive a percentage after your death.

Quicken Can Use Pre-retirement and After-retirement Tax Rates

In Quicken, you can enter your tax rate based on recent tax returns or use a demographic average. If you expect your income to drop in retirement, specify a lower after-retirement tax rate. To be on the safe side, use your pre-retirement rate as your after-retirement estimate.

All the retirement accounts that you fund, such as IRAs, 401(k)s, or Keogh accounts, appear in the **Investments** section. To create a new retirement account, click **Edit** to open the Investments window. Click **New** to create an account and select the account type. Because tax rules differ, you must pick the type of IRA on an IRA account.

If you make regular contributions to any of these retirement accounts, make sure to add a contribution. Select the retirement account in the top list and then click **New** under **Contributions**. For contributions, you can specify a percentage of your salary or a dollar amount, when the contribution starts and stops, and whether the employer matches your contribution and by how much.

For **Rate of Return**, enter the rates of return you expect to make on your investments before and after you retire. Over long periods, the stock market returns 11% on average. In general people invest more conservatively after they retire to protect their nest egg from drops in the market, so 6% or 7% is more appropriate. You also can specify different rates of return for taxable accounts and tax-deferred accounts. Because the taxable accounts are more for short-term goals, you might use a lower rate of return.

You Can Contribute More Than the Maximum to an IRA Account

The tax laws limit the amount you can contribute to an IRA with pre-tax dollars. But you can contribute to an IRA with after-tax dollars. Even though you contribute with after-tax dollars, the earnings grow tax deferred.

Don't Sell Your Stocks Just Because You Retire

With life expectancies today, retirement can last 20, 30, even 40 years. So, you should keep some of your money in long-term growth investments even after you retire.

Your current home and any other assets you might own can help fund your retirement. For instance, you might decide that the ski condo wouldn't be that useful when you turn 75, so don't forget to enter the date you expect to sell some of your assets. If you think you will sell your house to move into a smaller one, you can enter those events in the **Current Home** and **Assets** sections.

In the **Expenses** section, select **Living Expenses** to specify your expenses today. In **Adjustments**, you can define changes to your expenses, such as your children leaving home or retirement. You can set the start and end dates for the adjustment and set the change as a dollar amount or a percentage.

After you have all your information entered, click **Your Plan** to see how you're doing. The summary will tell you whether your plan works or not. You can also click **Check for Problems** to get a list of possible problems with your plan.

Course Corrections with Quicken What-if Scenarios

If your plan doesn't work, you can click **What-if** to experiment with changes. Some things you might try are

Check Your Plan If You Live to Be 100

What if you end up living to be 100? Will your funds hold up even then? Bump your life expectancy up to see what happens.

➤ Retiring at a later date

➤ Trying to save more money

➤ Planning to spend less after you retire

➤ Working part-time in retirement

➤ Making your kids pay for more of their college expenses

➤ Moving into a smaller house earlier

When you make changes in a what-if scenario, the Retirement Planner shows your original plan and the revised plan shown in Figure 12.3. If you like the results of the what-if changes, you can save them to your plan.

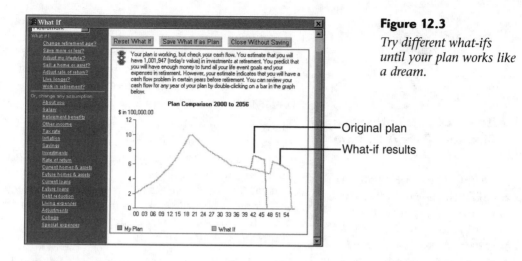

Figure 12.3
Try different what-ifs until your plan works like a dream.

Good Ways to Save Money for Retirement

Saving for your retirement might not be fun, but the government wants to help. In their eyes, they would rather tempt you to save for your own retirement, than pay your expenses when you run out of money. So, as you save for your retirement, you can save on taxes, too!

The good old days where companies provided pensions to all are gone. Defined contribution plans, where employers commit only to contributing a certain amount each year, are the rage. For employers, these plans are no risk. For employees, they are usually the wake-up call that makes you pay attention to your finances.

401(k) Plans to the Max

With 401(k) retirement plans, you put away a portion of your salary each year for retirement. You don't pay income taxes on the amount that you contribute. You can use the money you would have paid in taxes to help contribute to the plan. You also don't pay taxes on your earnings. You only pay taxes when you withdraw the money during retirement.

With a deal like that, contribute as much as you can. If you can't afford to contribute the maximum, plan to up your contribution each year until you max out.

Head of the Class

401(k) Plans and Salary Deductions Can't Be Beat!

401(k) plans are wonderful devices for saving. In addition to the tax advantages, your contributions come from payroll deductions. So, your nest egg grows, while you blissfully live on your paycheck.

After-tax Contributions Can Give Your Plan That Extra Push

Some 401(k) plans accept after-tax contributions. If you need to save more toward retirement, direct more of your pay to your 401(k). Your earnings grow tax deferred, even though you paid taxes on your contribution.

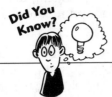

403(b) Is the Nonprofit Version of the 401(k)

Nonprofit organizations offer 403(b) plans instead of 401(k)s. The rules are just about the same.

In 1999, the maximum contribution was a percentage of your salary, which is set by each company (up to 15%), or $10,000, whichever is less. In addition, the maximum contribution to all your company savings plans is 25% of your salary, or $30,000, whichever is less.

Many employers match employee contributions. For example, a company might match 100% of your contribution up to 3% of your salary—or 50% of your contribution up to 8% of your salary. Even if you can't afford to contribute the maximum allowable, at least contribute to your 401(k) to the maximum that your employer matches. Otherwise, you're passing up free money.

Using Brook Smith as an example, let's see how the 401(k) works. Brook makes $35,000 a year and her company matches 100% of her contribution up to 3% of her salary. Brook contributes 12% of her salary—$350 each month out of her $2,916.66 salary. If her payroll taxes are 20% of her salary, she avoids 20% of $350, or $70, in taxes. For the year, she contributes $4,200 to her 401(k) plan. She avoids $840 in taxes. And, on top of that, her employer matches 3% of her salary, $1,050.

Individual Retirement Accounts (IRAs)

IRAs come in three flavors: deductible, non-deductible, and Roth (I'll get to the Roth IRA in a moment). If you don't participate in a company retirement plan, you can contribute up to $2,000 a year to a deductible IRA. Your contributions and earnings are tax deferred—you don't pay taxes until you withdraw the money. And you get a write-off on your tax return for your contribution. If you do participate in a company plan, you can still contribute to a deductible IRA, if your salary is low.

If you don't qualify for a deductible IRA, you can still contribute to a non-deductible IRA. You still pay taxes on your contributions, but your earnings grow tax deferred. When you withdraw money from a non-deductible IRA, your original contributions are not taxed, but your earnings and gains are.

Confused by all these options? Learn the ins and outs of IRAs at Quicken.com's Retirement page (www.quicken.com/retirement/IRA/basics), as shown in Figure 12.4.

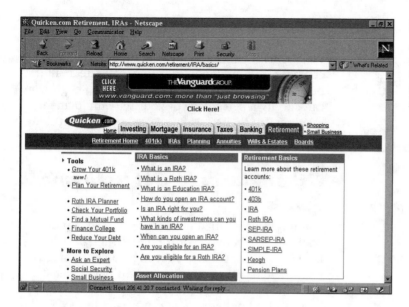

Figure 12.4
Learn the ABCs of IRAs and the rest of the letters in the retirement alphabet in Quicken.com's Retirement section.

The Roth IRA is a fairly new alternative. You pay taxes on your contribution to the Roth IRA, but you can withdraw all the money from the Roth after you retire without paying any taxes.

Retirement Plans for Small Businesses and the Self-Employed

Small businesses and self-employed folks have some other options for retirement plans. If you are self-employed, do not skip some form of retirement plan.

Whether you are completely self-employed or earn some money moonlighting, you can contribute to a Keogh plan. The maximum annual stash for a Keogh plan is 20% of your salary, or $30,000, whichever is less. To reach this maximum you have to have both a profit-sharing Keogh and a money-purchase Keogh.

Head of the Class

Rollover Your 401(k) If You Switch Jobs

You can roll your 401(k) savings into an IRA when you switch jobs. You won't pay taxes if you don't withdraw the money. And an IRA might give you more flexibility in investments than your previous employer's plan did.

You Can Withdraw Money from a Roth for Other Reasons

You also can withdraw money before retirement without paying taxes to buy your first house or pay for an education.

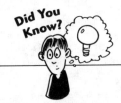

SEPs Are Simple for the Paperwork-Challenged

A Simplified Employee Pension has the same limits as a profit-sharing Keogh. But it is set up like an IRA so it's much easier to administer.

Crash Alert

Omit Your Social Security Benefits from Your Plan to Be Safe

To see whether your retirement plan works if Social Security goes bust, enter zero for Social Security in whichever retirement planner you use.

Profit-sharing Keoghs are flexible. You can contribute up to 13.04% of your annual self-employment earnings, but you can choose the percentage. You can choose not to contribute at all if business is bad. With a money-purchase Keogh, you can specify a percentage of your self-employment earnings, up to 20%. However, you must contribute that percentage, no matter what.

Other Places to Get Retirement Funds

You might be entitled to other retirement funds in addition to what you contribute. Although defined-benefit pension plans are getting scarcer than hen's teeth, one of your employers might have offered one. If so, check with the Human Resources department to find out what you can expect to receive.

According to the commissioner of the Social Security Administration, the trust funds for the Social Security program will be exhausted in 2032. At that point, income for the program will only cover three-quarters of the benefit obligations. However, because Social Security is so important, the President and other national leaders have proposed steps that would keep Social Security solvent at least through 2055, and possibly 2075. To learn more, read the commissioner's communication to Congress (www.ssa.gov/policy/congcomm/ testimony_022399.html).

Most of the online retirement planners can calculate your potential Social Security benefits. If you would like to get a Personal Earnings and Benefit Estimate Statement straight from the Social Security Administration, go to its Web site (www.ssa.gov). Click the **Top 10 Services** link and select **Request a Social Security Statement**. You answer the questions while connected to a secure server at the

Social Security Administration. However, if you use a library Internet connection or other public connection, make sure to log off when you're done. You receive the statement in the mail. The SSA has also made a commitment to send an annual Earnings and Benefit Estimate statement to all workers over age 25 in Social Security–covered work and not yet collecting benefits.

Head of the Class

Don't Lose Touch with Old Employers

Make sure to update previous employers on your whereabouts, particularly if you will get pension benefits. If they don't know where you are, they can't send that pension check!

The Least You Need to Know

➤ No matter how impossible it seems, start saving early for a big-time retirement payoff!

➤ If you haven't planned for retirement yet, start now. Online retirement planners lead you through step by step.

➤ 401(k) plans are a great way to save for retirement. Employer matching makes your job even easier.

➤ IRA accounts are tax-advantaged accounts for retirement savings. You can learn about which type works for you online.

➤ Keogh plans are great for the self-employed or even those who do a little moonlighting. You can stash up to 20% of your self-employment income into retirement savings.

➤ Pensions are nice if you can get them.

➤ Social Security might be around for you and maybe it won't. You can omit Social Security benefits to see if your plan works without them.

Chapter 13

Saving for the Rest of Your Wish List

In This Chapter

➤ Finding out how to save for the rest of your wish list

➤ Learning how investments for short-term savings differ from long-term savings

➤ Discovering ways to make saving for a house down payment easier

➤ A quick review of where to keep short-term savings

There are probably still a few things on your wish list after college education and retirement. A ski condo, a tropical vacation, a fancy sports car for your mid-life crisis. If you want a fighting chance of reaching them, these goals should be a part of your financial plan.

However, you plan for these goals a little differently than the essentials like retirement. There are no handy tax-advantaged accounts. You don't have as long to save. How do you do it?

The Web offers savings calculators to help you figure out how to save for your dreams. And refer to Chapter 10, "Saving Money," to find out what kind of rates you can earn on your short-term savings.

Online Calculators for Special Purchases

Getting your wish list down on paper is an important first step. Those letters in black and white show that you're serious about achieving your goals. But a total amount of money and a date when you need it doesn't tell you much about how to make it happen. What you really need is an amount of money that you should save each month and the return that you need to earn.

Using an Online Savings Calculator

The Strong Funds Web site has a Planning Center, `www.estrong.com/strong/pc/index.html`, which includes a host of tools for planning your finances. Figure 13.1 shows its calculator, Planning for a Major Purchase (`www.estrong.com/strong/pc/tools/purchase.htm`), which helps you figure out how much you need to save.

Figure 13.1

The Strong Funds Savings calculator helps you figure out how much you should save each month—and takes inflation and your tax rate into account as well.

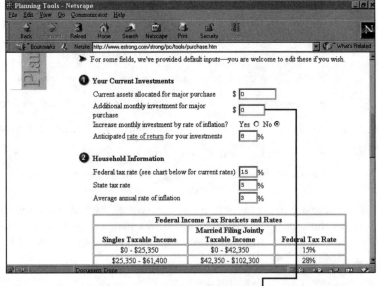

Use zero if you want the calculator to determine your monthly savings.

Start by entering the amount of money you currently have saved for your purchase. (You can enter zero if you are just starting.) Then, enter the amount of money you are saving each month. You can enter zero for the monthly saving if you want the calculator to figure the necessary monthly amount out for you.

You can specify whether you want to increase your monthly amount each year by the rate of inflation. Enter the investment return that you plan to achieve.

Your Potential Investment Return Drops as Your Savings Timeframe Shrinks

Use the following numbers as guidelines for the maximum likely returns based on the time until your goal:

Less than 1 year	4% (Money Market Account)
1 to 5 years	5–7% (CDs or Treasuries timed to purchase date)
More than 5 years	8% (Some stocks, some CDs)

Enter your federal and state tax rate. Use the tax table on the Web page to estimate your rates if you don't know what they are. If you think inflation will be higher or lower than the default of 3%, change that.

Next, enter the year that you plan to make your purchase and enter the amount that your purchase costs today. Click **Submit Query** to get your results. Our hypothetical family, the Smiths, want to take a month-long vacation to the South Pacific (without the kids) for their 20th anniversary, which is in 2011. Figure 13.2 shows how their vacation plans are working.

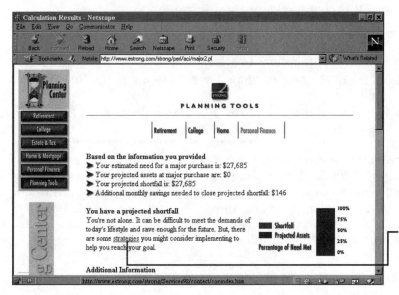

Figure 13.2

The Strong Funds Savings calculator projects your savings shortfall and gives you tips on how to make up the gap.

Click strategies to find out what you can do to meet your goal.

Putting the Savings Plan into Action

For the Smiths' vacation plan, they have over a decade to save, so they can use a variety of savings vehicles. Early in their savings plan, they can add 75% of their funds to a mutual fund, such as a Standard & Poor's 500 index fund, or perhaps a fund that covers the entire stock market. They can keep money they save each month in a money market fund, which earns 4% to 5%. At the end of each of the first five years they take money from the money market fund to buy a long-term CD. When those CDs mature, the Smiths roll them over into CDs that mature just before they start to pay for their vacation. Table 13.1 shows how the Smiths' vacation saving plan works.

Table 13.1   A Sample Savings Action Plan

Year	Action
1	$110 per month to Strong Index 500 Mutual Fund (SMF).
	$36 per month to Strong Money Market Fund (MMF).
2–5	At the beginning of each year, purchase 6-year CD with money in MMF.
	Continue monthly contributions to SMF and MMF.
6	At the beginning of the year, purchase 5-year CD with money in MMF and 25% of SMF.
	$146 per month to MMF.
7	At the beginning of the year, purchase 4-year CD with money in MMF and 25% of SMF.
	Continue monthly contributions to MMF.
8	At the beginning of the year, purchase 3-year CD with money in MMF, 25% of SMF, and money from maturing 6-year CD.
	Continue monthly contributions to MMF.
9	Purchase 2-year CD with money in MMF, all of SMF, and money from maturing 6-year CD.
	Continue monthly contributions to MMF.
10	At the beginning of the year, purchase 1-year CD with money in MMF and maturing 6-year CD.
11	Continue monthly contributions to MMF and move maturing CDs into MMF until vacation.

The Smiths use an automatic investment plan so they can start their saving plan without the usual Strong Funds $2,500 initial investment. Starting in the sixth year, the Smiths start adding 100% of their new savings to CDs timed to mature just before the vacation—a five-year CD, then a four-year, three-year, and so on. In addition, each year they move 25% of the funds in the growth fund into a CD so that all their funds are in CDs two years before the vacation.

Simplify Your Savings by Looking at the Big Picture

Planning CDs and investments separately for each of your goals could give you a headache to go along with a basketful of CDs and other accounts. Instead, look at the big picture—how much money do you need for goals less than a year away, how much for goals between one and five years, and how much for goals more than five years away? Set up your savings so you can meet the overall goal in each time period.

Using Quicken 2000 to Save for Special Purchases

The Quicken 2000 Planner Center includes a planner for other goals. But this planner works a little differently from the online calculator that we just used. Although it takes a few extra steps to get your special purchase plan right, Quicken 2000 can tell if you can afford this special purchase along with the rest of the goals in your overall plan.

Click **Create a Purchase Plan** under **Other Goals** to start your plan. Enter the name of the purchase. You can assign the purchase to a specific person if you want. Click **Next** to add the details about the purchase. Enter the date when you plan to purchase. You can specify a one-time expense or an expense that spans multiple years. Enter what you expect to pay for your purchase. The Quicken 2000 calculator is different here, because it wants the purchase price in the future. The Strong savings calculator uses the price today and calculates the increase due to inflation.

Inflation Makes the Difference Between Current Dollars and Future Dollars

Dollars in the future don't buy as much as dollars today because the price of things goes up each year with inflation. So, current dollars represent what your money can buy today. Future dollars are reduced in value by inflation. Future dollars don't buy as much, so you need more of them.

Click **Next** to see your Monthly Savings Target, as shown in Figure 13.3. Quicken uses the pre-retirement rate of return that you entered in your overall plan assumptions. If your pre-retirement return is high compared to a CD rate for your savings timeframe, you should lower your investment return. For example, you should consider a rate of return of 5% or 6% if your purchase is within five years.

Figure 13.3

The Quicken Special Purchase Planner shows the monthly savings amount needed based on the Smiths' 10% pre-retirement rate of return. They should recalculate their monthly savings amount with a more realistic 8% rate of return.

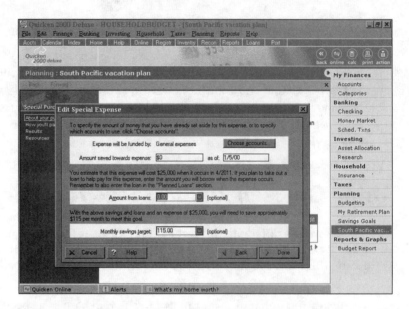

Finish adding the purchase. Then, go to your planning assumptions and change your investment return to reflect the timeframe for your purchase. When you edit the special purchase, the monthly savings target changes to reflect your lower investment return. You can move your rate of return back up after you get the monthly savings target added to your budget and scheduled transactions list.

Ways to Get a House with Little or No Down Payment

The American dream—owning your own home. A down payment on a house is one of the most common short-term savings goals around. Saving for a down payment is not much different than saving for other short-term goals—you have to save money each month for it. You stash your cash in the same types of savings.

One thing that you might do differently is change the inflation rate in the savings calculator. If you know that houses where you want to buy are increasing in price at a certain rate, put that number in for inflation.

Another thing you can do differently is to cut down on the down payment that you have to save. You can always go for a less expensive house—the lower the house price, the lower the down payment. Consider another part of the country. Or maybe areas further into the sticks.

You can buy private mortgage insurance through your lender. Instead of the typical 20% down payment, you can put down 5% or 10% when you buy private mortgage insurance. However, you have to pay up to 1% up front plus additional amounts each year, so you might try to find the funds for the down payment elsewhere.

You can look for mortgages backed by the Federal Housing Administration or the Department of Veterans Affairs, if you qualify for a VA loan. You can put down as little as 3% with an FHA loan. With VA loans, you might not need a down payment at all.

The Federal Housing Administration, Department of Veterans Affairs, and Federal National Mortgage Association (Fannie Mae) will accept low down payments on fore-closed houses that they hold. You also can expect reasonable prices and attractive mortgage rates.

> **Did You Know?**
>
> **You Build Sweat Equity with Your Time**
>
> If you have time to put in some extra labor, buy a handyman's special. With a little bit of money for supplies, you can build equity in your new house by fixing it up yourself!

The Least You Need to Know

➤ You need a plan even when you save for smaller goals, and online savings calculators can help you figure out how much you need.

➤ For shorter-term goals, estimate a rate of return between 4% and 8%, depending on the timeframe.

➤ You can reduce your savings goals by taking steps to lower the down payment you need for your house.

Part 4
Investing on the Internet

From your 401(k) retirement plan at work to your Aunt Sally telling you about her new fortune in tech stocks, it seems everyone is talking about investments. The secret to successful investing is following the tortoise on a straight, steady course. Use the Internet to plan, research, and manage your investments without some hare trying to talk you into the newest get-rich-quick scheme.

Chapter 14

Investing Made Easy

In This Chapter

➤ Learning about investment strategies that are easy and successful

➤ Finding out about the risks you take with your money

➤ Allocating your assets to achieve your goals

➤ Learning how diversified long-term investments along with reinvested dividends can make you a millionaire

---

Some folks (and a lot of investment newsletters) will tell you that they have a fool-proof method for getting rich quick. Others swear by complicated mathematical formulas while chanting unintelligible gibberish. Don't let these people fool you into trying to beat Wall Street—or scare you away from investing your money.

Investing, and growing rich from your investments, is actually an easy, leisurely journey. But attempts to speed it up usually result in a wild ride to a different destination.

The truth is that you don't have to beat the street. Wall Street is happy to work with you to make you wealthy. Successful investing relies on time, some simple investment choices, and a little bit of common sense. And you don't have to be a math wizard. The hardest part about the math that you do use is remembering it from way back in elementary school.

Investment Strategies

Simple and successful investment strategies all share some basic principles, which have held true for as long as there has been a stock market. Hold to these principles and your investments will grow over time with a minimum of effort:

➤ Invest regularly, regardless of whether the market is up or down.

Put money into your investments each month or quarter. When the market is down, you're getting a good buy. If the market is up, you don't buy as many shares.

➤ Reinvest all your dividends.

Even though investments grow over time, it's the reinvested dividends that make your results skyrocket! If your grandfather invested $100 in large-company stocks at the end of 1925 and spent the dividends, his portfolio would have grown to $9,636 by the end of 1998. But, if your grandmother invested that $100, and reinvested all the dividends that followed, her nest egg would have turned into $235,089 over the same period!

➤ Invest in good-quality growing companies.

Whether you invest in stocks or mutual funds, over the long term, the stock of good-quality growing companies almost always performs better than any other investment.

➤ Diversify your investments to reduce risk.

"Don't put all your eggs in one basket" applies as much on Wall Street as it does in the barnyard.

➤ Invest for the long term.

It's difficult and time consuming to try to predict the weather, or what the stock market will do tomorrow. But you can bank on the steady growth in the stock market over time.

➤ Have the courage and patience to stick to your investment plan.

If you sell out of fear when the market is down, and buy with exuberance when the market goes up, you'll end up with nothing. Remember that the long-term trend in the market is up, and stick to your plan.

Asset Allocation

The big picture of low-maintenance investing is *asset allocation*—putting your eggs into the right baskets! Different types of investments tend to do well under different circumstances and at different times. Some investment types go up just when others go down; others just grow at a different rate.

Asset allocation takes advantage of these differences to produce the returns you want without a stomach-jolting ride to get there. Stocks give higher returns, but are risky in the short term. Bonds usually have lower returns, but do better when stocks do badly. Cash is the lowest return, but also the lowest risk.

By allocating percentages of your investment money into different types of stocks, bonds, and cash, you can have a well-behaved portfolio that delivers through thick and thin. What's more, the only care your portfolio needs is some rearrangement once a year to keep the percentages on target.

Fundamental Stock Analysis

For the individual stocks that you purchase, fundamental analysis is one of the ways you can study a company to see if its stock is a good one to buy. Fundamental analysis focuses on the financial fundamentals of a company: its revenues, earnings, profit margin, prospects for future growth, and other measures.

Crash Alert

Technical Analysis Takes Time—And You Better Like Math

Technical analysis is another approach to studying stocks. People who apply technical analysis try to find patterns in the price chart of a stock to figure out which way the price might be headed. Technical analysis is a high-maintenance approach, because you have to keep watching your purchases. If you like math and computers and think technical analysis sounds interesting, you can find links to learn more about it at the InvestorGuide site (www.investorguide.com/ stocks-techanalysis-educationcontent.htm).

You can use fundamental analysis in two ways. The easiest approach is to look for growth companies. When a company steadily grows its revenues and earnings, earns a good profit on its sales, and has rosy prospects for the future, people want to own that stock. And the price of popular growth stocks tends to keep going up and up. After you find one of these gems, you can buy it and almost forget about it, because the best companies tend to keep growing and growing—and the price of your stock grows with it!

If you use fundamental analysis, you're in good company. Peter Lynch used fundamental analysis to pilot the Fidelity Magellan mutual fund to record performance. Warren Buffett, the genius behind Berkshire Hathaway, uses the fundamental approach to choose companies for the Berkshire Hathaway portfolio. You can learn more about Mr. Buffet's approach at the Berkshire Hathaway Web site (www.berkshirehathaway.com) shown in Figure 14.1. In addition, millions of successful investment club members have learned to use tools from the National Association of Investors Corporation (NAIC) to apply fundamental analysis to their stock selections. The NAIC Web site (www.better-investing.org) and Investorama (www.investorama.com) are both great places to learn about fundamental analysis using NAIC principles.

Value Investing Is Like Finding a Stock on Sale

With *value investing*, the other approach to fundamental analysis, you look for companies with good fundamentals that are on sale for some reason. Sometimes, the market overreacts to a piece of bad news. Or the investment masses just find the industry dull. Whatever the reason, the price of one of these value stocks is a steal. You can buy it and wait for the rest of the world to wake up.

Figure 14.1

Berkshire Hathaway invests in companies by making them part of the Berkshire Hathaway portfolio.

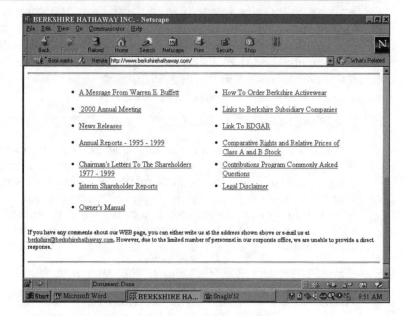

Peter Lynch is also a proponent of buying what you know. If you shop for discounts, you might invest in Wal-Mart. If your teenage daughters buy everything at the Gap, or Claire's Stores, look at those companies. Use the companies you know as a guide to potential investments. Then, study the companies' fundamentals to see if they warrant purchase.

Dollar-Cost Averaging

Dollar-cost averaging is another low-maintenance, boring technique that delivers. By investing a fixed amount of money at a regular interval in your investments, you are dollar-cost averaging. When the market, or your individual stocks' prices, are down, you buy more shares with your set amount of money. When prices are high, you buy fewer shares with your money. That's it!

For example, $100 buys five shares of stock, when the stock price is $20. If the stock price drops to $10, you can buy 10 shares with the same $100. When the price rises to $25, you only buy four shares. Because you buy more shares when prices are low, the average price of your purchases goes down. In our example, the average price for all the shares is $15.79, which is a lot closer to the low of $10 than it is to the high of $25.

Keep a Lid on Commissions

With dollar cost averaging, don't let commissions ruin your returns. With small regular contributions, focus your dollar-cost averaging in mutual funds (Chapter 17, "Investing in Mutual Funds") or dividend reinvestment programs (Chapter 16, "Buying Stocks Online"). As your regular contributions increase in size, you can dollar cost average in stocks using online discount brokers with low commissions.

The other advantage to dollar-cost averaging is that it keeps you focused on two of the investment principles: Invest regularly regardless whether the market is up or down, and stick to your plan.

Head of the Class

Stock Up on Stocks When They're on Sale

Many people end up doing things with investing that they wouldn't do anywhere else. Instead of stocking up (literally!) when the stock market is on sale, they assume they made a mistake when they bought the stock, and sell! With a regular investment in your holdings, you won't make that mistake.

Dogs of the Dow

If you haven't figured it out yet, low-maintenance investment strategies are in. Investing techniques that require hard work are out. Why make investing your money seem like a second job? The *Dogs of the Dow strategy* is about as simple as you can get—and the average annual return since 1973 has been 17.7%.

The Dogs of the Dow invests in the worst performers (the dogs) of the 30 stocks that make up the Dow Jones Industrial Average. Because the Dow Jones Industrial Average contains some of the largest and best-known companies in the country, even the poor performers tend to come back.

Crash Alert

Day Trading? Get a Life!

People who buy and sell large quantities of stock to take advantage of small changes in price during the day are called *day traders*. These folks might buy 500 shares of Youbetcha, Inc., at $100, and sell it an hour later when it hits $101. They make 500 bucks in an hour minus the commission. But, when prices drop, you can lose money faster than you made it. Plus, you can do almost nothing else while the market is open—eat, run errands, or take a bio-break.

To invest in the Dogs of the Dow, you start on January 1 each year by finding the 10 worst performers in the Dow. The worst performers are those that have the highest dividend yield—the annual dividend divided by the current share price. The lower the price, the higher the dividend yield. You don't have to do the math. The easiest way to find the dogs is to check the dog list on the Dogs of the Dow Web site (http://www.dogsofthedow.com/dogs2000.htm).

Purchase equal dollar amounts of stock for each of the dogs. Then, hold the stock until the following year, when you get a new list, and buy the new dogs. That's all you have to do.

Risk and Return

No matter what choice you make with your money, your money is at risk in some way. Even if you hide it in your mattress, it can burn up in a fire with the rest of your belongings! It is important to know what financial risks you face and choose among them wisely. But it is even more important to remember that doing nothing with your money is the biggest risk of all!

As we will see, the risks of the stock market shouldn't stop you from investing. But the risk of inflation slashing your buying power should get you started!

Market Risk: When Stock Picks Go Bad

Most people understand market risk, even if they don't know its name. *Market risk* is the risk that you will lose money on an investment gone bad. And this is the risk that people talk about when they justify not buying stocks.

But just how dangerous is market risk? It depends on how you invest and your time-frame. The bottom line: If you invest in a mix of different stocks and bonds and hold for the long term, your market risk is barely noticeable.

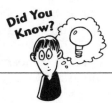

The Rule of Five

The Rule of Five, taught by NAIC in its investment classes, says that out of every five stocks that you select (using solid fundamental analysis), one will do far better than you expect, three will perform as you expect, and one will do worse. So, in buying five stocks, you have an 80% chance of being right. When you're right four out of five times, the occasional mistake won't kill you.

Looking at a one-year period, the return on stocks can be all over the map: from a high of 54% (in 1933) to a heart-stopping low of –43.3% (in 1931). But, for the past 73 years, the stock market with dividends reinvested has returned a compound annual growth rate of 11.2%.

Fine, you might say. What can I expect from stock performance in my lifetime? Based on past performance, if you invest in the stock market and hold your investments for 20 years—even the 20-year period with the worst performance—there is almost no chance of losing money.

Economic Risk: The Whole Kit and Caboodle Gets Sick

Economic risk is the danger you face when the entire economy hits a rough patch. For the younger folks reading this book, you might not even know what a recession is. But, from time to time, the whole economy does poorly. The good news is that recessions don't happen that often and don't last that long. More often than not, the economy does just fine.

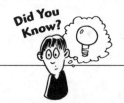

Cyclical Stocks Roll with the Economic Flow

People who invest in cyclical stocks depend on the natural cycle of the economy going up and down. By buying stocks affected by the economy (car companies, for example) when times are bad, you reap your rewards as the economy improves.

To avoid economic risk, don't speculate with your money. The current craze in dot-com stocks and initial public offerings (IPOs) might look glorious when things are good. But, when times get tough, those purchases will drop like a rock.

In the late 1980s, health care stock prices went sky high. When health care reform threatened the earnings of those companies, their stock prices plummeted. A couple of years ago, health care was back on top. And, in early 2000, they are out of favor again because investors want the recent sky-high returns of computer technology companies.

Interest rates going up, a war breaking out, or financial problems in another part of the world can all affect the stock market. When these situations arise, investors finally return to the basics: earnings. A dot-com company that looks hot today will still drop if it doesn't have enough earnings and steady earnings growth to support its sky-high price.

Playing It Safe Might Not Be So Safe (Inflation Risk)

Inflation risk is the worst of the bunch. Unlike market risk and economic risk, inflation risk just gets worse over time. A lot of people don't understand the danger it holds. Everybody over the age of five understands inflation: "I remember when a loaf of bread was only..." So, where does the risk come in?

If inflation is 3%, and your savings account at your bank pays 2% interest, you are losing money to inflation. Your bank balance doesn't go down; it still goes up by the 2%. It's your ability to buys things, your purchasing power that you lose. Just how much purchasing power can you lose? At the end of 30 years of 3% inflation, $1 is worth only about 40 cents.

Head of the Class

Bond Investors Face a Different Set of Risks

Bond investors have to put up with *interest-rate risk*. If interest rates go up, the value of bonds fall, and the bondholders lose money. Plus, the rate that the bond pays doesn't change, so it might not even make up for the bite from inflation and taxes. For short-term investments such as CDs, *reinvestment risk* is the risk that rates will be lower when your investment matures.

The danger of inflation risk is that people can squirrel their money away in safe investments for years, only to find that their savings amount to no more than a hill of beans.

Choosing the Right Risk

The right level and type of risk is different for everyone, because it depends on your circumstances and your tolerance for risk. If you skydive as a hobby, you would probably take more risk to get an investment return. But, if the thought of losing any of your money makes you squirm, you want to get your investment returns with as little risk as possible.

The risks you take with your money go hand in hand with your investment goals. When you want high investment returns, you accept higher risk—market risk and economic risk. When you're saving for retirement or college while your kids are still young, you have time on your side. Time reduces both market risk and economic risk. So, you can afford to go for the return that only stocks can give you.

When you want your money safe, because your goals are near, you want low risk. You don't care if your money doesn't grow that much. You can't afford to lose any of it. So, you buy those safe investments. In a year or two, inflation doesn't eat up too much of your stash.

Allocating Your Assets

Building your financial battle plan is all about allocating your assets. Before you burrow down into which stocks or mutual funds to buy, you figure out how big a return you want, and how much risk you can afford to take. From there you can get an overall allocation for each of the major asset classes: stocks, bonds, and cash.

How Asset Allocation Works

Asset allocation works because different investments produce results at different times. In the mid-1970s, when stocks barely moved at all, bonds returned 6%. In the late '70s, stocks returned 8%, while long-term bonds lost money. In the '80s, stocks and bonds both did well. And in the '90s, stocks have exploded, while bonds are back at 6%.

Stocks can go up or down quickly in the short term, but they provide the best long-term results. Bonds are more dependable than stocks, but don't offer as high a return over time. On the other hand, bonds can provide a steady source of income. Cash doesn't deliver much return at all. But it's handy in emergencies or when you want to buy more stocks and bonds. Don't cannibalize your three months of emergency funds to act on a hot stock tip!

By varying the percentages of these types of investments, you can balance the risks you take with your needs for growth of your money. Over time, asset allocation gives you a more predictable return without the wild one-year gyrations that stocks can go through.

One-year Returns for Stocks or Bonds Aren't Very Dependable

The single largest one-year gain for stocks was 52.6%. The single largest one-year loss for stocks was −26.5%. For the same period, the single largest one-year gain for bonds was 40.4, whereas the single largest one-year loss was −9.2%.

Choosing an Allocation That Meets Your Needs

For the risk-averse, or for goals in the near future, a low-risk mix might be 20% stocks, 40% bonds, and 40% cash equivalents (money market funds/CDs). An approach that works for conservative, income-oriented folks is more like 40% stocks, 40% bonds, and 20% cash. But, when goals are out in the future, a more aggressive mix perhaps to fund your retirement is 80% stocks, 15% bonds, and 5% cash.

The Charles Schwab Web site can suggest an asset allocation that's right for you if you answer the seven questions in its Investor Profile (`www.schwab.com/SchwabNOW/navigation/mainFrameSet/0,4528,540,00.html`). Click the

Planning tab on the site, and then click the link **Investor Profile**. The site's profile wants to know how soon you will need your savings, and how long those savings have to last. It asks some questions to determine your knowledge of investments and your tolerance for risk.

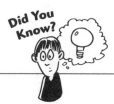

Your Risk Tolerance Also Depends on Your Income, Assets, and Level of Debt

If you're a novice at investing, you should lean toward lower risk. The price swings of higher-risk investments might scare you off your plan. If you don't earn much, or have a lot of debt, you should also keep your portfolio a little safer. On the other hand, when you make or have a lot of money, you can take more risks, because market setbacks don't endanger your lifestyle.

Click **Send** to see what type of investor you are, and what asset allocation percentages you should consider, as shown in Figure 14.2. The results not only break up your allocations into stocks, bonds, and cash, but also tell you what percentages of large company stocks, small company stocks, and international stocks you should use. You can click **Sample Portfolios** to see more detailed examples.

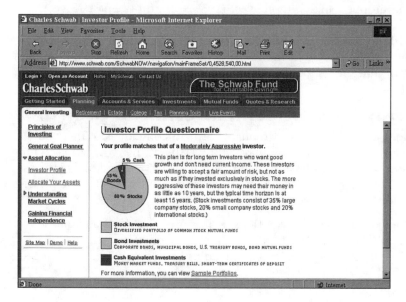

Figure 14.2

The Charles Schwab Web site can suggest an asset allocation based on your answers to its Investor Profile. You can see sample portfolios for short-term plans through aggressive plans.

Easy Ways to Allocate Your Investments

Using the Internet and mutual funds, asset allocation is a snap—and it doesn't cost an arm and a leg in commissions either. With index funds, you can allocate your assets using a handful of investments. A market index includes stocks that represent a part of the market, such as the S&P 500 index for large company stocks, or the Russell 2000 for small company stocks. *Index funds* are mutual funds that imitate a particular market index.

Asset Allocation Funds Do the Work for You

Many fund companies offer funds that provide asset allocation for you. For example, the Vanguard STAR fund keeps an allocation of about two-thirds stocks and one-third bonds.

There's an index fund for just about everything: large company stocks, small company stocks, the whole stock market, long-term bonds, intermediate-term bonds, international stocks, and many more. So, divvy up your loot, and put the right percentage of your dollars into each index that you need.

Asset allocation with index funds is more than convenient. Most index funds don't charge a fee when you purchase shares, so you can add your monthly contributions for little or no cost. It also doesn't cost much, if anything, to move your money around when you have to rebalance your allocations each year. In addition, with most fund companies, you can set up automatic withdrawals from a checking or savings account, so they automatically divide your monthly contribution between the funds you use.

Investing for the Long Term

Remember that stocks dropped 43.3% in one year (1931). But, for the past 73 years, stocks with dividends reinvested have returned an average compound annual-growth rate of 11.2%. The risks in stocks and bonds melt away with time, leaving you with a dependable and healthy return on your money. Any investment strategy can look awful at some point in time. You should care about the long-term return.

The Hazy, Lazy Days of Long-term Investing in Growth

You just can't beat long-term investments in quality growth companies. When you purchase a top-flight growth company, you have an investment that you can keep for years—those companies deliver results and investment returns for decades. As long as the company continues to grow its sales and earnings, and its prospects for the future look good, you can sit back on the weekends and let your portfolio do its work.

In addition to making your regular contributions, make sure to reinvest all your dividends. The average return from stocks on price appreciation alone over the past 73 years was 6.5%. The average return from stocks including reinvested dividends for the same period was 11.2%.

Long-term investing in growth stocks keeps your investments working for you. Every time you sell a stock, you pay a commission. And then, you have to pay a commission to buy another stock to replace it. Even with the low fees offered by online brokerages, those commissions amount to money that you can't invest.

Furthermore, unless you are investing in an IRA or other tax-deferred account, you have to pay taxes on your capital gains. With a capital-gains tax rate of 20% and commissions that might be 5% to buy and 5% to sell, a new investment has to increase 30% just to break even! The Investor's Toolkit, a stock analysis program from Investware, shown in Figure 14.3, tells you how much money a sale costs you, and how long your new investment will take to break even.

Reinvesting Dividends Is Easy!

Most brokerages can automatically reinvest any dividends you receive. And, because brokerages often don't charge a commission to reinvest dividends, you're getting a deal on the purchase of those new shares.

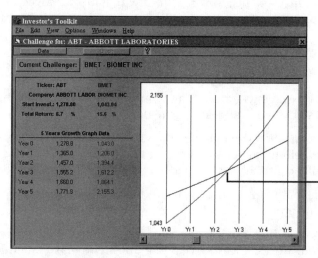

Figure 14.3

The Challenge feature in Investware's Investor's Toolkit software shows you how much you get from your sale, and how long it will take for the new purchase to break even.

With taxes and the broker's commission, this new purchase takes two and a half years to break even.

Using Mutual Funds to Invest Long Term

Mutual funds are a great way to invest for the long term. With one or two index funds or an asset allocation fund, you can allocate your investments across the entire market. You get diversification in your portfolio with just one mutual fund.

You can set up automatic transfers so that your regular contributions occur without your lifting a finger. With no-load funds, you can buy and sell your fund shares without a commission. As long as you stick with funds with low expense ratios, your investment dollars are almost 100% working for you.

Head of the Class

Some Mutual Funds Keep the Tax Bite to a Minimum

Most funds manage their business without much thought of the tax conse-
quences. Others, called *tax-managed funds*, take steps to minimize the impact of
taxes on total return. To keep the tax bite low, these funds tend to buy and
hold. But they also sell the shares with the lowest tax consequence, try to avoid
taxable income, and discourage short-term investors.

If your investments are in a retirement account, mutual funds are the perfect investment. Their only downfall is in taxable accounts. Mutual funds distribute dividends
and capital gains at least once a year, sometimes every quarter. Those distributions are
taxable, so you lose some of your investment to the government. If you want to protect your mutual fund investments, look for funds with a low turnover. By buying
and holding, these funds keep their expenses low, and minimize taxable capital gain
distributions.

Using Stocks to Invest Long Term

Stocks also are good investments for the long term. After you purchase a handful of
high-quality growth stocks, you can leave them alone for years.

You pay one commission when you purchase the shares, and might not pay another
commission until you sell the shares 40 years later in retirement. However, you do pay
commissions for regular contributions to your holdings, so a discount broker is a must.

Dividends are taxable, but many of the big technology companies don't pay dividends. They use all the profits to continue to grow the company.

A portfolio of stocks, even high-quality growth stocks, requires some maintenance.
You should review your stocks at least once a year, mostly to make sure that the fundamentals still look good.

Diversification

Diversification protects our portfolios from serious setbacks. By keeping eggs in several baskets, diversification makes sure that bad investments don't destroy our plans.

Asset allocation diversifies our investments between different types of stocks and
bonds. This type of diversification reduces the effect of bad performance by a whole
class of assets.

Diversifying Stocks

With stocks, you should invest in a number of companies of different sizes and in different industries. Smaller companies carry great risk, but usually provide the highest returns. Large companies are safer relative to small companies, but their returns are lower. And medium-sized companies fall somewhere in between. Table 14.1 shows the distribution by size that NAIC recommends, along with the returns you should look for. Many sources measure company size by *market capitalization*, which is the share price multiplied by the number of shares outstanding.

Table 14.1   Recommended Portfolio Distribution

Sales Volume	Size	% of Portfolio	Return
$0–$400 million	Small	25%	15% +
$400 million–$4 billion	Medium	50%	10%–15%
$4 billion +	Large	25%	7%–10%

Diversifying by industry helps you avoid setbacks that occur when something happens to throw an entire industry off. For example, when health care reform was a hot topic in the early 1990s, the entire health care industry lost value. If health care reform had gone through, the industry might never have recovered.

Because you can categorize each stock that you own by size and industry, you can build a diversified portfolio with about 10 stocks.

Using Mutual Funds to Diversify

A single mutual fund gives you a certain amount of diversification, because it might own hundreds of stocks and/or bonds. Depending on the fund's objective, it might own stocks of all size, in several industries. And it might include bonds and cash, as well.

You still have to be careful when you buy mutual funds. Different mutual funds could end up with very similar portfolios. Unless you check a fund's holding, you could end up buying a growth fund and a small-company growth fund that both invest in the same small-company stocks! One way to avoid this problem is to buy only one fund for each objective: one small-company growth, one large-company growth, one international, and so on.

Another pitfall that I have seen is buying too many mutual funds. People who buy several dozen funds have diversified themselves to distraction. They don't know if one fund is duplicating another. They probably don't know which funds are dogs. And managing asset allocation is a nightmare.

With mutual funds, less is more. If you buy index funds, you can allocate your assets easily and quite precisely with six funds: large-cap index, medium-cap index, small-cap index, international index, bond index, and one money-market fund. Of course, you can make it even easier with a total stock market index and a total bond market index or one asset allocation fund. The choice is yours.

The Least You Need to Know

➤ Invest regularly, regardless whether the market is up or down.

➤ Reinvest all your dividends.

➤ Diversify your investments to reduce risk.

➤ For stocks, invest in good-quality growing companies.

➤ Invest for the long term.

➤ Consider mutual funds, particularly index funds, if you are short on time or investment know-how.

Chapter 15

Finding and Researching Stocks Online

In This Chapter

➤ Using an online stock screen to find stocks to study

➤ Other online information sources and what sources to avoid

➤ Finding company news and financial data online

➤ Learning about software tools that help with stock analysis

➤ Finding places online where you can learn more about investing

Many people new to investing wonder where they will get ideas for stocks to purchase. As you start to invest, you find out that ideas for stocks aren't the problem—it's figuring out which stocks you should pursue.

The Internet is a great source for investment ideas. But it also helps you weed out the losers. After you decide on some stocks to study, you can download all the financial data and news you need, while still in your pajamas.

Finding Stocks on the Web

There are stock tips everywhere that you look on the Internet: investment newsletters, chat rooms, email lists, and investment companies selling their wares. In addition, you also can use stock screening tools that search through thousands of stocks to screen for the ones that fit your criteria.

The Needle in the Haystack: How to Use a Stock Screen

Trying to find 10 stocks out of the 10,000 or so on the major stock exchanges sounds like looking for a needle in a haystack. Fortunately, a stock screen is like a magnet for stocks with the features you want. With a stock screen, you can search for big companies, little companies, companies that pay dividends, those with steady earnings growth, and many other criteria.

Crash Alert

Garbage In, Garbage Out!

A screening tool dutifully delivers a list of stocks that match your request. But that doesn't mean it's a great list of candidates. To get the best out of a stock screen, you have to know what to look for.

The stock screen on the Wall Street Research Net (WSRN) Web site (http://www.wsrn.com) has categories for price and yield, growth, ratio, and size. Most of the criteria have minimum and maximum values, so you can search for companies with values within a range. The WSRN screen provides more than a dozen criteria, as shown in Figure 15.1, including price, PE, dividend yield, five-year EPS growth rate, sales, market cap, and which index it belongs to.

Stocks screens come in many shapes and sizes. One approach to screening is to look for companies with a record of at least five years of growth in sales and earnings, low debt, and low Price/Earnings (PE) ratios relative to their growth. In addition, you might want a small-cap company for your portfolio, but you don't want it too small because of the risk. If you want to look for companies in an industry, select an industry group.

You don't have to fill in every box. If you don't care about a minimum or maximum number, just leave it blank. A screen for this kind of company might use the criteria listed in Table 15.1.

Table 15.1   Criteria for a Stock Screen

Criteria	Minimum	Maximum
PE trailing 12 months	15	30
Yield		1%
Five-year growth rate	15%	
Debt-to-equity ratio		33%
Sales in millions	$400	$1,000

If you want a company that pays a dividend, you enter values for yield and dividend payout ratio. Select an industry group if you want to search a specific industry.

Another criterion that is good to check is the last quarter % Change in EPS (earnings per share). By using the same number in the last quarter criteria and the five-year criteria, you can see whether the screened companies are still on their growth track.

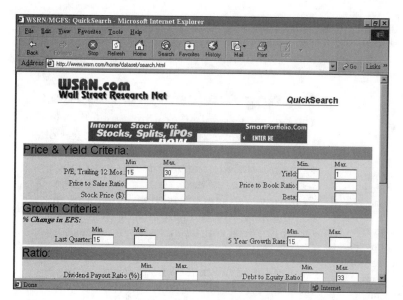

Figure 15.1

The Wall Street Research Net stock screen uses more than a dozen criteria that you enter.

When you click **Submit Query** for the screen in Table 15.1, only 20 companies fit the bill. That's still more stocks than you want to research, but far better than the thousands that you started with. Click **Refine Search** to make your stock screen even tougher. For example, bumping the EPS growth rates to 25% and decreasing the maximum PE to 25 narrows the field to only seven stocks, displayed in Figure 15.2.

Click one of the headings in the stock screen results to sort the results by that criterion. You also can click a stock name if you want to see more information about the company.

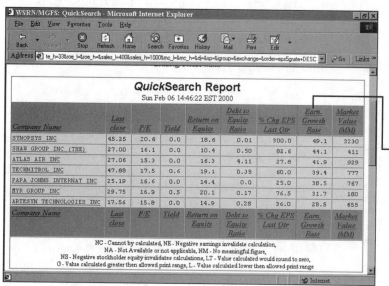

Figure 15.2

You can sort the results of the stock screen by clicking the headings. Click a company name to find out more about that company.

Sorted by Earnings Growth Rate

Company Name	Last close	P/E	Yield	Return on Equity	Debt to Equity Ratio	% Chg EPS Last Qtr	Earn. Growth Rate	Market Value (MM)
SYNOPSYS INC	45.25	20.6	0.0	18.6	0.01	300.0	49.1	3230
SHAW GROUP INC (THE)	27.00	16.1	0.0	10.4	0.50	82.6	44.1	411
ATLAS AIR INC	27.06	15.3	0.0	16.3	4.11	27.8	41.9	929
TECHNITROL INC	47.88	17.5	0.6	19.1	0.35	60.0	39.4	777
PAPA JOHNS INTERNAT INC	25.19	16.6	0.0	14.4	0.0	25.0	38.5	767
MYR GROUP INC	29.75	16.9	0.5	20.1	0.17	76.5	31.7	180
ARTESYN TECHNOLOGIES INC	17.56	15.8	0.0	14.9	0.28	36.0	28.5	655
Company Name	Last close	P/E	Yield	Return on Equity	Debt to Equity Ratio	% Chg EPS Last Qtr	Earn. Growth Rate	Market Value (MM)

NC - Cannot by calculated, NE - Negative earnings invalidate calculation,
NA - Not Available or not applicable, NM - No meaningful figure,
NS - Negative stockholder equity invalidates calculations, LT - Value calculated would round to zero,
G - Value calculated greater then allowed print range, L - Value calculated lower then allowed print range

If you want a lot of options for screening, Market Guide's Stock Quest (www.marketguide.com/mgi/STOCKQUEST/sq-about.html) screens by 75 variables. You also can create your own screening variables and custom reports.

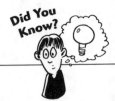

You Can Get Advice for Free!

Before you pay someone to give you investment advice, check to see if your broker provides these services for free! Many of the larger firms help with financial and investment planning at no charge. They make money when you invest in their products.

Getting Advice from the Pros

You can gather a lot of great investment advice on the Web—for free. Folks in financial services often give away some information to try to turn you into a client. Newsletters might provide one of their recent issues, or excerpts of their current issue. Company Web sites often publish opinions and commentary, which might include stock picks. Other financial consultants present model portfolios.

The Investorama directory includes a host of sources for advice and commentaries (www.investorama.com/directory/News,_Advice,_and_Talk/). With links and short descriptions, you can check out advisory services, newsletters, and other publications. Some are free. Others offer samples before the fees start. Many newsletters, magazines, and publications now offer delivery via email or print.

Talking About Stocks

Another way to get ideas for investments is to discuss stocks online. The Web hosts thousands of email discussion lists, Web discussion boards, and newsgroups about stocks. You can find discussion groups for a single stock, an industry, or investments in general.

Etiquette Is More Important on the Web

Because people do not communicate face-to-face on the Internet, *netiquette* is particularly important. Others can take your words the wrong way. No one can see your wink. CAPITAL LETTERS SEEM LIKE YOU'RE SHOUTING! And sometimes it is easy to mouth off at someone you don't know and can't see. As a member of an online community, don't escalate discourtesy. Be polite!

The NAIC I-Club-List (www.better-investing.org/computer/maillist.html) is an email discussion list where people discuss a range of subjects. From fundamental analysis to problems in investment clubs to opinions on particular stocks prospects, thousands of subscribers help each other learn and invest successfully. In addition to discussions, presenters frequently lead workshops on the email list. These workshops are thorough, thoughtful, and always educational. Those who follow along can ask questions throughout the series of presentations. To read some of the past workshops, go to the NAIC Web site (www.better-investing.org/iclub/workshop.html).

Crash Alert

It's on the Web, It Must Be True—Not!

Just because you read something on your computer screen, doesn't mean it's true. In discussion groups and even some questionable Web sites, people might post information that isn't true, to advance their own agendas. Always verify information that you get from the Internet before investing your hard-earned cash. Don't take someone else's word about the value of an investment. Do your own research, and come to your own conclusions! See Chapter 21, "Security and Safety," for more tips on protecting yourself from the bum steers in a bull market.

The Motley Fool message boards (http://boards.fool.com/), shown in Figure 15.3, include discussions on stocks from A to Z. They also host boards for other investment topics, international investing, personal finance, and more. You can read the most popular posts by clicking **Recommended Posts**. Yahoo! Finance (messages. yahoo.com/yahoo/Business_Finance/) hosts almost 8,000 message boards for individual stocks as well as more general investment topics. If you like tech stocks, don't miss the Silicon Investor Web site discussion groups (www.siliconinvestor.com/stocktalk/).

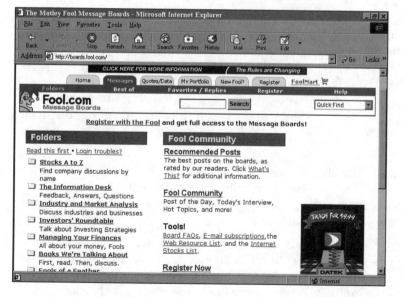

Figure 15.3

You can find groups that discuss every investment topic imaginable in message boards on the Web.

Researching Stocks

Getting the names of some stock prospects should be your first step toward buying a stock. The second step is research. Whether you get your stock tips from your eccentric Aunt Sally who picks the winners at the race track, or from your own custom stock screen, it's the research you do that increases your chances of investment success.

It doesn't matter whether you use fundamental analysis or technical analysis. Stock research needs data. And the Internet is a great place to get it!

Software Tools for Stock Analysis

If you are new to investing, how do you know what to research, what to study, or even which results are good and which are bad? Stock analysis tools help you by asking for the important data and showing you results. In addition, these tools save you a ton of time punching on a calculator, so you can spend less time calculating and more time making good decisions.

Crash Alert

Check Your Data Entry!

A good stock analysis depends on accurate information and common sense. Always check that you entered all the data correctly. If a number looks way off, double-check to make sure it is correct.

There are two software packages that analyze stocks using the NAIC investment approach. Investware (www.investware.com) offers Investor's Toolkit. STB Software (www.stbinvestorsoftware.com) offers Stock Analyst Plus! Both of these packages use sales, earning per share, profit margins, and other fundamental measurements to determine whether a company is growing, of good quality, and a good investment at the current price.

The packages include tools to select stocks and to manage your portfolio. The Stock Selection Guide helps you determine whether a company is a good investment. The Stock Comparison Guide compares the results of several Stock Selection Guides. For instance, you can compare several prospects in an industry to see which stock has the most potential.

The packages also include tools to keep track of your portfolio, and help with buying and selling decisions.

The Value Point Analysis Model (www.eduvest.com) uses 13 criteria to evaluate a stock. At the eduvest Web site, you can enter criteria to evaluate the fair value of a prospect. You also can see an existing analysis, which might be helpful as a double-check of your own research and conclusions.

For technical analysis, MetaStock 7.0 Professional (www.equis.com) implements trading strategies for all types of securities. In addition, you can download real-time and historical data automatically from the Web for your analyses. If you just use basic charting, you can try the online version of MetaStock (www.equis.com/java).

Your Judgment Is a Key to Success

In many cases, the company's future is very different from its past. Never accept the results of a computer program without making sure that they make sense. For example, a company whose earnings are growing at 100% a year won't continue like that for very long. In this case, you should estimate the growth in the future at a slower rate.

Using EDGAR to Get Company Financial Data

EDGAR (Electronic Data Gathering, Analysis, and Research) is the database of company financial data maintained by the SEC. The best way to find and download SEC filings is through FreeEDGAR (www.freeedgar.com). FreeEDGAR is easier to use, and the filings are posted sooner.

On FreeEDGAR, you can enter a company name, or up to 10 ticker symbols, to see a list of SEC filings for those companies. You can click the hyperlink for a report to view it on the screen. If you want to download a file, click the **RTF** button. The FreeEDGAR site also provides a glossary of the different types of SEC filings (http://www.freeedgar.com/Reference/tools/filingtypes.htm).

The Alphabet Soup of SEC Filings

A 10-Q report is a quarterly report that includes unaudited financial statements and information about the company's performance during the year. A 10-K is a comprehensive annual report of the company's business and finances.

Investment Reports

Some companies gather financial data about companies, and sell the data in a concise, standard format so that it is easier to compare different companies. Value Line (www.valueline.com) presents company financial information on more than 6,000 stocks in a concise one-page format. You can subscribe to the Value Line service and receive hardcopy reports or a compact disc. Using the CD, you can sort, screen, graph, and report on the data. Or you can transfer the data to your software stock analysis program. If the subscription cost is too high for you, most libraries keep the hardcopy reports in the reference area.

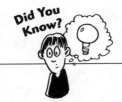

Normalizing Data Helps You Compare Apples to Apples

Value Line normalizes the data in its reports. To normalize data, it removes certain numbers, such as one-time charges, to better reflect the true performance of the company.

Standard & Poor's Compustat database (www.compustat.com) offers reports on more than 11,000 companies in the United States and Canada, plus information on indexes, and more.

Going Online to Snag Annual and Quarterly Reports

As a shareholder in a company, you should receive copies of the annual and quarterly reports of the companies that you own. Getting reports for companies that you don't own used to be tedious. But, with the Internet, it's a snap. Most companies include a section where you can download their financial reports and SEC filings.

Check Things Out with Investor Relations

The Investor Relations departments at most companies are there to answer your questions. Most company Web sites have a link to Investor Relations, so you can email your questions to them. For example, find out why their profit margins have dropped during the last five years. Just remember you won't get any insider information.

The Annual Report Service site (www.annualreportservice.com) offers annual reports for many companies online. First, pick the link for the section of the alphabet for the company name. Then, click **Online** to view an online version. Or click **Hardcopy** to request a hardcopy report. In many cases, you can download a copy of the online annual report. You can also click the company's name to go to its Web site.

If a company doesn't offer its annual report through the online Annual Report Service, you can contact the Public Register's Annual Report Service (www.prars.com) to request a hardcopy annual report. On the PRARS site, you can search for companies by industry, state, stock exchange, or by the first letter of the company name.

All the News That's Fit to Post

The Internet is a tremendous place for news. With online news, you can search for certain words, or set up an alert so that you get an email when a news item comes out on a particular company.

Wall Street Research Net (www.wsrn.com) is a great place to start for information on companies. On the WSRN home page, enter a company ticker symbol and click **Get Research**. You get a whole page of links for information on that company, displayed in Figure 15.4. WSRN provides links to the company home page, SEC filings, stock quotes, graphs and charts, summaries, and news. You also can link to sites for historical data, research reports, spreadsheets, and earnings estimates. If a link takes you to a site that charges a fee, you see a dollar sign ($) after the link name.

Use the Web Sites That You Like

Many sites on the Web provide financial news, quotes, charts, and more. Web sites come in all sorts of styles. Some have a lot of ads and glitzy pictures. Others are plain and simple. Find Web sites that you like, and use them.

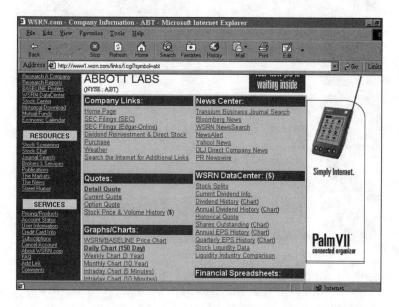

Figure 15.4

Wall Street Research Net gives you links to all kinds of information about a company from one Web page.

Did You Know?

Some Sites Charge Extra for Information

The WSRN Data Center is a subscription service. For a small monthly fee, you can get information such as dividends, stock splits, historical prices, and historical annual and quarterly earnings.

The WSRN NewsSearch can search for news about a company in newspapers, such as the *Wall Street Journal*, or online magazines, such as *Forbes* and *Fortune*. WSRN NewsSearch also searches Web sites, such as CNNfn, Silicon Investor Discussion, or Yahoo!.

Financial Charts

Charts can be handy for fundamental stock analysis. But they are critical for technical analysis. MoneyCentral Investor on MSN (www.moneycentral.com/investor), shown in Figure 15.5, provides a lot of information on companies, including charts. To see charts in MoneyCentral, you must download the MSN MoneyCentral software. It's free, and downloads in about five minutes.

Figure 15.5

You can view price charts for time periods from one day to more than 10 years, display technical indicators or market indexes, and even download data into an Excel spreadsheet.

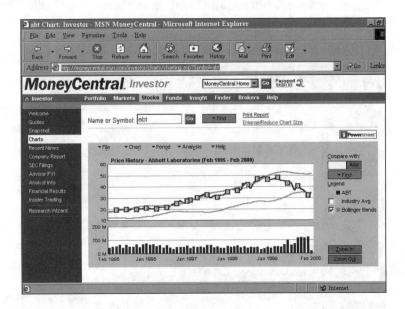

You can select a chart of price history, price performance, or investment growth. Click **Period** to set the time period from as short as one day to more than 10 years. If you want technical indicators on the chart, click **Analysis**, and select the analysis items you want. In Analysis, you also can show indexes or moving averages. To download the data into an Excel spreadsheet, click **File** and select **Export Data**.

WSRN also has links to several charting sites. BigCharts (www.bigcharts.com) has easy-to-read charts for us idiots who have ruined our eyes on the computer. If you click **Quick Chart**, you can see a price history from one day to more than 10 years. Click **Interactive Chart** to customize the chart. You can set the length of time, as well as the reporting frequency, such as quarterly reports for five years.

You also can control what indicators appear on the chart, and which chart style to use. If you click **Compare To**, you can view charts for two companies at a time. When you click **email this chart**, you can send the chart to yourself (or a friend). You can even pick the days of the week that you want the chart sent.

Other People's Analyses

Even with analysis software, entering data can be a chore. On top of that, if you're new to investing, you might not trust your judgment. Or you don't even know what judgment is!

In the NAIC Data File library (www.better-investing.org/content/filelib.html), you can download analyses of stocks posted to the site by NAIC members. These files work with the NAIC approved software, Investor's Toolkit, and Stock Analyst Plus. By using these files, you can see what others think about a company, and you don't have to enter data by hand.

However, you should double-check to make sure that the other person entered the data correctly. You also want to check the assumptions that the other person made. Did they estimate the future growth rates too liberally? Did they apply some judgment that you disagree with?

Learning More About Stocks

The Internet contains a wealth of information about investing for beginners to professionals. As you learn, you can surf on the Web to continually increase your knowledge. But all that information can be intimidating at the beginning.

Getting Started

The Motley Fool Web site (www.fool.com) is the best site to start. The Motley Fool motto is "To educate, amuse, enrich." Fools believe that us mere mortals can succeed at investing—even outperform the professionals on Wall Street. At the Fool's School (see Figure 15.6), you can learn to invest your money "Foolishly," and have fun at the same time (www.fool.com/School/Basics/InvestingBasics.htm). Thirteen steps take you from the basics to advanced topics. It won't hurt a bit!

Figure 15.6

The Motley Fool is a fun place to start learning about investing in seriously making money.

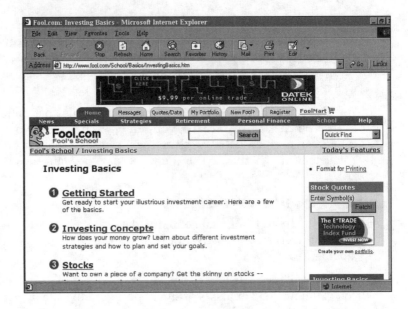

NAIC is a not-for-profit organization that has taught millions of people to invest successfully. With more than 50 years of practice, NAIC investment clubs and their members regularly beat the pros.

The NAIC Web site offers education, tools, software, and services to help you invest successfully. Its online workshops cover investment topics, such as reading financial statements or questioning Investor Relations. They also present workshops of stock studies so you can follow what the more experienced NAIC folks do. Those who follow along on the email presentations can post questions or opinions. NAIC chapters around the country also teach face-to-face classes.

Head of the Class

Do Your Homework

When you belong to an investment club, you can't put off doing your homework. The monthly meeting is an incentive to spend some time learning about investments.

Try an Investment Club—You'll Like It!

Investment clubs are another great place to start. Even with a group of beginners, an investment club gives you the opportunity to discuss your reasoning and decisions. If each person researches an investment topic, and presents it to the club, everyone learns at a faster pace. Plus, by dividing up the work, a club can study and follow more stocks than you can by yourself.

If you want to learn more about investment clubs, the NAIC Web site is the place to go (www. better-investing.org/clubs/clubs.html).

The Least You Need to Know

➤ You can use a stock screen to find investments that suit your needs and investing style.

➤ You can learn a lot with online discussion groups. But don't believe everything you hear! Always do your own homework.

➤ Stock analysis software helps you find a good investment. But you still have to think!

➤ The Internet provides financial data, financial reports, news, research, and more. A lot of information is free. But some companies charge for their information.

➤ You can learn about investing online. You also might try an investment club for a lot of learning and support.

Chapter 16

Buying Stocks Online

In This Chapter

➤ Services that brokers offer

➤ Choosing an online broker

➤ How to buy or sell stocks online

➤ Setting up a watch list for stocks

You can't go down to the corner store to buy stock in a company. You must purchase your investments through a brokerage firm. However, with the advent of online brokers, you can place orders at any time of day. And, in many cases, you use most of your cash for investments, instead of paying the broker's commission.

Today, you can choose from all styles of brokerage firms: full-service, discount, online, or one somewhere in between. Once again, the Internet comes to the rescue, so you can surf through all these choices and companies to find the broker just right for you!

Picking a Broker

Whether you work with a broker in person, or place your orders in cyberspace, you entrust your portfolio and your investment decisions to your brokerage firm. They hold your investment assets, and they execute your orders. They should be trustworthy. And they should place your orders correctly and in a timely fashion.

Price Versus Service

In the past, brokers were one size fits all. They offered full service and charged full commissions. Full-service firms do not only place your buy and sell orders for you. With a full-service firm, you might start by working with a planner to review your finances and prepare a financial plan. You might work with the planner to put together an estate plan, or figure out how to minimize the taxes you pay.

A Full-Service Broker Can Be a Great Deal!

A full-service broker's commission might seem high. If you buy and hold for the long term, though, you might only make one or two trades a year. That means you could get his other services for a song.

Full-service firms have their own research staffs. You can get investment recommendations, research, and advice only available to the firm's clients. In addition, you might work with one individual, who knows your financial situation, can answer all your questions, and can recommend investments that fit. To pay for all these services, you pay quite a commission on each trade that you make.

To find a full-service broker, take a look at the list on the Yahoo! Web site (http://dir.yahoo.com/ Business_and_Economy/Companies/ Financial_Services/Investment_Services/ Brokerages/Full_Service/). SmartMoney.com ranks seven of the largest full-service brokers (http://www.smartmoney.com/si/brokers/fullserv/). Click **Complete Rankings: A Sortable Table** to see who comes out on top depending on what you want.

Discount brokers focus on low commissions. Their commissions might be 10% of those charged by a full-service firm. You won't get the support, recommendations, or one-on-one planning services. But some discount brokers do offer services and might have higher commissions. Others offer no extra services, but bargain-basement commissions. Read on to find the best broker for you.

Things to Consider Before Selecting an Online Broker

Before you can decide on a broker, you need to know what's available. And you have to decide what is important to you. Each broker offers a different combination of features, whether it's low commissions, a dependable Web site, a lot of products, or good customer service.

Here are some of the things you should consider before you make your choice:

➤ **How much money do you need to open an account?** Some firms do not require a minimum to open an account. Others might want $1,000 or more. If you're just getting started, look for firms with no minimum balance. Also, check to see if a firm waives the minimum if you agree to an automatic monthly investment plan.

➤ **How much do trades cost?** A trade could cost anywhere from $5 to more than $100, depending on which broker you use. However, discount brokers might charge different amounts for online orders, versus telephone orders, market orders, or limit orders. Some brokers offer higher discounts if you trade frequently. If you use market or limit orders, check the trade costs for the type of orders you use.

Commissions might vary depending on the number of shares you trade, or whether you buy stocks listed on an exchange or over-the-counter.

Head of the Class

Two Brokers Might Be Better Than One

If your IRA account meets the minimum for a broker with great research, or services such as automatic reinvestment of dividends, transfer your IRA account to them. Open your regular brokerage account with a firm with no minimum balance.

Did You Know?

Choosing Between Market and Limit Orders

When you place a market order, the broker buys or sells the shares at the going price in the market. That price could be quite different from the price when you placed your order. You know that your order will be filled, but you don't know exactly what the buy or sell price is.

With a limit order, you specify what price you want to buy or sell at. The order won't execute unless the price hits the limit. So, you know what the trade price is, but you don't know if the order will be filled.

➤ **What other fees do they charge?** Some firms charge fees for other services, such as an account maintenance fee, issuing a stock certificate, getting a copy of a statement, wiring funds, or even closing your account. If you use those services, make sure you know how much they will add to your costs.

➤ **How is their customer service?** There are quite a few horror stories about discount brokers taking months to correct an error, or telling their customers to stop calling so much. Even a discount broker should answer the phone in a reasonable period of time. Make sure that the broker provides the level of support that you want.

➤ **What kind of access do they provide?**   Some brokers only offer online access; some offer access at their offices; the majority offer online and telephone access. Check that the broker offers the type of access that you want. Also, check to see whether a trade costs more if you use the telephone or show up in person, instead of using the Web.

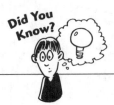

Buying on Margin Can Be Dangerous

With a margin account, you can borrow up to 50% of your total account value to buy more shares. If your investments do well, margin can increase your return, because you can buy more. But you pay interest on your margin loan, which reduces the return on your investment.

In addition, when the value of your account drops, so does the amount you can borrow. When the amount you borrowed exceeds 50% of your account, the broker makes a *margin call*, and you have to deposit more money into your account, or sell shares to cover your margin loan.

➤ **What services do they offer?**   Brokers offer more than buying and selling shares. Some offer news, research, or unlimited free quotes, as shown in Figure 16.1. For example, you might want to be able to write checks on your account, roll cash over into a money market account, or transfer funds automatically from your bank to your money market each month. See if the broker automatically reinvests dividends and fractional shares, and whether he charges a commission for these reinvestments. If you do want to buy on margin, see if the broker offers margin accounts.

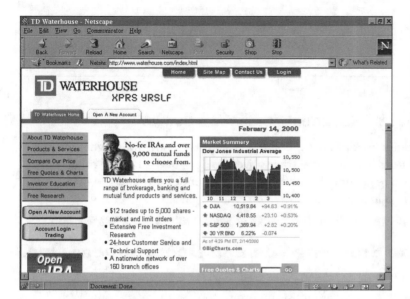

Figure 16.1

Waterhouse Securities (www.waterhouse.com) is one of SmartMoney.com's top-ranked discount brokers. It offers online trading, research, news, quotes, charts, earnings estimates, S&P reports, and more.

➤ **Do they offer mutual funds?**
Some brokerages act as supermarkets where you can invest in mutual funds from many different mutual fund companies. You might have to pay a transaction fee to buy some funds. If mutual funds are a part of your plan, find out whether the broker offers the funds you want, and whether he or she charges a transaction fee.

➤ **What other types of securities do they sell besides stocks?** Not all firms sell other types of investments, such as options, foreign stocks, penny stocks, IPOs, or bonds. If you plan to invest in securities other than stocks, check whether the firm sells those securities.

➤ **How reliable are they at executing trades when the market heats up?** Whether you use market or limit orders, you want your broker to execute your orders quickly. When the market experiences heavy trading volume, brokerage firms sometimes get bogged down. If you are trading online, you might not even get logged in to place a trade. Find out how well the firm performs on busy days. Also, look into their policies. They might give you the online trade rate whenever you can't log in to their site.

Head of the Class

A Lot of Information Is Free on the Web

Don't pay a broker for research, news, and quotes that you can find free on the Web!

Crash Alert

Exotic Securities Could Cost You a Bundle

There are other securities besides stocks, bonds, and mutual funds. You might have heard about options, commodities, derivatives, Spiders, and a host of other investments. Unless you really understand what these securities do—and the risks that they carry—you're a lot better off sticking to the basics.

Do You Want the Brokerage Behind Door Number One, Two, or Three?

After you decide which features are most important to you, there are some Web sites that can help you weed out the potential winners.

All Online Brokers Keep Your Transactions Secure

All online brokers require that you use a secure Web browser on your computer when you enter your financial data. The brokers use special software at their end so that they can unscramble the code. Go to Chapter 21, "Security and Safety," to learn more about online security.

The Gomez Advisors Web site offers several great features for choosing a broker. It rates every broker that offers Internet trading. You can view the 20 best Internet brokers for categories, including ease of use, customer confidence, on-site resources, relationship services, and overall cost. The site also rates the firms by best overall score.

The Gomez Advisors Web site also rates the firms by how well they serve the needs of different types of investors. Investor types include the Hyper-Active Trader, the Serious Investor, the Life-Goal Planner, and One-Stop Shoppers. As you get close to a decision, you also can compare the features for two brokers side by side. Or you can read broker ratings and reviews by consumers.

SmartMoney.com offers a survey of 21 well-known discount brokers, shown in Figure 16.3. It rates these brokers by several criteria, such as trading costs, the products they sell, their mutual fund offerings, services, reliability, responsiveness, and complaints. Click **Complete Rankings: A Sortable Table** to see how these brokers perform in the criteria important to you.

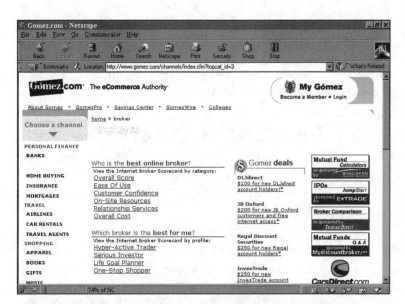

Figure 16.2

Gomez Advisors offers several great tools on its Web site for choosing the right broker.

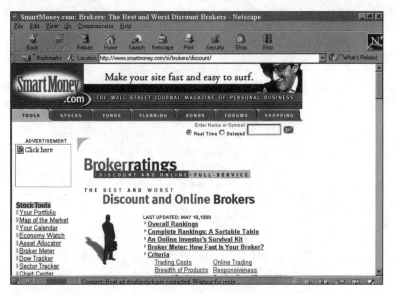

Figure 16.3

The SmartMoney.com surveys ranks 21 well-known discount brokers by several criteria. You can sort the brokers based on the criteria that are important to you.

Opening an Account

Most brokers have an account application that you can download from their Web site. Usually, the main page of the Web site has a hard-to-miss link: Open a New Account, or something similar. In some cases, you can fill in the blanks on an online application, and then print the application out. Either way, you sign the form and send in your application, along with a check to open the account.

A few online brokers have simplified the application process even more. For example, when you apply online for an account with DLJDirect, they electronically review your application. As soon as the review is complete, and they approve your application, you get an account number and a password. You might be able to start trading immediately. Of course, you must send a check in within three days to cover any trade.

Tool Tips

The Internet Ticker Is Universal

You don't have to be at your broker's site to get a quote. Most portal and search sites provide stock quotes using an identical system.

Crash Alert

Review Twice, Click Once

When you click the button to send the order, don't get impatient. When they're busy, Web sites are slow to react. If you click the Send Order button twice, you might end up sending two orders to buy those 1,000 shares of Microsoft! Give the Web site a little time.

Investing in Cyberspace

Online trading is quick, convenient, and cheap. In addition to these advantages, other online tools give you the edge to make your investments a success.

Online Investment Transactions

Each broker's online procedures are different. But, to buy or sell shares of stock, they all need the same information. You enter the ticker symbol or the company name. Often, you can click a **Quote** button, to get a current quote. If you enter the company name, click **Lookup** to find the ticker symbol for the stock.

You specify whether you want to buy or sell, and the number of shares. You select whether you want a market order or a limit order. Your broker might have other types of orders as well. For a limit order, you enter the limit price. If you place a stop order, which sells your stocks if the price drops to the stop price, you must enter the stop price. Finally, you specify whether you want the order good for the day, or good until you cancel it.

Many sites give you a chance to review your order before you send it. Read through the order carefully, before you click the button that actually sends the order. If you see a mistake, click a button to cancel or edit the order! If you send a market order with an error, chances are good the order will execute before you can go back in and change it.

You might be able to check status, cancel, or change orders that have not been executed. Look for buttons such as **Change Order**, **Review Order**, or **Status**.

Watch for a Bargain

With the market sky high, you might have a list of stocks that you would like to buy. The only problem is that their price is higher than you want to pay. One way to solve this problem is to place a *good until cancelled limit order*. For example, if Cool-E-Commerce shares are selling for $50, but you only want to pay $30, you can place a limit order for $30 a share. By setting the order as good until cancelled, the order will stand for three months, or until it executes, whichever comes first. If Cool-E-Commerce doesn't drop to $30 within the three months, the order cancels automatically.

The Problem with Good Until Cancelled Limit Orders

Sometimes, bad news comes out about the company. The price might drop—for a very good reason! Cool-e-Commerce's young and geeky CEO, the brains behind the business, leaves to study Buddhism in Tibet. With a limit order, you buy the stock when it hits your limit price, regardless of the reason.

A watch list is a better way to watch for a drop in a stock price. With a watch list, you can see if a stock has dropped to your buy price or lower. But you decide whether it is still a buy!

You can trick most of the online portfolio trackers into being watch lists. The trick goes like this. Tell the portfolio tracker that you purchased one share of stock. But, instead of an actual purchase price, put the price at which you would like to buy the stock. When the portfolio tracker shows that you lost money on your purchase, the stock has dropped below your buy price.

For example, let's create a watch list on Quicken.com. Click the **Portfolio** link on the Quicken.com Investing page (`www.quicken.com/investments/`). Then click **Create New Portfolio**. Let's say that we would like to buy Abbott Labs at $40. In the form, enter **ABT** for the ticker, **1** for the number of shares, and **40** for the purchase price. In Figure 16.4, the current price for Abbott Labs is $35.06, below our desired price of $40. And the gain/loss column shows a negative number. That's our buy sign!

Figure 16.4

A loss in the gain/loss column of our Watch List means that the stock price has dropped below our desired purchase price.

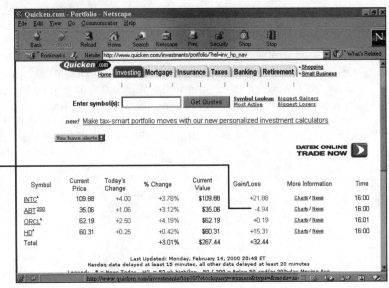

Abbott Labs is below our desired buy price, because the gain/loss number is negative.

Buying Stocks Without a Broker

If you're ready to invest in stocks, but only have a few dollars a month, don't worry! Dividend Reinvestment Plans (DRIPs) enable you to buy shares in many well-known companies, such as Coca-Cola, Intel, and Johnson & Johnson.

What Are DRIPs?

Many companies offer dividend reinvestment plans so that they don't have to pay their dividends out in cash. Current shareholders enrolled in a DRIP can get their dividends reinvested in shares of the company for little or no commission.

Did You Know?

More Companies Offer Direct Stock Plans Every Year

In 1999, more than 600 companies offered direct stock purchase plans. More than 1,600 offer DRIPs or DPPs.

The real steal with DRIPs is that most allow you to purchase additional shares without paying commissions. With a minimum investment of $25 and no commission, even the leanest budget has room for investing!

If you're interested in learning more about DRIPs, go to DRIP Central (www.dripcentral.com). Click **Guide to DRIP Investing** to find out the details to this low-cost technique. The DRIP Central site also has links to articles, books, and newsletters on DRIP investing, as well as directories of companies that offer DRIPs.

Find That DRIP!

At NetStock Direct (www.netstockdirect.com) you can enter a company name or ticker symbol. Click **Find!** to see if the company offers a DRIP or direct stock purchase plan (DPP or DSP). If they do offer a plan, you can click **Plan Summary** to learn the details.

If you want to see what companies offer plans, you can click **Find Plans** to search for plans, as shown in Figure 16.5. You can search by industry, by minimum investment, or several other features. From the main page, you can also click **All Plans A to Z** to see all the plans available.

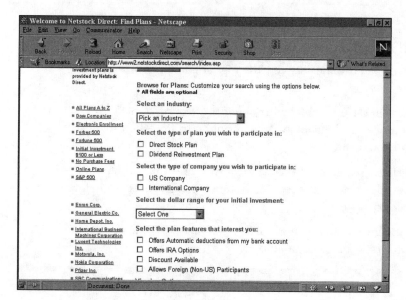

Figure 16.5

With NetStock Direct you can search for DRIP plans by several criteria.

How to Buy a DRIP

The one snag in the DRIP scheme is that you must own at least one share to participate in the plan. You can buy that share through a discount broker, but you might pay a commission on $5 to over $50 for that share. In addition, the broker might charge you a fee to issue the stock certificate—and that could cost another $25.

Click **DRIP Services** on the DRIP Central Web site to get a list of companies that can help you get started with DRIP investing, and buy that first share without spending a bundle.

Did You Know?

Some Plans Are Raising Their Fees

As more and more plans appear, you might find that some charge higher fees or require higher minimums. Read the details of the company's plan to make sure that its fees fit your budget.

The National Association of Investors Corporation offers a low-cost investment plan (http://www.better-investing.org/store/lcp.html). You must be a member of NAIC to participate ($39 per year). For a one-time $7 charge and the cost of one share for each company you buy, the NAIC plan buys your first share and sets up your DRIP account with the company. After that, you work directly with the company.

With companies that offer Direct Purchase Plans, you can buy shares right from the company. You don't pay commission, and you don't need someone to help you get your first share.

The Least You Need to Know

➤ Full-service brokers offer a lot of hand-holding and services, such as research and planning. If you need these services, the higher commissions might be worth it.

➤ Discount brokers offer differing degrees of service, discount commissions, customer service, products, and reliability. Search online to find the broker that offers the features you want.

➤ You can place orders, change orders, or check order status online. Always double-check an order before you send it, because it might execute before you have a chance to correct it.

➤ Dividend Reinvestment Plans and Direct Stock Purchase Plans help you buy shares of stock with little or no commissions.

Chapter 17

Investing in Mutual Funds

In This Chapter

➤ Why mutual funds might make more sense for you than individual stocks

➤ Finding funds online that meet your objectives

➤ What to look for in a mutual fund and what to avoid

➤ Learning more about mutual funds online

The thought of investing in stocks stops many people in their tracks. Some of us don't have the time to spend finding and researching stocks. Others prefer time with their families, or enjoying a hobby, to managing their investments. Then again, some of us are intimidated by the financial markets and want someone experienced to help. New investors wonder how they can afford to buy individual stocks without paying most of their money to a broker. How can you build a diversified portfolio when you can only afford to invest $30 a month?

Mutual funds are the answer to all these issues. They're a good fit for a portfolio, whether you are a beginner with a little money to invest or an expert with limited time—or anyone in between!

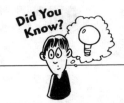

Did You Know?

Closed-end Funds Are Like Stocks

A closed-end fund issues a fixed number of shares. You can only buy shares if someone else sells them. Like stocks, the share price depends on what someone will pay, as opposed to the value of the fund's investments.

What You Really Need to Know About Mutual Funds

A mutual fund is an investment vehicle that pools money from many investors. Each mutual fund has an investment objective that guides how the fund invests, such as small-company growth stocks, short-term corporate bonds, or an S&P 500 index. The manager or managers for the mutual fund invest and oversee the pool of money to achieve the investment objective. If the manager is successful (and unfortunately, there is no guarantee that he or she will be), your mutual fund gets you where you want to go financially. In addition, mutual funds have the clout of a big investor and obtain better commission rates, slightly better purchase prices, and higher priority than you could get as a small individual investor.

The mutual funds that most people are familiar with are called *open-end mutual funds*. With open-end funds, you can send money to the fund any time you want, and new members can join any time. The fund creates shares when you add cash, and eliminates shares when you withdraw your money.

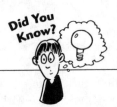

Did You Know?

Other People's Purchases Don't Affect Your Investment

When other people add money to the mutual fund, the NAV doesn't change. The value of the fund goes up, but so does the number of shares.

Each day, an open-end mutual fund calculates its net asset value (NAV). The net asset value is the market value of the securities the fund holds, minus costs, divided by the number of shares outstanding. You buy or sell shares at the most recent NAV. The price of a fund share goes up or down depending on how its investments do.

Seven Reasons to Love Mutual Funds

Mutual funds earn a place in every investor's heart—and portfolio—because they offer so much for a (usually) small price. Here are some of the reasons you should consider mutual funds for some, if not all, of your investment portfolio:

➤ **Match your objectives to your investments.** Mutual funds pack a punch. With mutual funds, you can achieve all your investment objectives—from long-term growth to short-term savings—and diversify—by market sector, company size, and individual holdings—by investing in half-a-dozen mutual funds. In addition, you can achieve any specific investment objective by buying one fund that shares that objective. You might need more individual stocks and bonds than you can handle to achieve those same objectives.

➤ **Get professional money management.** Mutual fund managers are experienced professionals. Although there is no guarantee that a fund manager will achieve the fund's objective, the manager's full-time job is managing the fund's assets to achieve the fund's objective. Fund managers carry the burden of finding and buying good investments. They watch the fund's investments and weed out the dogs. Depending on the type of fund, they might move to other types of investments as market conditions change. In short, they spend their working hours trying to earn you the best return for your investment objective.

Few of us can afford to work full-time managing our investments. Furthermore, if you want a professional to manage your money for you, but can't afford an investment advisor, mutual funds are one solution.

Crash Alert

Churn Butter, Not Stocks

Good stockbrokers sell you on good stocks, and suggest investments appropriate for your goals. Bad stockbrokers might be few in number, but they can cost you money by churning your account—trading securities to generate commissions. Some brokers might recommend investments not suitable for your goals. Others might even buy or sell without permission, or even steal from your account.

➤ **Spend less time following your investments.** Let's face it. Investing in stocks takes some time to do right. You have to find potential investments. Then, you gather your data, research a company's prospects, and decide whether it is a good investment. As a shareholder, you have to follow your stocks to make sure they will continue to perform. Managing a well-rounded portfolio of stocks can take several hours a month.

Instead of finding, researching, and tracking numerous individual stocks and bonds, you can find a handful of mutual funds that match your objectives. Then, you can sit back, relax, and let the fund managers take care of the rest. All you need is a quick quarterly check-up to make sure that your funds still are performing. You also can look at moving your money around once a year if one fund's huge success has skewed your allocations.

➤ **Follow the investment principles without even trying.** Mutual funds make it easy to follow the basic steps to financial success: buy and hold for the long term, reinvest your earnings, and diversify to limit risk. You invest in your portfolio of mutual funds and mostly leave them alone. The fund manager takes care of any investment changes that are needed. You can set your funds up to reinvest all earnings, so you reap the benefits of compounding. And, each mutual fund owns many different securities, so you diversify by buying just one investment.

➤ **Follow your non-investment principles.** Socially responsible, or *green*, mutual funds only invest in companies that meet certain criteria for principles, such as environmental friendliness and equal opportunity for minorities, or avoid companies with products such as tobacco or alcohol. The mutual fund does the research so you can concentrate on investing without worrying about company policies counter to your principles.

➤ **Start investing without big bucks.** Some mutual funds do require minimum initial deposits and minimum monthly deposits. But, with automatic investment plans, you can begin investing in many funds with no initial deposit and regular monthly contributions of as little as $25. Automatic investment plans also give you dollar-cost averaging at no extra charge!

➤ **Pick good funds without a lot of work.** Good mutual funds are much easier to find than good stocks. See the section "What to Look for in a Fund," later in this chapter.

A Fund for All Seasons

According to the Investment Company Institute, investors could choose from 7,314 mutual funds in 1998, compared to the 505 mutual funds available in 1978. No matter what your investment objectives, there are mutual funds to satisfy them.

Many mutual funds have very specific objectives, such as a sector fund, which invests in a particular sector of the market (such as technology or health care). A short-term corporate bond fund invests primarily in short-term corporate bonds. Other mutual funds embrace broad objectives, such as a capital appreciation or income. A capital appreciation fund seeks to increase its value. The manager invests in almost any investment that he or she thinks will produce results. Table 17.1 lists major fund categories in order of increasing risk, and shows their investment objectives.

Table 17.1   Mutual Funds Come in All Shapes and Sizes

Fund Category	Capital Risk	Objective
Money market	Low	Short-term interest rates
Short-term bond	Low	Higher income than money markets

Fund Category	Capital Risk	Objective
Intermediate-term bond	Medium-low	Higher income than short-term bonds
Long-term bond	Medium	High income; capital gains on interest rate declines
Mixed income	Medium	High income from bonds and dividend-paying stocks; some growth from stocks
Balanced	Medium	Some income; some growth
Equity income	Medium-high	More growth with some income from high dividend paying stocks
Growth and income	Medium-high	Mostly growth with some income
Asset allocation	Medium-high	Good growth while limiting risk
Global equity	Medium-high+	Capital gains from U.S. and foreign companies
Growth	Medium-high+	Capital gains from growth companies
International equity	Medium-high+	Capital gains from foreign companies
Sector	High	Capital gains from companies in a market sector
Capital appreciation	High	Above-average gains from any investments that produce
Small-company growth	High	Above-average capital gains from small companies
Index	Same as index	Mirrors the performance of a market index

Distributions and Taxes

One downside to mutual funds that you can avoid with stocks is distributions. Some stocks pay dividends. If you hold those stocks in a taxable account, you will pay taxes on those dividends. However, you don't pay taxes on the capital gains until you sell the stock. In addition, if you buy growth stocks that don't pay any dividends, and hold them for the long term, you could avoid paying taxes on your investments for years.

When a mutual fund makes a distribution, it's paying out cash to the shareholders (or possibly creating new shares for those who reinvest earnings). As the cash goes out, the NAV of the fund goes down. The value of your investments doesn't change. You just have some of it in cash or additional shares instead of in the NAV of the fund.

Income distributions are made up of interest and dividends paid by a fund's securities. When a mutual fund sells securities at a profit, it also makes capital gains distributions. You might receive an income distribution every quarter. Capital-gains distributions usually occur at the end of the year. Mutual funds usually do more buying and selling than an individual investor does. So, with mutual funds in a taxable account, you end up paying taxes on capital gains as you go.

Head of the Class

Beware the Ides of March—And the End of June and December

Capital gains distributions commonly occur at the end of June and the end of December. The record date of a distribution is the day that the fund identifies everyone who owns shares in the fund. Then, several days later, the fund makes the distribution on the payable date. If you buy between the record date and the payable date, you immediately lose money. You won't receive the distribution because you weren't an owner on the record date. But, your investment value drops along with the fund NAV on the payable date.

If your mutual funds are in an IRA or other tax-deferred account, you don't have to worry about paying taxes on distributions. However, there is a way to reduce the tax bite for funds in a taxable account. Tax-managed mutual funds manage the fund investments not only to achieve the investment objective, but also to minimize taxes. These funds hold stocks longer, so they don't realize as many capital gains. In addition, fewer capital gains means lower taxable distributions. In general, funds with low portfolio turnover are best for avoiding current taxes.

Index Funds for the Lazy Over-Achievers

Index funds are mutual funds that strive to mirror the investments and performance of a market index. Refer to Chapter 14, "Investing Made Easy," for the basics on index funds. Actively managed funds are funds where the fund managers pick stocks in an attempt to beat the market averages.

Despite all the claims you might see about different mutual funds' performance, over time it is very difficult for actively managed funds to outperform a corresponding market index fund, as shown in Figure 17.1. Index funds are easy—and cheap—to manage. An index fund owns the same securities that make up the market index, and it has to change stocks only when the composition of the index changes. Index funds can have expense ratios as low as 2/10ths of a percent.

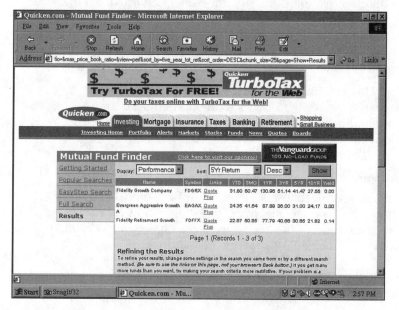

Figure 17.1

Only three mutual funds out of the 2,263 in the Morningstar large-company categories beat the S&P 500 over all measured periods up to the past 10 years.

One disadvantage that actively managed funds face is the fact that they are actively managed. Actively managed often means active trading, which in turn means broker commissions. Actively managed funds might have higher expenses to pay for all those commissions, as well as the expertise of the manager. If a fund has an expense ratio of 2%, the fund performance has to beat the index by 2% just to stay even!

It's true that some actively managed funds consistently outperform their market index. But, if you look at long-term results, you might find that the difference in return is small. Index funds provide good performance at a low cost. In addition, picking index funds is easy.

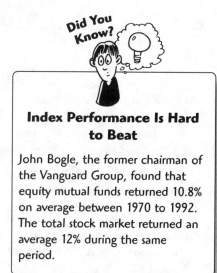

Did You Know?

Index Performance Is Hard to Beat

John Bogle, the former chairman of the Vanguard Group, found that equity mutual funds returned 10.8% on average between 1970 to 1992. The total stock market returned an average 12% during the same period.

What to Look for in a Fund

So, what should you look for in a fund? Some things are obvious, such as performance. However, there are other considerations that you shouldn't ignore.

Fund Objective

Of course, the most important feature is that the investment objective fits in your plan. If you're in the market for a lower-risk, medium-return investment, say for college tuition four years out, look for intermediate-term bond funds. If you're looking for above-average returns for your retirement, search for growth, international equity, and small-company growth funds.

It isn't enough to say, "This fund invests in junk bonds." You should read the prospectus closely enough to understand that a junk-bond fund can provide high yields—and also understand that junk bonds provide high yields because they carry a high risk of default.

The Road They Travel

Read the section in the prospectus that talks about what the fund will buy to meet its goals. For example, find out what percentages of stocks and bonds an asset allocation fund uses. Does the asset allocation fund keep a fixed percentage in stocks and bonds, or does it vary the percentage depending on market conditions?

Funds Should Invest

Many funds try to time the market, stocking up on cash at times, investing completely at other times. Market timing is difficult to get right. If you use asset allocation to protect yourself from downturns in a portion of the market, you should look for funds that mainly stay invested in their objective. However, funds will always have some percentage of cash to cover share redemption.

Pay careful attention to the extra risks a fund chooses. Some funds might invest a small portion of their holdings in higher-risk investments to achieve a higher return. They might invest in complicated derivative securities. Many international and global funds speculate on currency exchange rates. Bond funds might include lower-quality bonds or even some junk bonds to bump their performance up.

Brother, Can You Spare a Dime?

It costs money to run a mutual fund. However, every dime a fund charges in fees, or spends in expenses, drags down the earnings that you receive. A fund that achieves a 16% return, but charges 3% fees and expenses, earns you, the investor, 13%. A fund that earns a 14% return, but only charges .5% for expenses, is actually better with a return of 13.5%. One or two percent might not sound like much, but it can add up to big bucks.

Crash Alert

STAY ALERT TO CAPITAL LETTERS

Fund prospectuses put critical information in capital letters. Capital letters can mean trouble, such as particularly risky investments or high expenses.

For example, let's use Mr. Bogle's example of the average equity mutual fund versus the total stock market from 1970 to 1992. Ten thousand dollars invested in the average equity fund in 1970 with an average annual return of 10.8% turned into $95,500 by 1992. Ten thousand dollars invested in the total stock market in 1970 with an average annual return of 12% resulted in $121,300 in 1992. That 1.2% that the equity fund missed cost $25,800 over 22 years—almost three times the original investment!

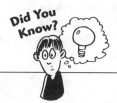

Did You Know?

Hit the Road, Jack

There are times when you might consider selling a mutual fund. If your fund delivers below–average performance for its investment objective for two years straight, look elsewhere. If your fund falls, when the market goes up, find another fund. Watch carefully if your fund's top performing manager leaves. His or her replacement might be great, and then again, might not.

Some funds that charge loads might produce performance that makes the fees worthwhile. However, past performance is no guarantee of future results. If a hot fund turns cool, those fees make it downright cold.

Loads come in many forms. Front-end loads are sales commissions and can be as high as 8.5%. With the Web resources at your disposal, there is no reason to pay anyone a commission to buy a mutual fund. Some funds charge an exit fee if you sell the fund within six years. If you sell in the first year, that exit fee could be as high as 6%. Other funds charge redemption fees of 1% or 2% no matter when you sell the fund. 12b-1 fees cover brokers' commissions and marketing expenses. These fees can really hurt over the long term, because funds usually charge them every year.

Your best shot at a winner is a no-load fund with a good performance history. No-load funds don't charge any sales fees.

Every mutual fund charges management fees, which is what the fund managers get paid to run the fund. Sometimes, funds reduce, or even waive, their management fees to make their performance look better. Check the prospectus and the fund's annual report for this information. When the fund reinstates the management fee, the fund performance might drop.

Operating expenses are the costs to run the fund, expressed as a percentage of the total assets of the fund. A high expense ratio drags down the return you earn from a fund. There are plenty of mutual funds with good performance that don't cost an arm and a leg. You can expect average expense ratios for no-load funds around 1.2%. International funds and small-company funds might have higher expense ratios because they incur higher costs of trading. The Vanguard Group is the premier example of low-cost funds, with expense ratios of .5% or less. Some index funds have operating expenses as low as .2%.

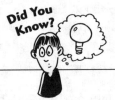

What's It Gonna Cost?

A fund prospectus will include a section on hypothetical costs. This section shows what you might pay in fees and expenses per $1,000 invested over several timeframes, assuming an annual fund gain of 5%.

Performance

One important measure of performance is the annual total return. If you can't find that figure in the prospectus or the annual report, you can find it online or by calling and asking the fund company.

Did You Know?

Performance Can Be Deceiving

Most performance figures don't deduct front-end sales charges. If a fund charges a front-end load, it might take several years of superior performance to beat a no-load fund with lower returns. Morningstar mutual fund reports include load-adjusted returns that show the actual performance including the effect of the loads.

Consistency counts! Over time, funds that perform more consistently from year to year beat out funds that return 40% one year and 1% the next. Check the prospectus and annual report to compare the annual total return for the past 10 years. Morningstar reports, available at your library or online for a fee, show a fund's ranking compared to similar funds. Look for funds that stay in the top rankings consistently over time.

Check the average annual return for a 10-year period or longer to see how good performance is over the long-term. Compare the fund's return to the return of the corresponding market index over the same period. If a fund has great long-term performance, check to see if the fund managers that produced that performance still are running the fund.

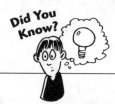

Roses Are Red, and Daisies Aren't

Remember risk versus reward? Higher returns usually mean riskier investments. Always compare funds with similar objectives, so that you're comparing the performance of funds with similar levels of risk. The performance of a small-company growth fund might look great compared to a balanced fund, but you buy them for different reasons.

Also, check recent years' returns to make sure that the fund still is a top performer. You might find a fund that had several hot years in the past, while the last few years were downright dogs!

Finding Funds on the Web

With more than 7,000 funds to choose from, we could all use some help finding the right funds. Many mutual funds and mutual fund families have Web sites. In addition, the Internet comes to the rescue with fund searches of all kinds.

Searching for Funds That Meet Criteria

The Yahoo! Finance section on mutual fund screeners (`http://dir.yahoo.com/ Business_and_Economy/Companies/Financial_Services/Investment_Services/ Mutual_Funds/Screeners/`) includes two links to Web sites that provide free fund screens. FundFocus (`http://fundfocus.com/index.html`) and the Quicken.com

Mutual Fund Finder (`http://www.quicken.com/investments/mutualfunds/finder/`) provide slightly different search criteria. Check both sites to see which one fits your search the best.

The Quicken.com Mutual Fund Finder provides several approaches to finding mutual funds, displayed in Figure 17.2. You can click **Popular Searches** if you want to search for funds that meet broad criteria, such as 5- or 10-year performance, equity or bond funds, company capitalization, or minimum initial investment. Click **Top 25 Funds** to see the top 25 funds in each of Morningstar's 50 fund categories.

Figure 17.2

Quicken.com Mutual Fund Finder offers several pre-packaged fund screens. You also can screen for the funds that meet your specific criteria.

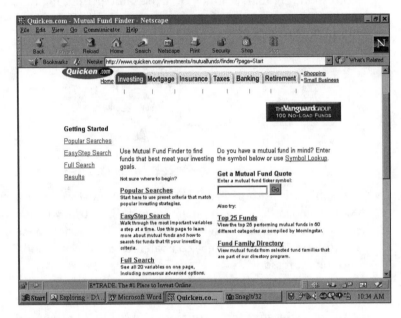

If you want to learn a little bit more about what to look for in a fund as you screen, use the Quicken.com **EasyStep Search**. This screen steps you through selections for category, Morningstar rating, five-year return, front load, expense ratio, total net assets, and manager tenure. Each step includes a brief description of what you might want to look for in those criteria.

Click **Full Search** if you want to specify up to 20 criteria. You can select category, Morningstar rating, values for four types of sales loads, expense ratio, initial minimum, manager tenure, and total net assets. With full search, you can specify total return for periods from three months to 10 years. A nice feature of full search is you can specify a minimum value for the total return or specify that the return beat a particular market index, such as the S&P 500 or the long bond aggregate. For dividend yield, PE ratio, price/book ratio, and median market cap, you can select a value from a drop-down list or enter specific minimum and maximum values.

As an example, let's try a search with these criteria:

➤ Large growth

➤ Morningstar rating of four stars or better

➤ Total return that beats the S&P 500 over all periods

➤ Any dividend yield

➤ No loads

➤ Expense ratio less than .75%

➤ Any minimum initial investment

➤ Manager tenure five years or more

Harbor Capital Appreciation comes out on top of a field of only three funds ranked by performance. If you select **Operations** from the **Display** drop-down list, you can see in Figure 17.3 that Harbor Capital Appreciation also has the lowest minimum initial investment ($2,000). You might be interested to notice that the number-two entry, GMO Growth III, has a minimum initial investment of $1,000,000!

Depending on what information is available online, you can click **Fact Sheet** for a brief overview, **Prospectus** to see the fund prospectus, **Family Page** for the fund's Web page, or **Quote Plus** to see the current NAV.

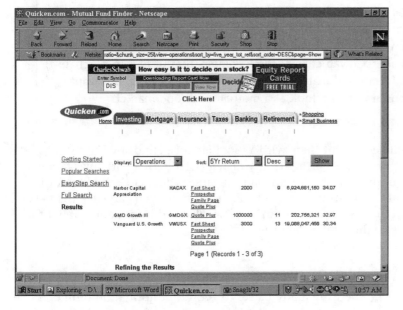

Figure 17.3

On Quicken.com, you can use 20 criteria to screen down to a small number of funds that meet your needs.

Searching for a Specific Fund

The Quicken.com Mutual Fund Finder is also the first place to look for information about a specific fund. If you know it, you can enter the ticker symbol for the fund and click **Go**. If you only know the fund name, click **Symbol Lookup**. Select **Mutual Fund**, and enter the full or partial name. Click **Search** to see the results.

All in the Family

Many mutual fund companies offer more than one mutual fund. The funds within one company are called fund families and can number from two or three to hundreds of funds in the large families. With fund families, you usually can transfer your money easily between different funds in the family.

Shop at a Mutual Fund Supermarket

Some brokerages offer one-stop shopping for stocks and mutual funds. For example, Charles Schwab offers hundreds of fund families. You can purchase funds in its OneSource program (which still covers over 200 fund families) without a load or transaction fee. Charles Schwab charges some combination of fees to purchase the rest. If you prefer to mix and match funds from different families, but want the convenience of one statement, look at a mutual fund supermarket.

You can see what families are out there with Yahoo! Finance Funds by Family (http://biz.yahoo.com/p/fam/a-b.html). If you are looking for a particular family, click on the portion of the alphabet for the family name. Then, click the link for the family name to see all the funds in the family. For each fund, you can click the ticker symbol to see current quotes. Or, click **Profile** to see detailed information about the fund, as well as a link to the family Web page.

Getting Fund Information

As with individual stocks, there are many places to get fund information online. If you're hunting for a prospectus, the results from Quicken.com fund searches have links to fund prospectuses. You can search the SEC EDGAR database specifically for a mutual fund prospectus (http://www.sec.gov/edaux/prospect.htm). But some Web sites provide other useful information about funds.

Show Me the Money

The Yahoo! Finance Profiles provide a wealth of information about a fund. Click the **Overview** display to see the category, the Morningstar rating, net assets, a performance snapshot compared to the appropriate index, turnover, manager and tenure, a phone number, fees, expense ratio, and minimum investments.

Click **Performance** and you can look at performance for periods from three months to 10 years compared to the appropriate index, plus performance in the last bull market and the last bear market. As displayed in Figure 17.4, the performance profile also shows the annual return for the past 10 years—an excellent way to see how consistent the fund is. You also can look at return statistics, risk measures, and rankings. Click **Top 10 in Category** to see the top performers in this fund's category over different periods.

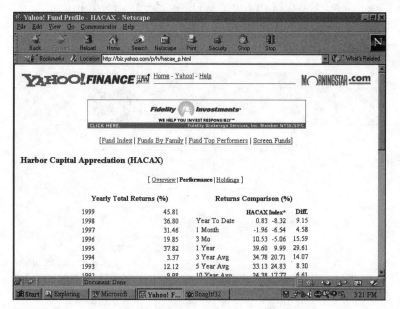

Figure 17.4

Yahoo! Finance mutual fund performance compares past performance to a corresponding market index, and shows how well the fund performed during the last bull and bear markets.

Click **Holdings** to see the portfolio composition (stocks, bonds, and so on) and the sector weightings (technology, financial, and so on). This page shows the top holdings for the fund. In addition, you can see the average PE and the median market cap for the fund's holdings.

Go to the Back of the Line

Don't be enticed into buying the top performer for the past three months, or even the past year. The number-one fund for a short period rarely delivers a back-to-back win like the Denver Broncos. Look for top performers over the past five, and even 10, years.

Comparing Funds Online

Access Vanguard has a great fund comparison tool. You can compare two different Vanguard funds or two funds from non-Vanguard fund families. Click the **Funds** tab on the Access Vanguard main page to see the tools that Vanguard offers for mutual funds (http://majestic.vanguard.com/FP/DA/0.0.funds_intro). In the Non-Vanguard Funds section, click **Fund Comparison Tool**. Enter the two fund families you want to compare and click **Select**. Then, select the funds that you want to compare from the drop-down lists, and click **Compare**. The results show all the pertinent data about both funds side by side, as shown in Figure 17.5.

Figure 17.5

Access Vanguard shows comparisons between Vanguard or non-Vanguard funds measure by measure.

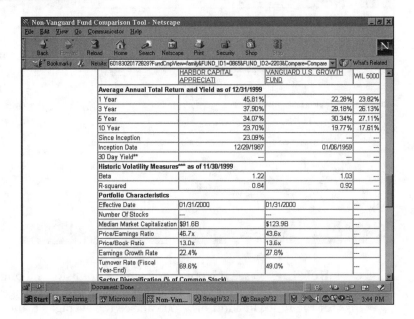

Learning More About Mutual Funds

Whether you want to learn more about the basics of mutual fund investing, or want the complete low-down on a particular fund, the Web is a great place to start.

Mutual Fund Education

Most fund family Web sites provide educational material on mutual funds. The more you know, the more they hope you will invest in their products. Although this educational material might have a marketing motivation, some of it is excellent.

The Strong Funds investment firm offers an excellent introduction to mutual funds with its Mutual Fund Basics (`http://www.estrong.com/strong/LearningCenter98/basics/whatmf.htm`). You can focus on the features that mutual funds offer or focus on stock funds or bond funds.

The Investorama Mutual Fund Info Center (`http://www.investorama.com/infocenter/funds`) offers great information on numerous mutual fund topics. You can go from beginner to advanced with Mutual Fund Basics; Types of Funds: What, Where, and How; Investing in the Stock Market the Easy Way: Index Funds; and the Essentials of Global and International Funds, to name a few.

Mutual Fund Reports

Morningstar is the king of mutual fund reporting. Just as Value Line presents stocks, Morningstar publishes comprehensive, concise, and standardized reports on thousands of mutual funds. In addition, its rating system is widely used as a measure of a fund's quality and potential performance.

Morningstar's Web site (`www.morningstar.net`) provides articles, columns, message boards, and more about mutual funds and stocks. The Expert Q & A section has some of the most well-known fund managers available to answer your questions.

You can look at its QuickTake reports online for any mutual fund. Enter the fund ticker symbol on the site home page and click **Go**. The QuickTake report includes information on performance, risk, return, fees, expenses, the Morningstar rating, top holdings, the manager, and investing details.

For downloadable Morningstar fund reports, you could subscribe if you want to spend $495 a year. Another alternative is to purchase the reports you want for $5 apiece from InvestTools (`www.investools.com`). But, even those charges can add up if you want to study several dozen funds. Of course, you can always get the paper version at your local library free!

The Least You Need to Know

➤ You can find mutual funds to meet almost every investment objective without spending a ton of time to find a good one.

➤ Mutual funds make it easy to buy-and-hold for the long term and use dollar-cost averaging. And, you can get started with less than $100 when you invest automatically each month.

➤ Index funds provide performance that is hard to beat, and they usually have the lowest fees and expenses.

➤ If you buy mutual funds through a broker, you pay a sales load that can drag down your earnings. With many funds, you can buy directly through the fund company or a fund supermarket, often with no load or fees.

➤ You can search online for mutual funds that meet your requirements. After you find a fund, you can learn everything about it online.

Chapter 18

Keeping Financial Records Electronically

In This Chapter

➤ The records you need to keep and for how long

➤ Information for tax reporting and portfolio performance

➤ Understanding the basic tax rules for your investments

➤ Learning how to track your finances on your computer

Whenever you deal with money, you can expect a trail of paper to follow. Most people like to know where their money is and how much they have. Even if you don't care what's going on with the trust fund that your nerdy Uncle Bill set up for you, the Internal Revenue Service does.

When it comes to keeping records, the Internet isn't that much help. No Web sites exist to track all your financial transactions. You don't want a dead telephone line, or a busy Internet service provider, to keep you from working with your finances. Besides, the IRS, insurance companies, and other financial firms like to see paper proof.

Everything You Wanted to Know About Your Finances, But Were Afraid to Track

Keeping good records does more than make the IRS happy. In addition to saving time searching for papers, good records make it easy for your heirs to find and collect the inheritance you leave when you're gone. If you toss deeds to vacation properties into cookie jars, and leave no instructions, your heirs could spend big bucks on lawyers to straighten things out—or even lose part of their inheritance because no one knows about it.

Right There in Black and White

Paper records are a fact of life. Almost every company and government agency wants to see original paper copies. In addition to setting up a good filing system, you should get a safety deposit box and a fireproof safe.

Signed, Sealed, and Delivered

Some states seal safety deposit boxes when the owner dies until someone inventories the contents. Others allow the executor or a spouse access to the box. Make sure that your state's rules don't delay access to the safety deposit box before you store your will there.

Keep your will, powers of attorney, living will, life insurance policies, deeds, titles, surveys, and such in a fireproof safe in your house. Personal papers, such as birth certificates, passports, and Social Security cards can go in the fireproof safe or the safe deposit box.

Your household inventory, including a printed list, photographs, or videotape, should go in your safety deposit box. Your inventory isn't much good if it burns up with your belongings. Keep receipts for big-ticket items as well as physical stock certificates, valuable coins, and jewelry with your inventory.

If you have a fax machine or a scanner at your house, you can make copies of your papers before you put them in the safety deposit box. Or stop by the local copy shop on the way to the box. You have copies at the house as reference, as well as a backup of the original documents.

Cancelled checks, receipts, credit card statements, bank statements, tax returns and supporting data, investment statements, and confirmations can go in a regular filing cabinet. Whenever you receive annual statements from your accounts, you can throw away the monthly statements. However, you should keep your investment transaction confirmations.

If you use Quicken to track your finances, use the Emergency Records Organizer to tell people who to contact and where to find your records. You can enter emergency contacts, doctors, dentists, medical history, and hospital information. You can include employment or business information, education, marriage, or military records. As shown in Figure 18.1, you can include where you keep your personal and legal documents. You can keep information about all your financial accounts, income, investments, retirement, possessions, insurance, and loans. If you don't have Quicken, you can still create a list with this information with pencil and paper. Update this information whenever it changes, and give copies to your emergency contact, a close friend, and perhaps your lawyer.

If You Could Turn Back Time

You should keep tax records and supporting data for at least three years. The IRS has six years to audit, if you underreport your income by more than 25%. There is no statue of limitation for tax fraud.

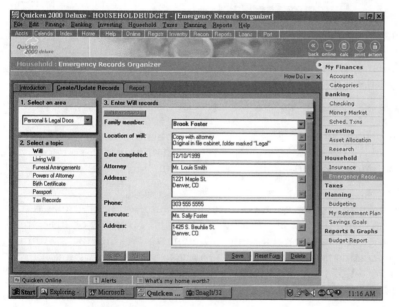

Figure 18.1

With your information in the Quicken Emergency Records Organizer, your emergency contacts, caretakers, or survivors will know what to do.

Investment Information

Investment records test your diligence. For tax reporting and portfolio performance calculations, you have to keep track of your investments for years. If your money is in a nontaxable account, such as an IRA, you don't have to worry about taxes until you take money out. In taxable accounts, the IRS taxes you on your capital gains when you sell a stock and on your dividends every time you receive one.

For example, let's say you bought 100 shares of Affiliated Freeblesnaps at $20 per share. Using an online broker, you paid $10 commission for the trade. Your *cost basis*—the amount you paid for the stock—is the purchase price plus the commission, or $2,010. You have invested your capital in this stock.

Over the next three years, Affiliated Freeblesnaps shares increase to $35 a share. Your investment is now worth $3,500. Your capital has grown for a capital gain of $1,490! As long as you hold onto the stock, your capital gain is only on paper—an unrealized capital gain. If the stock drops back down, your unrealized capital gain could disappear.

Dumping the Dogs

When you sell a stock that drops below your purchase price, you realize a capital loss. You end up with less capital than when you purchased the stock. Many people check their portfolios for dogs near the end of the year. They can sell the dogs for a capital loss, which offsets any of their capital gains.

Finally, after 10 years you sell your stock at $80 a share, with a $10 commission. Because the capital gain is now safely in your hands instead of on paper, you now have a realized capital gain of $5,980—minus the $2,000 purchase and the $20 in commissions.

The government jumps in to enjoy your good fortune. Because you held Affiliated Freeblesnaps for 10 years, you pay tax at the long-term capital gains rate of 20%, or $1,196. If you had earned the same capital gains by buying and selling stocks within 12 months, your capital gains tax rate would be the same as your ordinary income tax rate, at 28%, a tax of $1,674.40. Short-term trading costs not only in brokers' commissions, but in taxes, too!

If you sell only a portion of a stock or mutual fund, you can calculate your capital gains a couple of ways. By default with stocks, the first shares that you sell are the first shares that you bought. This method is called *first-in/first-out* or FIFO for short. You do have the option to specify specific shares to sell. By specifying shares, you can control the capital gains, or losses, that you receive. To sell specific shares, you must tell your broker which shares you want to sell. If you hold the certificates, you take those certificates to your broker.

With mutual funds, you can use FIFO or specific shares to figure your capital gains. But you also have a third option. With the average share price method, you calculate your cost basis by dividing the total value of your shares in the fund by the number of shares.

Capital Gains Have the Advantage

If you're trying to hold down the taxes you pay on a taxable investment account, go for stocks that don't pay dividends. Even if you reinvest your dividends, you have to pay taxes on those dividends each year. With capital gains, you won't pay taxes on those gains until you sell the stock, which could be years away.

In addition, the tax rate on dividends is the same as ordinary income, which can be as high as 39%. The tax rate on capital gains on stocks held more than one year is only 20%!

If Affiliated Freeblesnaps pays a 20-cent dividend each quarter, you would receive $20.00 each quarter for the dividend on your 100 shares. At the end of each year, your $80 in dividends adds to your ordinary income: your salary and a few other items. If your tax rate were 28%, you would pay $22.40 in tax on those dividends.

Now, let's say that you reinvest your dividends. First, you have to pay the $22.40 in taxes on the dividends from some other source, because the $80 went to buy more shares. In addition, you have to keep track of each reinvestment purchase: how many shares, what price, and when it was purchased.

Computers to the Rescue

If all those investment transactions sound like a lot of work, you don't want to even think about calculating your portfolio performance. Fortunately, you don't have to! Software tools can keep track of all your investment transactions and spit out what you need to know for your taxes in a jiffy. In addition, they can keep you posted on other aspects of your finances, such as how much you owe on your mortgage. In Chapter 19, "Managing Your Portfolio," you can see how software can handle portfolio performance without a pause.

On the Right Track

If you have taken your personal finances into cyberspace already, a personal finance program, such as Quicken, can keep track of your investments, in addition to your checkbook, mortgage, and the rest of your finances. But, if you're focusing on investments, and don't use Quicken or one of its kin, you might want to check out an investment-only program, such as NAIC's Personal Record Keeper (www. better-investing.org/computer/prk.html).

These programs track your investment purchases and sales. They also provide the tools to handle the nagging details of investments: stock splits, corporate name changes, spin-offs, and acquisitions.

The Big Buy

Your investment journey starts with a single buy. As Figure 18.2 shows, the essential information for a purchase is the security name, the number of shares, the purchase price, and the commission. However, when you use Quicken's Buy/Add Shares, you also can specify the type of security (stock, mutual fund, index, and so on), the asset class (domestic bonds, large-cap stocks, international stocks, and so on), and the investment goal (income, growth, and so on).

Figure 18.2

Quicken makes it easy to enter your investment transactions.

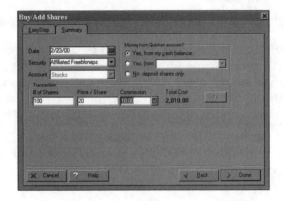

In addition, you can download the asset class information from the Internet. You can specify whether you want to use average cost or specific lots to determine your capital gains. You can even enter high and low alert prices, so that Quicken notifies you when you might want to buy or sell.

When you sell your shares, you specify which security to sell, the number of shares, the selling price, the date, and the commission. In addition, you specify the method to use for calculating your cost basis, as shown in Figure 18.3. If you specify lots, Quicken displays all the lots that you purchased, and you select which ones you want to sell.

Figure 18.3

In addition to the basics, you have to tell Quicken which cost basis method you want to use when you sell.

Reinvesting Made Easy

Whether you receive a dividend from a stock or a flurry of mutual fund distributions at the end of the year, Quicken's Easy Action, Reinvest Income, handles it all at once. Enter the date and the security. For a stock dividend, enter the dividend amount and the number of shares purchased with the dividend. For a mutual fund distribution, you can enter the dollar amounts and the number of shares purchased for dividends, interest, long-term capital gains, medium-term capital gains, and short-term capital gains in one window, as in the example in Figure 18.4.

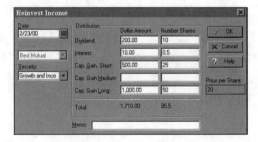

Figure 18.4

Quicken's Reinvest Income action makes reinvesting mutual fund distributions a breeze.

Other Investment Transactions

Unless you invest in Warren Buffett's Berkshire Hathaway stock, your stocks will split from time to time. Companies split their shares, so that the share price stays within the means of the average investor. If you own 100 shares, and the stock splits 2 for 1, you would end up with 200 shares. In this case, the share price is cut in half, so that the value of your stock stays the same. A Berkshire Hathaway share sold for $81,100 at one point in 1999.

To enter a stock split in Quicken, select **Stock Split** from the **Investing Easy Actions** drop-down menu. Enter the security, the number of shares before the split, the number of shares after the split, and the price after the split.

If an investment pays a dividend in stock instead of cash, go to **Advanced** on the **Easy Actions** menu, and select **Stock Dividend**. You can enter the number of shares that you received as a dividend.

The Day of Reckoning

After New Year's most of us start thinking about or dreading preparing our tax returns. With capital gains, dividends, cost basis method, and other foolishness, our taxes could be a nightmare if we still used pencil, paper, and calculator.

But, if you keep your transactions in Quicken, collecting your investment information for tax season is easy. To produce a report of your capital gains for a year, select **Investing**, **Capital Gains Report** from the **Reports** menu. If you run this report for your previous year's taxes, select **Last Year** for the period. You can subtotal the report by asset class, account, month, and several other items. But, for tax reporting, select **Short/Long-Term**. Click **Update** to see your capital gains report. You can see in the capital gains report in Figure 18.5 that the Growth Fund shares were sold using the FIFO method.

Figure 18.5

Quicken's Reinvest Income action makes reinvesting mutual fund distributions a breeze.

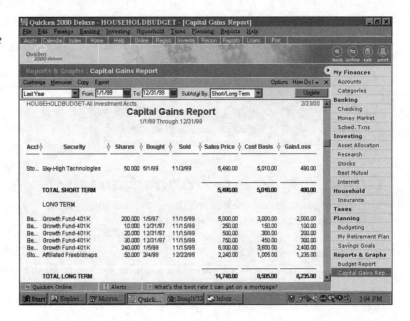

For a report on your investment income, including dividends, interest, and capital gains, select **Investing, Investment Income Report** from the **Reports** menu. This report shows dividends, interest, capital gain distributions, and realized capital gains for one or all your investment accounts.

Quicken provides a Net Worth report that shows what you own and what you owe. Your assets minus your liabilities show your financial net worth. Quicken's spending reports can show you how much you spend in a variety of ways. Click **Reports** on the Quicken toolbar to explore the other reports that you can use.

The Least You Need to Know

➤ Good record keeping not only makes tax season easier, but also helps your loved ones take care of your finances when you can't.

➤ The computer age hasn't eliminated the need for paper records. Get a safety deposit box and a fireproof safe for your important records.

➤ You should keep your paper investment account statements and confirmations. When you track your investment transactions on your computer, you can prepare for tax season by printing a couple of reports.

Managing Your Portfolio

In Chapter 14, "Investing Made Easy," we talked about investment strategies that almost take care of themselves. Did you hear the story about the young mother who left the wheel of her car to attend to her child, because the car salesman said the car practically drove itself? Many investors buy a stock, and then think that their portfolio will manage itself. Others pay plenty of attention to their stocks—going online to check prices every 30 minutes, bragging to their co-workers every time a holding goes up a dollar (keeping quiet when another holding goes down).

But investment professionals know that portfolio management is much different. Portfolio management means feeding the flowers and pulling the weeds in your portfolio. You increase your return by improving the quality of your portfolio.

Did You Ever Have to Make Up Your Mind? Picking Up on One and Leaving Another Behind

Portfolio managers watch stock prices, but they concentrate on a company's performance. When a company delivers sales and earnings growth that continues to meet or exceed your expectations, a run-up in the stock price is no reason to sell. On the other hand, significant signs that a company won't perform as you expected might be a good reason to sell.

Head of the Class

Reasons to Sell

According to Warren Buffett, the best time to sell is never! However, there are a few circumstances where selling makes sense:

➤ You want to use your investment dollars for the goal you invested for.

➤ You want to maintain the proper asset allocation in your portfolio.

➤ Another company of equal or greater quality offers a higher potential for return.

➤ The company has a declining financial condition or profit margins.

➤ The company has disappointing growth rate and deteriorating fundamentals.

➤ The company's competition heats up.

➤ The company only has one product or customer.

The Internet can be noisy! One problem with the Internet's wealth of information is that you can go into information overload. Sometimes, it's hard to tell whether information is relevant or not. Whenever you read news about a company, focus on the effect the news might really have on your investment.

Pay attention if the news could affect the company's long-term profitability. If bad news only affects the short term, you might even consider buying more stock if the price drops when the market overreacts. Think about whether the news affects only your company or the entire market. Once again, if the entire market is affected, you might consider buying more stock while it is on sale. Management changes might only be a transition to replace a retiring chairperson. But be cautious of quick management changes. The company might be trying to salvage a weak market position or recover from bad strategic decisions.

Head of the Class

Is It a Rocket—Or a Drop in the Bucket?

You might see news or an online message about a hot new product for some company. Hot new products can catch the world on fire, but they might not affect a company's fortunes. Ten million dollars in annual revenues are only a drop in the bucket for a company with annual revenues of $40 billion. In addition, competition can release its hot new product at the same time.

Checking Up on Your Investments

If you use asset allocation and mutual funds for your investments, you can get by with an annual checkup. If you own stocks, you should monitor your portfolio at least once a quarter.

If you track your investment transactions in Quicken, you can do most of your portfolio management on your computer. If you don't have Quicken, Morningstar.net provides a very capable online portfolio management tool (`http://portfolio.morningstar.com/x.xs/PortCover/CoverPage`) if you register for a free membership. Morningstar even provides two versions of its tool. In the Quick Portfolio, you just enter the ticker, the number of shares, the purchase price, and the commission. Or you can use the Transaction Portfolio to include dates for your purchases, plus complete transaction information on sales, dividend reinvestments, and more. You can import your transactions from Quicken or Microsoft Money. After you create a portfolio, you can select a view, such as Performance shown in Figure 19.1, to see different information about your holdings.

Juggling Eggs and Baskets

As we discussed in Chapter 14, much of your portfolio's return is due to the asset allocation you choose. From day to day, or year to year, some types of investment do well, while others languish. You want to make sure that your asset allocation hasn't been thrown off by big winners (or losers) in your investment stable.

Figure 19.1

Morningstar.net provides a portfolio tool that can track all your investment transactions

Select a view such as Performance, Fundamentals, or Snapshot to see different information about your holdings.

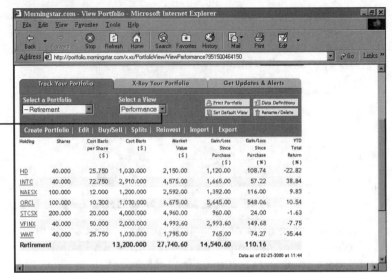

You can manage your asset allocation online or in Quicken. On the Morningstar Portfolio page, click **X-Ray Your Portfolio** to see the underlying asset allocation of your portfolio, as well as a breakdown of your portfolio by stock sector, stock type, and the Morningstar stylebox, as in the example in Figure 19.2. The stock sector portion of the X-Ray is a good way to see how well you have diversified by industry. The stylebox is a great way to check for diversification by company size.

Figure 19.2

Use the Morningstar X-Ray to see the true allocation for your stocks and mutual funds.

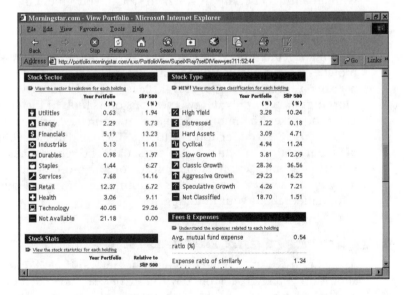

The Morningstar X-Ray looks at your stocks as well as the holdings within any mutual funds you own. The X-Ray also shows stock stats, such as the PE for your portfolio, yield, and market cap. You also can see what kind of expenses you are paying for the mutual funds that you own. As a premium member of Morningstar, you can even see the overlaps of stocks between mutual funds that you own.

In Quicken, select **Asset Allocation Guide** from the **Investing** menu. After you read up on asset allocation and decide the allocation that you want, click **Set Your Target Allocation**. Quicken displays the asset classes for the investments you own. You can enter percentages for any asset class that you plan to use, as long as the total equals 100%! If you have added stocks or mutual funds to your portfolio, click **How do I update asset classes** on the side menu and then **Go Online and update asset classes** in the content area.

After you have a target allocation, select **Portfolio Rebalancer** from the **Investing** menu. The Portfolio Rebalancer shows a chart of your current allocation compared to your target allocation, as displayed in Figure 19.3. It also provides a list of your asset classes, indicating how far off your allocation percentages are from your target, and tells you how much money you have to add or subtract from each class to reach your target.

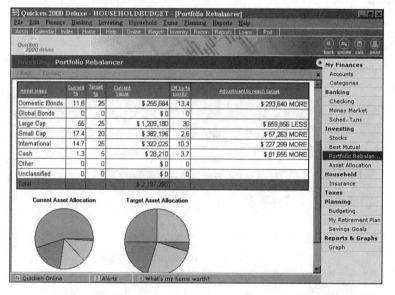

Figure 19.3

Quicken's Portfolio Rebalancer shows you what you have to do to reach your target allocation.

Double-click your current asset allocation pie to see a graph of your asset classes. Then double-click a slice of the pie to see which investments make up that asset class. After you know which investments make up each class, you can decide to sell some of the investments in the over-allocated classes and buy more of the investments in the under-allocated classes.

Check Under the Hood

Mutual funds often invest in a variety of asset classes, which can make it difficult to rebalance your portfolio with precision. Use Morningstar's X-Ray tool to really see what your mutual funds invest in. And don't worry if your allocations are a few percentage points off.

Checking Out Mutual Fund Performance

Once a year, it's a good idea to make sure that your mutual funds are performing well for their investment objective. With index funds, this test really comes down to whether the fund keeps its expenses low and performs within a few tenths of a percent of the corresponding index.

For example, if you look at the Morningstar QuickTake report for the Vanguard 500 Index fund, as in Figure 19.4, you can see that the fund's performance approximates the index. The QuickTake report shows that the Vanguard 500 Index fund has an expense ratio of .18%, which is extremely low.

Figure 19.4

With index funds, check that their performance mirrors the index and that the fund expenses are low.

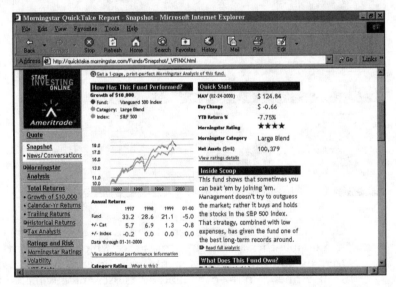

If you invest in actively managed funds, you should make sure that your fund continues to produce above average performance. As you see in Figure 19.5, a mutual fund's performance can vary considerably from year to year compared to its peers. In this example, this fund was usually in the top third of its category over the past six years. In addition, it ranked in the top 20% for the 3-, 5-, and 10-year annualized returns.

On the other hand, if your fund underperforms its category for a couple of years, start looking for a better fund. The fund shown in Figure 19.6 looked great from 1993 through 1995. But, from 1996 through 1998, it came in almost dead last. By the third year of bottom dwelling, you should sell the fund. In this case, the fund came back in 1999 and 2000. However, it is better to invest in funds that perform consistently. The wild swings in performance take away from your return.

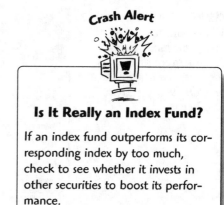

Crash Alert

Is It Really an Index Fund?

If an index fund outperforms its corresponding index by too much, check to see whether it invests in other securities to boost its performance.

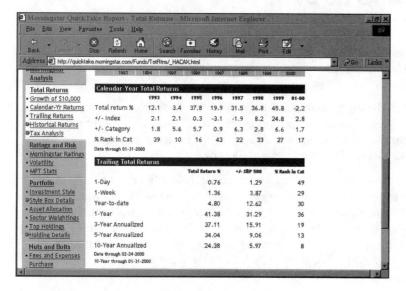

Figure 19.5

Use a Morningstar QuickTake report to see how your fund has performed compared to its peers.

Calendar-Year Total Returns

	1993	1994	1995	1996	1997	1998	1999	01-00
Total return %	12.1	3.4	37.8	19.9	31.5	36.8	45.8	-2.2
+/- Index	2.1	2.1	0.3	-3.1	-1.9	8.2	24.8	2.8
+/- Category	1.8	5.6	5.7	0.9	6.3	2.8	6.6	1.7
% Rank in Cat	39	10	16	43	22	33	27	17

Data through 01-31-2000

Trailing Total Returns

	Total Return %	+/- S&P 500	% Rank in Cat
1-Day	0.76	1.29	49
1-Week	1.36	3.87	29
Year-to-date	4.80	12.62	30
1-Year	41.38	31.29	36
3-Year Annualized	37.11	15.91	19
5-Year Annualized	34.04	9.06	13
10-Year Annualized	24.38	5.97	8

Data through 02-24-2000
10-Year through 01-31-2000

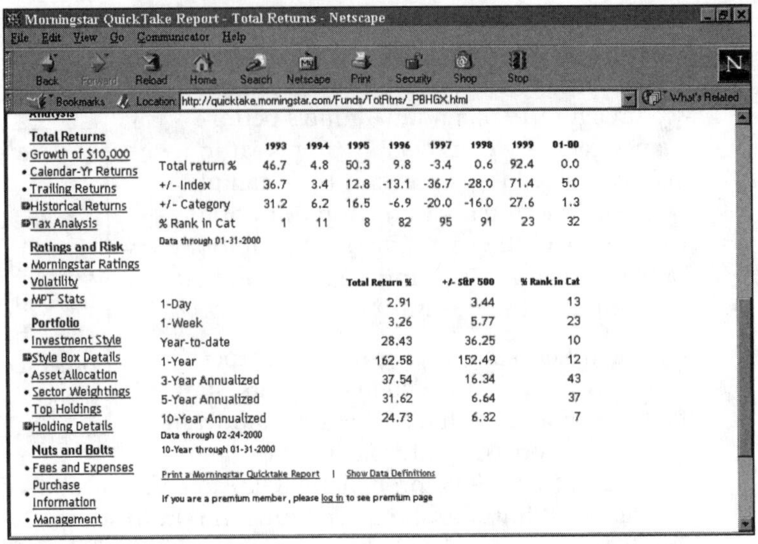

Figure 19.6

You should find replacements for funds that underperform their peers for more than two years, or swing between great and lousy.

Watching the Stocks Go By

Stock checkups require a little more work than mutual funds. Plus, you should check in with your stocks every quarter. If a stock shows signs of deteriorating fundamentals for two quarters, that might be the warning you need to get out before the price dives. It's a good idea to check the company news, stock price, and Price-Earnings ratio each month as well.

Of course, you should always investigate the root of a stock's performance before you decide to buy or sell. Reading the annual report, the 10-K, recent quarterly reports, and 10-Qs can indicate whether a company's recent hot performance might continue for a while, or whether its recent problems are temporary or cause for concern.

Check the news about your stocks at Wall Street Research Net (www.wsrn.com) or any of the other stock sites mentioned in other sections of this book. If you want a service that sends you email with news about your stock holdings, create up to three portfolios at Infobeat Finance (www.infobeat.com). You can get emails several times a day, after market close, or once a week, with recent prices as well as news summaries. The news items include links to the full story. You also can ask for a file that you can use to import prices into your portfolio tracker.

If you use fundamental analysis to pick stocks, you probably have an expectation for the company's revenue and earnings growth rates. Whenever a company issues a quarterly report, it's time to see how they're doing. You can get an overview of a stock's annual growth rates at Quicken.com (www.quicken.com/investments). Enter the ticker symbol and click **Go**. Then click **Fundamentals** and scroll down to the annual revenue and earnings rates.

Don't Sugarcoat It

Many annual reports have a lot of glossy pictures and sections that are meant to make you feel good about the company. But you can find the straight scoop in the management's discussion, the financial statements, and footnotes. For example, in the management's discussion, you might find information about competition, impact of costs (positive or negative), and management's outlook for the future. You also could find out that ordinary expenses are included in restructuring charges. This tactic can make future earnings look better than they are. By looking at the income statement and balance sheet, you can see if inventories are growing faster than sales, which indicates that sales are slowing.

For a closer look at the trends in a company's revenues and earnings, use a fundamental analysis tool, such as Investor's Toolkit. One of the reports in Investor's Toolkit uses past quarterly data to show trends in the sales, pre-tax profit, and EPS growth rates, as in the example in Figure 19.7. If the company's growth rates are slowing, or do not meet your expectations, the stock price performance is likely to disappoint you as well.

Figure 19.7

Investor's Toolkit reports show trends in sales, earnings, and pre-tax profit.

PERT Worksheet-A

Company MICROSOFT CORP   (MSFT)

PERIOD	**%GE**	**SALES $MIL**	**%CHANGE**	**INCOME TAX RATE**	**EPS $**	**PRE-TAX PROFIT $MIL**	**%SALES**	**SALES MIL**	**INCOME TAX $MIL**	**%RATE**	**EPS**	**PRE-TAX PROFIT**	**SALES**
09/93		983.00		33.5						32.3			
12/93		1,129.00		33.5						32.7			
03/94		1,244.00		33.5						33.1			
06/94		1,293.00		33.5	0.99	1,728.60	37.2	4,649.0	578.2	33.5			
09/94	.6	1,247.00	26.9	33.0	1.05	1,835.40	37.4	4,913.0	611.6	33.3			
12/94	.6	1,482.00	31.3	33.0	1.11	1,942.52	36.9	5,266.0	644.9	33.2			
03/95	.8	1,507.00	27.6	33.0	1.15	2,014.88	35.9	5,609.0	666.4	33.1			
06/95	.2	1,621.00	25.4	33.0	1.16	2,034.54	34.3	5,937.0	670.4	33.0	17.2	17.7	27.7
09/95	.9	2,016.00	61.7	35.2	1.29	2,348.52	35.0	6,706.0	787.0	33.5	22.9	28.0	36.5
12/95	.2	2,195.00	48.1	35.0	1.44	2,707.35	36.5	7,419.0	921.1	34.0	29.7	39.4	40.9
03/96	.9	2,205.00	38.9	35.0	1.56	3,010.10	37.5	8,037.0	1,039.4	34.5	35.7	49.4	43.3
06/96	.1	2,255.00	39.1	35.0	1.72	3,379.00	39.0	8,671.0	1,184.1	35.0	48.3	66.1	46.1
09/96	.7	2,295.00	13.8	35.0	1.81	3,554.00	39.7	8,950.0	1,244.0	35.0	40.3	51.3	33.5
12/96	.0	2,680.00	22.1	35.0	1.93	3,809.00	40.4	9,435.0	1,333.0	35.0	34.0	40.7	27.2
03/97	.5	3,208.00	45.5	35.0	2.20	4,548.00	43.6	10,430.0	1,592.1	35.0	46.2	51.1	29.9
06/97	.1	3,175.00	40.8	35.0	2.64	5,314.00	46.8	11,358.0	1,860.1	35.0	53.5	57.3	31.0

With consistently high EPS growth rates, you can see why Microsoft has done well.

The Bottom Line

If you are a diligent portfolio manager, your portfolio's performance should be a cause for celebration. But figuring out that performance is beyond us mere mortals. A stock might have grown 300%. Over one year, that feat is amazing. But, if it took 30 years for the stock price to triple, it isn't so incredible. On top of that, you might have to consider dividend reinvestments or regular purchases.

Quicken provides reports that show the average annual total return for your stocks and your entire portfolio. From the **Reports** menu, select **Investing**, **Investment Performance Report**. You can pick different date ranges for the drop-down date list, or you can enter specific start and end dates. If you want to see the performance for each security, select **Security** from the **Subtotal** drop-down list. Click **Customize** if you want to select certain accounts or securities for your report. Click **Update** to see the results, as in Figure 19.8.

Figure 19.8

Quicken can show you the average annual total return for each security.

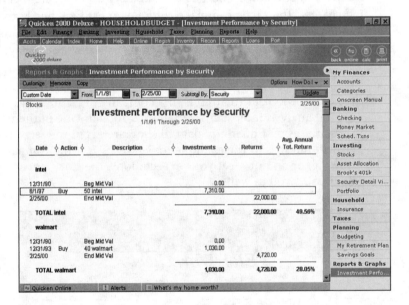

262

The Least You Need to Know

➤ Portfolio management means making changes to your portfolio to increase the quality of your investments as well as your potential return.

➤ Making sure that a company continues to deliver sales and earnings growth is more important than what the stock's price is doing.

➤ Check in on your mutual funds once a quarter and make sure that the funds you own are consistent above-average performers.

➤ Check up on the news and fundamental measures for your stocks each month to make sure that your holdings will continue to meet your expectations.

Part 5
Don't Be an Idiot

There are wolves out on the Internet that seem to use your grandmother's email address to give you helpful investment advice. But in hyperspace, it's hard to see the hairs on their chinny chinny chins. So, protect that basket of investments and only give your data to someone you know.

Chapter 20

Avoiding Scams and Ploys

In This Chapter

➤ How to recognize a rip-off

➤ Why hot tips aren't hot

➤ Don't believe everything you read on the Web

➤ Learning how to check references online

Scams and con artists have been around for years. Scams rely on people's desires—whether it's a miracle cure or an instant fortune. Investments have always been fertile ground for scams because greed drives both the con artists and their victims.

In the past, scams often required some effort and up-front money. Go back and watch the movie *The Sting* (or the recent offering *The Boiler Room*). Today, anyone with a computer, a good printer, and some software, can set up a snazzy, legitimate-looking Web site and letterhead. In fact, many scams are pulled off with just a telephone!

Fortunately, it's easy to avoid becoming a victim. Following a few simple guidelines should keep you out of trouble. In addition, the more knowledge you have about a finance product, the harder it is to fool you. And con artists like easy prey. Above all, remember the adage, "If it sounds too good to be true, it probably is."

How to Stay Out of Trouble

There's no point in getting paranoid. It's easy to steer clear of fraud—as long as you take the time to educate yourself. The National Fraud Information Center (www.fraud.org) is a nonprofit organization that fights fraud by educating the public and helping law enforcement agencies track down the crooks. Its Web site has helpful tips for avoiding fraud, whether it's through telemarketing or the Internet, as displayed in Figure 20.1.

Figure 20.1

The National Fraud Information Center can educate you about tele-marketing fraud, Internet fraud, or scams targeted at certain groups, such as the elderly.

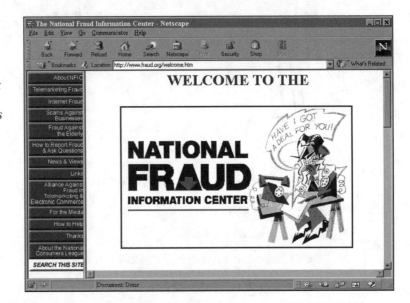

The National Fraud Information Center also has information about fraud against the elderly, and business scams. You can fill out a form online to report fraud. You also can call a toll-free hotline if you think you are the target of fraud. Just remember— call before you sign any deals or pass out financial information!

The Consumer Protection section on the Federal Trade Commission Web site (www.ftc.gov/ftc/consumer.htm) also has good advice for protecting yourself from all kinds of fraud, including e-commerce and the Internet. It also covers some of the legal, but annoying, tricks out there, such as pay-per-call services.

The tips in this section can help you sidestep scams not only on the Internet, but also over the telephone, and even in person.

Crash Alert

Sometimes You Shouldn't Be a Good Samaritan

I once received an email from someone who claimed to a refugee from some-where. He said that his money was still back home. He needed my bank account number, Social Security number, and a few other odds and ends, so that he could transfer his money to the United States. If you get an email like this, delete it as I did. In fact, variations on this con game are as old as the hills; it's called the Spanish Prisoner ploy.

Knowing Who You're Dealing With

If you aren't familiar with a company, do some homework before you deal with it. Find out about the company, and where it is physically located. You can check with your state or local consumer protection agency to see if the company has to be licensed or registered. Make sure it is licensed or registered.

Crash Alert

Web Site Names Can Be Misleading

If a Web site is well known, such as amazon.com, or represents a known company, such as BarnesandNoble.com, you're probably okay. However, beware of slight differences in domain names (Web addresses). For example, someone runs the commercial site amazom.com, which users looking for Amazon might inadvertently type. You should check to make sure that the site truly represents the company that the URL implies. For example, www.whitehouse.com is a site for pornography. The URL for the White House that the President lives in is www.whitehouse.gov.

You can check with the Better Business Bureau or the consumer agencies to see if a company has any complaints registered. However, sham companies tend to appear quickly and disappear just as fast. They might not have any complaints on the record.

They've Got an Offer You Can't Refuse—or Not!

Ask for any offer in writing. This gives you a chance to check out the company, and keeps you from being buffaloed by a high-pressure salesperson.

Read through the offer carefully, and ask questions about anything you don't understand. Make sure you know what you're getting, how much you are paying for all the charges, when it will be delivered, the return and cancellation policy, and terms of any guarantees.

Head of the Class

Take Your Time

Some offers are only good for a certain time. But high-pressure sales are a red flag for fraud. A deal that you must take right away could be a fabulous steal—but it also might be someone stealing your money. During your lifetime, you should come out ahead by "sleeping on it."

If persistence isn't your strong suit, pretend you're Colombo on a case. If a company won't provide information or an offer in writing, it might be a fraud. If you get an offer on the Internet, print out a copy in case you need it.

Don't Talk (or Deal) with Strangers

One piece of information here. Another there. Crooks can use pieces of your personal and financial information to charge things to your accounts, deduct money from your accounts, or get credit in your name. Only give out your information to companies you know are legitimate, and only if it's necessary for the transaction.

Some con artists don't even have to set up a Web site. A scam might be as simple as posting a friendly tip about a great deal, or an easy way to make a bundle. Keep in mind that you don't know these people. You don't even know where they live or what they look like. If something sounds too good to be true, it probably is!

The Online Financial Bag of Tricks

According to the Internet Fraud Watch, operated by the National Consumers League, Internet fraud increased by 600% from 1997 to 1998. Sixty-eight percent of the complaints concerned online auctions. However, con artists have several games they play.

It Doesn't Take Much to Look Good on the Web

Cyberspace does make fraud a little easier. With a personal computer and a little time, almost anyone can build a flashy, professional-looking Web site. Even crooks! Don't think a company is legit, just because they have a cool-looking site.

These games have one rule in common: Get the victims to pay up front. Whether someone sells something they don't own, or offers to repair your credit, find scholarship money, discover bargain basement travel, or allow access to a hidden job market, paying a fee up front is a *big* red flag! If they want cash up front, run away as fast as you can.

Going Once, Going Twice, Your Money's Gone!

Online auctions are very popular. Someone says she wants to sell something. Someone else buys it. Somewhere in between, the merchandise might not show up, or it isn't as described. The seller disappears—along with your money.

Sometimes Credit Cards Are the Safest Way to Pay

In general, it's better not to give your credit card number to strangers. But, for businesses that you are comfortable with, paying by credit card can be better than paying by check or with cash. If a problem arises, you can dispute a charge on your credit card. You hold off paying the charge. And the credit card company helps get the dispute resolved.

If you plan to use an online auction, check to see if the auction company verifies that the merchandise exists and is described accurately. Many online auctions just list items. Check out the seller, and get a physical address and telephone number for him. Get a delivery date and any information about return policies and warranties. Some online auctions use escrow services so that the seller doesn't get the money until the goods arrive in satisfactory condition—if so, take advantage of this service. Again, although auction sites keep a list of complaints against sellers, a con artist can easily create a fresh online identity.

Did You Know?

Get Your Own Credit Card, or Do Without

If you can't get a credit card on your own, no one else is going to get you one. Besides, if your credit is that bad, you might be wise to switch to cash, and repair your credit yourself.

Paying for Credit

In addition to protecting your credit card from online theft, watch out for online credit scams. Targeted at people who are credit risks, these scams offer to repair your credit, or find you a credit card—after you pay a fee up front.

It's illegal for a company to ask for payment for credit repair before the services are performed. No one can legally remove negative information from your credit report, anyway. You can correct mistakes on your credit report without someone's help. You also can repair your credit by starting to use your credit responsibly. If you need help, take a look at Chapter 4, "Getting Out of Debt."

Getting Rich with Little or No Work

A classic scam for years, pyramid (or Ponzi) schemes work by paying people at the top with the money from the recruits below them. And for some people, the scheme works—until it runs out of suckers and the bottom drops out. In some cases, the pitch is that you won't have to work. You'll just reap the rewards of those that you recruit. If you have never worked in sales or management, take my word for it: Sales and management is hard work.

Plans that pay you just for recruiting more distributors are questionable. Avoid any plan where you aren't paid mainly for your own sales, or the sales of distributors under you. In addition, if a plan requires a large purchase of inventory, you might get stuck with it if the plan folds.

Scholarship Scams

Scholarship search services aren't illegal. If you read Chapter 11, "Saving Money for College," you might not need one. But, some scholarship search services are scams.

Crash Alert

Sitting on the Dock of the Bay

Don't fall for Web sites or emails that offer free or low-cost travel packages. These deals might be a complete scam—or they might disguise the true cost of the trip with hidden fees. High-pressure tactics are always suspect. But so is stalling. Some companies keep stalling you until the offer expires before you take the trip. Or they give you two years to take the trip—and they conveniently go out of business.

You might see an incredible deal on a cruise. Then, you find out that you have to buy airfare from the same company, at an incredible markup.

The easiest way to avoid a scholarship scam is to work with your college financial aid office, or try the Web sites in Chapter 11. If you do talk to a search service, don't do business with anyone who requires a large fee in advance. Also, beware if a service guarantees a scholarship, or a certain amount of financial aid.

On a related topic, you might receive offers from modeling services—especially if you're a proud parent who thinks your baby is the cutest ever. Although many agencies legitimately charge a consulting fee to restrict inquiries to serious ones, it shouldn't be excessive, and you shouldn't have to pay them for an expensive photo portfolio.

Investment Schemes: Teaching an Old Dog New Tricks

Online investment schemes are generally electronic versions of the low-tech ploys used in the past. Many people can't help believing everything that appears on their computer screen. They are lured by emails, bulletin board posts, newsletters, and fancy Web pages that promise "an easy way to get rich quick."

The Securities and Exchange Commission has the scoop on Internet investment fraud. Go to its Investor Education and Assistance Web page (`http://www.sec.gov/oiea1.htm`), shown in Figure 20.2, to learn about investing, and how to avoid online scams.

Figure 20.2

The Securities and Exchange Commission can warn you about investment fraud before you're duped, or can help if the worst has already happened.

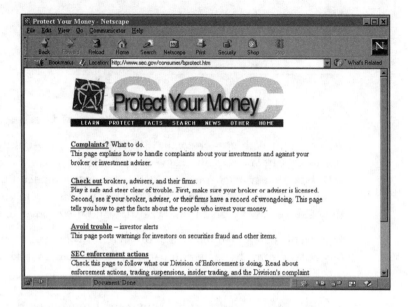

The Pump and Dump

Someone talks about the "next" Microsoft on a message board, urging you to buy before the price skyrockets (the pump). On the Internet, one person can build interest in a stock with very little effort. Under a variety of aliases, he can reach thousands of potential investors with a handful of email messages or a bogus research report. That's why you should beware of emails from people you don't know touting a great stock deal.

With thinly traded stocks, a handful of buys can pump up the price of a stock. As greedy investors buy the stock, the price goes up. Wow! The pumper was right! The frenzy begins. More people buy the stock. The price goes higher.

Did You Know?

Money Changes Everything

Our extended bull market has driven people to desperate acts. Some folks have even taken to slamming a company on the Internet to try to make the price drop so they can buy the stock at a lower price.

The person who posted the message sells his shares at a handy profit (the dump), sometimes 400% or more. When the hype stops, the price usually drops like a rock. Investors who bought late in the frenzy, and are late getting out, can lose 80% in no time.

Risk-free Investments

In Chapter 14, "Investing Made Easy," you learned that risk and reward go hand in hand. The higher the reward, the higher the risk. So, what about the investment you see on the Web that offers unbelievable profits, and guaranteed returns? It sounds too good to be true. Well, it probably is. When someone on the Internet offers a low-risk, high-return investment, the low risk and high return are for that person—not you.

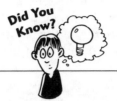

Don't Eat Spam

Junk email is known as *spam*. Con artists increasingly use spam, because they can reach more investors than with mass mailings or cold calls—and for a fraction of the cost. With bulk email programs, they tout their sham investments or spread false company information to millions of potential investors at a time.

Some of these schemes involve offshore investments. These are even more dangerous. Any opportunities outside U.S. borders are difficult for U.S. law enforcement agencies to investigate or prosecute.

Online Newsletters

Online newsletters are easy to produce and cheap to distribute. Anyone can do it. Many online investment newsletters discuss their stock picks with glowing reports of the stocks most likely to succeed. But, in some cases, the companies featured in the newsletter actually paid the newsletter to promote them.

It's not illegal. But by federal securities laws, the newsletters should disclose who paid them, how much, and whether the payment was cash or stock. This information is usually buried in fine print, so get out your reading glasses. In some cases, the newsletters falsely proclaim their independence, while collecting payments or making money on their holdings in the stocks they feature.

Checking Those References

Because it is so easy for crooks to build a legitimate appearance on the Web, you should always check an organization's references. Whether you're about to open a brokerage account, buy a piano for $50 on an online auction, or plunk your money down on the next Microsoft, find out everything you can about the business or person you are dealing with.

Brokers and Financial Advisors

To find out about brokers and securities firms, go to the National Association of Securities Dealers (NASD) Web site (www.nasdr.com). Click **Perform an Online Search**. Click **Agree** to agree with their terms and conditions. Then, select **General Public/Individual Investor** from the requestor type list. Click **Broker** or **Firm**. Then, enter the name you are looking for. Click the name of the company in the list.

Check with EDGAR on Your Investments

Many online investment scams use unregistered securities. Start your research with the SEC EDGAR database to see if the security is registered. Companies with less than $10 million in assets don't have to register with the SEC. But you can check with your state's securities regulator.

You can find out general information about the company, what businesses it can transact legally, and where and when it was registered. Disclosure Events include criminal events, bankruptcies, regulator actions, customer complaints, injunctions, and more. As shown in Figure 20.3, zero would be a good number to see under Disclosure Events.

Figure 20.3

You can look for problems with criminal events, legal actions, and customer complaints for a broker or securities firm under Disclosures at the National Association of Securities Dealers Web site.

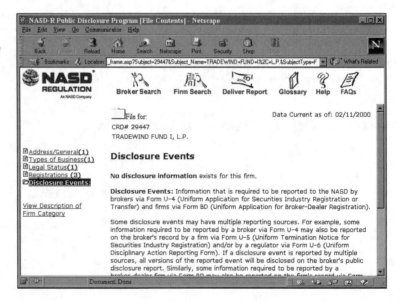

Being Careful of the Company You Keep

Before dealing with a company, check with the Better Business Bureau (www.bbb.org/reports). Company reports might be in the national Better Business Bureau database, in a local database, or still on paper. You can access reports for the offices that store their data online by clicking the link to the local office. If a Web site displays a Better Business Bureau online seal or a Trust-e symbol, it has passed an independent audit and is deemed trustworthy. Remember, though, that it's easy to change identities online, so just because the BBB has no record of complaints doesn't mean an unfamiliar company is squeaky clean.

Head of the Class

Check Several Sources for Information

You also can check with the National Fraud Information Center (www.fraud.org) to see if there are any complaints. State or local consumer protection agencies also are good sources.

If you are looking into a franchise or business opportunity, the seller must provide a detailed disclosure document at least 10 days before you fork over any cash. Check with the Federal Trade Commission (www.ftc.gov) if a seller says he doesn't have to comply with the FTC Franchise rule.

The Least You Need to Know

➤ Check with regulatory agencies, the Better Business Bureau, or the National Fraud Information Center on companies you aren't familiar with.

➤ Always get offers in writing.

➤ Don't give out information to strangers. Don't give information to companies you know, if it isn't required.

➤ If a deal seems too good to be true, it probably is.

➤ Be very wary of any deal that requires you to pay up front or offers fabulous returns with little or no risk.

Chapter 21

Security and Safety

In This Chapter

➤ How to set up your computer to keep your data secure

➤ How to set up your Internet browser to keep your online transactions secure

➤ Learning to avoid the tricks people use to steal your personal information

➤ How to avoid losing data because of hardware failure

When children start to crawl, parents zoom around childproofing the house. They put protectors in the electrical outlets, place the fancy crystal out of reach, and do anything else they can think of to keep their child—and their belongings—safe.

You can do the same thing with your computer. By adding some protections to keep others out, locking up the things you want to keep safe, and by using common sense, you can surf, buy, and invest on the Internet without worrying.

But, don't forget, you have to think about safety on the computer and off. Crooks and con artists can get to you through the telephone, your mail, or on the street.

Keeping Your Transactions Secure

Computer security can get pretty complicated. But, in many cases, people who steal your information use the easiest approaches. A few simple security measures can protect your data from most hackers.

What's the Secret Word?

Whether you keep your financial information on your computer at home or at work, there are a couple of computer settings that can help keep others away from your personal data. With a password on your user profile, you can log on to your computer only if you know the password.

Head of the Class

What's in a Name?

Don't pick passwords that are easy to guess. Your spouse's name, birthdays, and your anniversary are common passwords, and the first things a hacker would guess. If you must choose an easily remembered password, replace a letter with a number—for example, *bonnie* might become *bonn1e*.

And, don't tell anyone your password—even a system administrator. Some hackers pose as technical support, claiming to need your password to test the system. Don't buy it! Finally, never leave a password written down where someone else can find it.

If you are using Windows 98, and you don't have a password set up, click **Start** on the Windows menu bar. Then, scroll the mouse to select **Settings**, **Control Panel**. In the Control Panel window, double-click **Passwords**. On the Change Passwords tab in the Passwords window, click **Change Windows Password**. Finally, enter your old password if you had one, and your new password. Retype your new password in the third box to make sure that you typed it correctly, as in the example in Figure 21.1. Click **OK**. The next time you log on to your computer, you enter your username and your Windows password.

Another password that you can use is a screensaver password. A screensaver starts after your computer has been idle for a certain amount of time. You can set up the screensaver to ask for a password when you come back to use the computer again. A screensaver password is handy if you stay logged on to your computer all day at work, and don't want anyone to touch it while you're gone. Beware, though, that a determined intruder can get past your screensaver password by rebooting your computer, so use it in conjunction with a logon password.

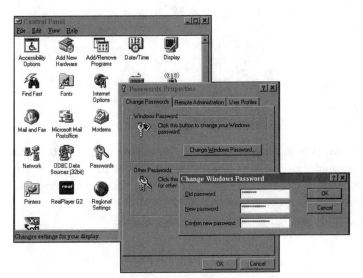

Figure 21.1

Set a Windows password so that others can't access your computer.

To set up a screensaver password, go to the Control Panel window. Double-click **Display**. Click the **Screensaver** tab and check the **Password Protected** check box. Click the **Change** button. Enter your new password, and retype your password in the **Confirm New Password** box. To remove the password, leave both boxes blank.

If you use Quicken, you can set passwords on Quicken files, as well as transactions. To set a password on your Quicken file, click **File** on the Quicken menu bar. Select **Passwords**, **File** and enter the password for the file. Retype the password to confirm it. Each time you open that Quicken file, you must enter the password.

Did You Know?

You Have to Log Off for Windows Passwords to Work

You can set up a password on your computer. But, if you never log off, the computer never gets the chance to ask for the Windows password. Anyone can walk up and start using your computer.

If you want to protect existing transactions, you can set up a password to modify existing transactions. Select **Passwords**, **Transaction** and enter the password. You can specify a date so that any transactions before that date require the password. If you want to avoid changing transactions from previous years by mistake, the transaction password can help.

You also can apply passwords to your Excel spreadsheets. To require a password to open a spreadsheet, select **Save As** from the Excel **File** menu. Select **General Options** from the **Tools** menu. Enter the password in the **Password to Open** text box and click **OK**. Re-enter the password to confirm, and click **OK**. Click **Save** and the file is saved with the password protection. Be careful, though! If you forget the password, that spreadsheet is lost to you forever!

Tool Tips

Adjust the Screensaver Wait Time to Your Schedule

If you tend to stay near your computer or work at home, set the wait time on the screensaver to 15 minutes or even more. You won't have to enter your password as often. However, if you aren't in your office more than five minutes at a time, set the wait time so that the screensaver kicks in quickly.

Crash Alert

Don't Let Someone Sniff Out Your Personal Information

Never send credit card numbers, account numbers, or other sensitive information by email. Sniffer software can read email traffic and looks for patterns such as credit card numbers.

Scrambled Data

The Internet isn't secure. It's like a telephone party line. Anyone with *sniffer* software can listen in on the data sent around the Internet. Well, if the Internet isn't secure, why would you send personal and financial data across it?

As long as your data is encrypted (encoded with a complicated key), you can send it across the Internet safely. The encryption used on the Web is called *Secure Sockets Layer*, or SSL. You want the highest level of encryption possible, which, for now, is 128-bit encryption. Information encrypted with 128-bit codes would take centuries to decode. If you use versions of Microsoft Internet Explorer or Netscape Navigator later than 3.0, you're okay.

So, your browser supports 128-bit encryption. Great! Before you start your buying spree or investing, be sure that you are on a secure site. To show that a site is secure, Internet Explorer and Netscape Navigator show a locked padlock symbol in the status bar at the bottom of the window as illustrated in Figure 21.2. If the site isn't secure, the padlock is open. The Web address is another way to tell whether the site is on a secure server. If the URL begins with `https://` instead of `http://`, your connection is secure.

Figure 21.2

Netscape Navigator and Internet Explorer use a locked padlock to show that a site is secure.

	Document: Done	

Cookies

Computer geeks go to great lengths to amuse themselves when they work late into the night. Some hungry Web nerd named the little package of data that some Web sites store on your computer a *cookie*.

By storing basic information about you and the things you like, cookies help Web sites customize themselves to your preferences. Web sites use cookies to show where you have been on the site, which ads you have seen, or perhaps the products you have purchased from the site. Cookies also can hold information such as your logon information, or your name and address so that you don't have to re-enter them each time you visit or buy.

A Public Place Is No Place to Stay Logged On!

If you go to the library or other public places with Internet access, log off your Internet session, and the computer, when you're done. Be sure that logon information isn't saved to the computer. On a public computer, you might want to set the browser to disable cookies, so that your personal information for a Web site isn't saved to the computer.

On your own computer, cookies are okay. Besides, the Web practically doesn't work without them. I tried disabling cookies once. The constant prompts about whether to accept a cookie turns a surfing session into a nightmare.

What's Mine Is Mine

Privacy is something that only you can protect. Whether you are online or off, you should think twice before giving someone else private information about yourself.

Many Web sites make their money through advertising. And, advertisers like to know the demographics of the people they're reaching.

Look for a Privacy Policy

Because of the Federal Trade Commission, many Web sites publish their privacy policy, which includes how they use the information that they collect about you. Take the time to read a site's privacy policy. If you don't like what you see, don't spill the beans!

You might have been asked to register on a Web site or enter information about yourself to qualify for a prize. This information is just what the advertisers want to know: your age, your level of education, your salary range, your marital status, your hobbies, and other items.

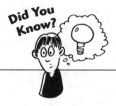

Just Say No

Your Social Security number is a key to your identity. Protect it at all costs. Companies, other than your bank, broker, or other financial institution, don't need to know your Social Security number. If they ask for it, politely refuse. If it's required, use another site. If someone, such as your health insurance company, uses your Social Security number as an identifier, you can ask them to use another number.

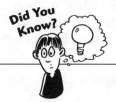

He Wrote the Book on Security

For more easy-to-understand information on computer security for the whole family, check out *The Complete Idiot's Guide to Protecting Yourself Online* by Preston Gralla.

One option for limiting the information that you give out is to answer only the required fields (often indicated with an asterisk). If a site requires a personal item that you want to keep private, try to find another site that isn't so nosy. Another trick to watch for is check boxes that are checked by default giving the site permission to use or sell your personal information.

To learn more about protecting your privacy—or possibly regaining it—go to the Consumer Protection section of the Federal Trade Commission Web site (http://www.ftc.gov/privacy/protect.htm). It provides links to the credit bureau, Department of Motor Vehicles, and Direct Marketing sites. By following those links, you can find out how those organizations use your information, and how you can stop them.

Protecting Your Data

It isn't enough to protect your data from someone trying to steal it. Losing your data might be even worse. With a small bit of prevention, recovering your data is only a slight inconvenience, instead of a full-blown crisis.

Infections Don't Have to Be Fatal

Now that computers can talk, it's no wonder that they get sick, too. Computer viruses are small programs that infect your computer, just as real viruses infect us humans. Sometimes computer viruses cause mischief; but, sometimes they can wipe out your hard drive. These viruses hide in other files and they spread when you download an infected file to your computer.

Head of the Class

Avoid Germs

The best way to avoid a virus infection is to keep infectious files off your computer. Don't download files from Web sites that you aren't familiar with. If someone you don't know sends you an email with an attachment, delete the email without opening the attachment. If you read your email before you download it, don't download that message.

However, with few exceptions, you can't get a virus simply from *reading* email. Email warnings about such viruses abound, but they are hoaxes—in fact, they are themselves a sort of virus, as well-intentioned people forward the messages, which annoy the recipients and clutter up the Internet.

Macro viruses are viruses that hide in macros within Word documents or Excel spreadsheets. Someone you know or work with might give you an infected file without knowing it. When you open the document, the macro runs, often infecting your Word or Excel template, and then the rest of your documents.

Eventually, you will get a computer virus on your machine, no matter how careful you are. So, you should buy an antivirus software package. These packages scan files on your computer for signs of viruses, can eliminate them, or tell you what to do to get rid of them. McAfee VirusScan (www.mcafee.com) and Norton AntiVirus (www.symantec.com) are two popular and effective virus scan programs.

Tool Tips

Keep Your Virus Protection Running

Sometimes, you have to turn off antivirus software to install new software on your computer. If you do turn it off, remember to turn it back on when you are done with your installation.

Hackers create new viruses every day. The antivirus folks keep creating new antidotes, which they put into data files. It's vital to update your antivirus data files regularly, so some new virus doesn't infect your computer. You can update your antivirus data files by visiting the Web site for your antivirus software to download the new files. Sometimes you can just click a button on your virus program and it will update itself.

When You Are Your Own Worst Enemy

When it comes to losing data, it's a question of when it will happen, not if. A virus infects your computer, and before you know it, your hard drive is empty. Or you delete a file you didn't mean to, or save one with changes you didn't want. Even if you're extremely careful, a hard drive packed with data can fail at the most inopportune time. Every time this happens, you get a sick feeling in your stomach, when you realize what it takes to rebuild that file—or your entire computer!

However, if you back up your computer regularly, these problems become minor inconveniences. When you lose a file, Murphy's Law says that it will happen at the worst possible time—right before a big presentation or your taxes are due. Then, even restoring files from a backup can seem to take forever.

Tool Tips

Back Up Your Entire Computer Whenever You Install Software

After you install software on your computer, you should back up your entire computer. If you don't, you might have to reinstall software if your hard disk crashes. It is a good idea to back up your entire computer *before* you install software—just in case the installation causes major problems.

Often, the hard work is figuring out where your data is. Many applications end up saving your files and data in the folder for the application. When this happens, your data could be in more than a dozen different places. If an application gives you the option of where to save your files, keep them in a special folder for your data. For example, in Word, click **Tools** on the menu bar, and select **Options**. Click the **File Locations** tab, and select **Documents**. Click **Modify** and enter the folder where you want your documents to go by default, as in the example in Figure 21.3.

It Won't Hurt to Learn More About Your Computer

If you're using your computer to track your financial life, and all this talk of back-ups, finding files, and folders is complete gibberish, your safest step is to learn a little bit more about how to use your computer. Consider taking a beginner class at your local community college. Or read *The Complete Idiot's Guide to Windows 98* by Paul McFedries, or *The Complete Idiot's Guide to PCs* by Joe Kraynak.

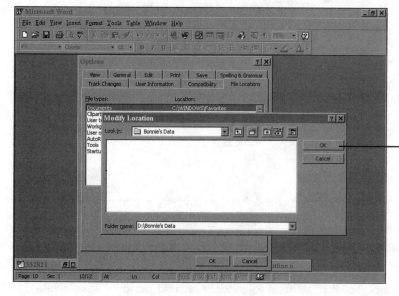

Figure 21.3

In Microsoft Word, you can choose where your documents go by default.

Click **OK** to change the default document location.

If you have more than one hard drive, consider keeping all your software on your C: drive, and all your data on another hard drive. If you have only a C: drive, one top-level folder that contains all your data makes backing up your data easy. For example, you can create a folder on your C: drive called "Data."

If you want to keep different folders for different types of documents, create subfolders under the top level. You also can create subfolders for business files versus personal files. Figure 21.4 shows both approaches to storing your data.

Figure 21.4

You can store your data on a separate hard drive, as in the D: drive. Or you can create a top-level folder on your C: drive, such as the folder "Bonnie's Data."

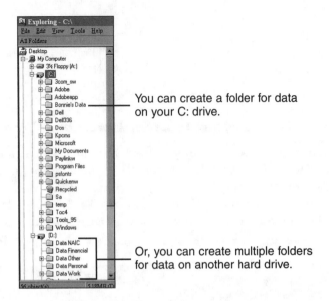

You can create a folder for data on your C: drive.

Or, you can create multiple folders for data on another hard drive.

It's a good idea to keep a copy of a recent backup somewhere else, in case your house burns or floods. You can keep the copy with your important papers in a safe deposit box. Or just keep a copy of your personal data at the office—locked up, please—and vice versa.

Personal Data at Work Might Not Be Private

According to U.S. law, employers can monitor all traffic traveling over their networks, personal or not. So, if you check your stocks or send personal email while at work, you should beware that someone at the company could listen in. Indeed, such personal traffic might be forbidden; make a discreet inquiry about your company's policy, if any.

Data Backups Are Like Insurance

Some people take chances and go without insurance. They're okay as long as nothing happens. Backups are the same way. Most people don't back up their data until they lose something important. At the very least, back up your data once a week.

To be safe, you should set up a backup plan. In your backup plan, you set a schedule for backups, and rotate your backup media (tapes, zip drives, floppy disks, CDs). Backups are no good unless you can restore your data. If the media is bad, the backup is worthless. Rotating media is extra protection that you can restore at least one copy of your lost file.

Here's one possible backup plan if you use your computer mainly on the weekend:

1. Keep and label a set of media for two days of the week, Friday and Saturday. Back up your data to the media for the day. The following week, reuse these sets of media. Write the backup date on the label each time that you perform a backup on that media.

2. Keep a set of media for each Sunday of a month (five sets). Each Sunday, back up your data to the appropriate media (Sunday 1, Sunday 2, and so on). The following month, reuse those sets of media. Write the backup date on the label each time that you perform a backup on that media.

3. Save the backup from the first Sunday as an archive, and label it by month and year—for example, July 2000. Create a new set of media for the first Sunday.

4. Every year, create new sets of media for your daily and weekly backups. Store your archives someplace cool and dry.

With these precautions, you might lose some data, but recovering should take minutes instead of days.

The Least You Need to Know

➤ Use passwords to keep unauthorized persons away from your data.

➤ Use an Internet Browser that supports 128-bit encryption (Netscape Navigator or Microsoft Internet Explorer 3.0 or later).

➤ Don't enter private information on an insecure site. Look for the padlock in your browser, or an address that begins with https://.

➤ Provide only required information. If a site wants information that you don't want to give out, withhold it or find another site.

➤ Don't download programs, videos, or music from unfamiliar sites. Don't open email attachments from people you don't know.

➤ Use antivirus software to protect your computer against viruses.

➤ Back up your data frequently.

Appendixes

If computers and the Internet make you feel like Alice in Wonderland, learn what you need on a computer. Find out how easy it is to get online. Then, you can surf the Web like a madhatter.

Getting Online

In This Appendix

➤ Background on the Internet and the World Wide Web

➤ Three quick steps to getting online

➤ Customizing your Internet browser

The Internet and the World Wide Web are hard to ignore. Almost every TV commercial seems to include a reference to "dot-com." If you have kids older than six, they might know more about the Internet than you do. If you're tired of feeling left behind, here's the place to start.

What's Online, Anyway?

To be completely accurate, you are *online* anytime you connect to another computer, whether you use a telephone line or another type of communication network. But most people mean the Internet when they talk about being online.

What Are the Internet and the World Wide Web?

Computer networks connect computers so that they can share information. For example, I have a small network in my house so that I can share information between my desktop computer and my laptop computer. If you work for a large company, it might have a network that connects computers around the country, or even around the world.

Just as the interstate highway system is a series of roadways that connect the states in our country, the Internet is a system that connects computer networks around the world. It is really a network of networks, very much like the connections between our telephone network here in the United States and the telephone networks in every other country in the world.

Most of us don't want to know how to connect computers with cables and network hardware. We just want to get the information that we need. That's where the World Wide Web comes in. The World Wide Web uses the Internet. The Web is a way of sending information across the Internet that is very easy to use.

Read All About It

You can learn more about the history of the Internet from several sources. One good source is *The Complete Idiot's Guide to the Internet,* by Peter Kent, which contains everything you need to know to understand and get started with all aspects of the Net, from Web surfing to email to online chat. The Pubic Broadcasting Service provides an interactive Internet timeline and links to beginners' resources at http://www.pbs.org/internet/timeline/.

There are also plenty of online primers to help you get started. Try the Electronic Frontier Foundation's Extended Guide to the Internet at http://www.eff.org/papers/eegtti/eegtti.html. Or check out Beginners' Central at http://www.northernwebs.com/bc/.

Dial-up Versus Network

When you connect to the Internet from your home, you are probably using a dial-up connection. You use your telephone to dial up your Internet service provider, which in turn connects you to the Internet.

The computer network at your workplace might connect to the Internet. In that case, you can get to the Internet directly from your computer. You don't have to dial a telephone number.

If your company computer network doesn't connect to the Internet, you are back to dialing up an Internet service provider. However, the digital phone systems in many companies don't play well with modems and Internet connections. If you need access to the Internet, talk to your boss or the computer folks at your company about getting a special phone line for Internet access.

Online Before You Know It

When you buy a computer today, chances are that it has almost everything you need to get online. This section describes what you need, and how to choose between the available options.

The Well-Mannered Computer

Computers are relatively cheap these days. It makes sense to spend a little more when you buy a computer. Upgrading pieces later costs as much, if not more, as buying a new machine.

The minimum features for a PC running Windows, Microsoft Office, and accessing the Internet are a 133-megahertz (MHz) processor, 32 megabytes (MB) of memory, 1-gigabyte (GB) hard disk space, and a 28.8-kilobaud (kb) modem. If you're buying a new computer, consider at least the following:

➤ 300MHz processor

➤ 64MB memory

➤ 4GB hard disk space

➤ 56kb modem

The processor speed and memory don't affect your Web sessions too much, but Quicken, Excel, and other applications will run much faster with a faster processor and more memory. Software takes up a lot of room these days. Microsoft Office needs hundreds of megabytes of disk space if you install all the options. And, if you like to download graphics from the Web or keep your digital photos on your computer, get 8GB of hard disk space or even more.

If you use a regular telephone for Internet access, get a 56kb modem. Uploading and downloading data from the Web takes the most time, so you want the fastest modem you can get.

Tool Tips

The Web Is a Standard

The prefix to every Web address starts with http, which stands for *Hypertext Transfer Protocol*. The World Wide Web exists because a hypertext link can point to anything, whether it is a Web page on your computer or on a Web site on the other side of the world.

Crash Alert

There's No Free Lunch—Or Computer Either

You might notice marketing efforts offering free or inexpensive computers. There's a catch, though—usually a long-term contract with an Internet service provider, or you might agree to receive lots and lots of electronic advertising. In addition, the computer you receive is probably not very expensive—and therefore not very powerful—to begin with.

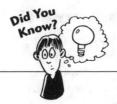

Older Computers Can Get Online, But They're Better for Other Things

Computers that are five or six years old can connect to the Internet. But, you might find the experience unpleasant. With new computers often costing less than an upgrade, you could try to give your older computer to your kids. But, kids seem to want (or need) the fastest computers. So, consider giving your old computer to your parents! Also, charities often are delighted to get older computers.

One of the larger expenses for a computer these days is the monitor, but even these prices are beginning to drop. Fourteen-inch and 15-inch monitors are standard for many computers. For a small upgrade fee, you can get a 17-inch, 19-inch, or even 21-inch monitor. The upgrade fee is a small price to pay compared to bifocals!

Getting an Internet Service Provider

Because the Internet connects networks, you need to belong to a network to get on the Internet. Online services and Internet service providers have those networks. When you dial in to your Internet service, you get a temporary network address from them, and off you go!

Online services, such as America Online or CompuServe, offer entire communities of services and information without even touching the Internet. The major online services have telephone access numbers around the country, so your telephone calls probably are local calls. You get an email address as part of your service, but sometimes the services' email programs have trouble with email from other places, or with attachments.

Internet service providers (ISPs) usually have a Web site that you can use as a starting point for your Web surfing. But you use an Internet browser, such as Internet Explorer or Netscape Navigator, as your interface, and these programs might take you to their own start pages, or *portals,* instead. You also get an email address with an ISP. If you use an email program, such as Microsoft Exchange or Outlook, you might have less trouble exchanging emails with others.

Online Services Cater to the Beginner

When you connect to the Internet through a major online service, you see the Internet through its interface. These interfaces are often very easy-to-use, but sometimes Web pages won't display properly. Online services also might provide more handholding for beginners.

Some ISPs are local, and some are national. If you travel on business, you might want a national ISP, so you can get local telephone access numbers around the country. It's a good idea to take advantage of trial periods, if you sign up with a local service provider. Some ISPs outgrow their resources, which leads to trouble getting connected, slow response times, or busy Web pages.

If you plan to surf a lot, look for good prices on unlimited monthly access ($20 a month or less). Otherwise, you can get an hourly plan. You get a number of hours each month for the base fee. Then you pay $1 or more for each additional hour you spend connected each month. Some services offer discounts if you pay for a year at a time up front.

Finding Internet Service Providers Online

It might seem like the chicken before the egg, but you can find a list of ISPs online at http://thelist.internet.com or http://www.isps.com.

Telephone Service

You can use your home telephone line to connect to the Internet. Many telephone companies now offer special deals if you get a second line for your computer. A second telephone line is a good idea if you spend more than an hour or so a day online. Otherwise, you might find that your friends and family wonder where you are.

With a regular telephone connection, you might find yourself tapping your fingers waiting for Web pages to load. A few new, faster options have appeared.

An *Integrated Services Digital Network (ISDN)* line can transfer data much faster than a regular line. Getting an ISDN line to work can be a challenge. ISDN lines need special equipment. And the installation fee and per-minute charge are steep.

Turn Off Call Waiting Before You Get Online

With call waiting, an incoming call kicks you off your connection to the Internet. To turn off call waiting during your call to your ISP, enter ***70** in your computer's telephone dialer before the phone number for the ISP. Sometimes your modem setup program will ask about call waiting and supply this code for you.

Internet Access by Cable or Satellite

Cable modems use your television cable to provide fast connection to the Internet. Because the bulk of data for an online session comes into your computer, you can speed up your Internet connection by downloading information by using a satellite dish. The data that you send back still goes through your telephone line.

Asymmetric Digital Subscriber Line (ADSL) is a new technology that can increase transfer speeds over regular telephone lines up to 50 times without additional telephone cable. ADSL isn't available everywhere at this point. But it's a cost-effective alternative, if it's available in your area.

Using an Internet Browser

Internet Explorer and Netscape Navigator are the most popular Internet browsers on the market. A browser is software that can navigate through Web sites and Web pages. Version 4.0 and later of both Internet Explorer and Netscape Navigator offer 128-bit encryption for secure surfing.

Download the Current Version of Your Browser

You might experience some problems with certain Web sites with earlier versions of these browsers, or with other browser software. Download the current version of your browser. Internet Explorer and Netscape are both free; you can look for them at `http://www.microsoft.com/windows/ie/default.htm` and `http://www.netscape.com/computing/download/index.html`, respectively.

Most of the time, your surfing consists of typing an address for a Web page or clicking a link on the current Web page. But setting up a few features in your browser can make your sessions even easier.

The home page or portal is the first place your browser goes when you get online. If you find a Web page that you go to often, you can set that as your home page in your browser. In Netscape Navigator, click **Edit**, **Preferences**. You can type the address of the page (Uniform Resource Locator or URL) in the **Location** text box, or click **Use Current Page** if your browser is on that page.

The Portal Wars

Competition is fierce among sites to be the one at which you start your surfing. As a result, these portals offer more and more services so that popular items such as news, weather, stock quotes, and searching are available with just a click on the first page you see.

When you return to Web pages frequently, use bookmarks to save the URLs. You can click a bookmark and go right to a favorite page. Because you might end up with many bookmarks, it's a good idea to create folders for different types of sites. For example, you might create folders for shopping, investments, and entertainment.

Click **Bookmarks** in Netscape Navigator, and select **Edit Bookmarks**. Click **File**, **New Folder**. Enter the name for the folder, as shown in Figure A.1.

Figure A.1

You can create folders in Netscape Navigator or Internet Explorer to group bookmarks, and make them easier to find.

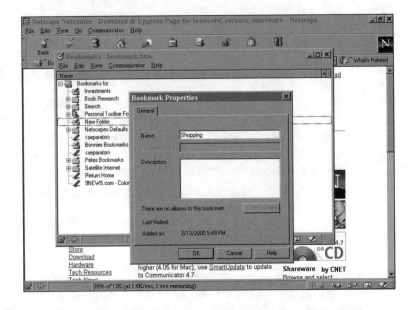

To add a new bookmark in one of your folders, click **Bookmarks**, and select **File Bookmark**. You can then select the folder for the bookmark. Sometimes the bookmark's name is confusing. If you want to change the name of the bookmark, use **Edit Bookmark**. Select the bookmark. Click **Edit** from the menu bar, and select **Bookmark Properties**. Enter the name you want to use in the **Name** text box.

Internet Explorer uses a similar process, but it calls the sites you save Favorites. Still, you can create folders and arrange your favorites in a similar fashion by clicking the **Favorites** menu and selecting the appropriate option.

Happy surfing!

Personal Finance Web Sites

The Web is chock full of Web sites to help you with your online personal finance. This appendix includes some of the best. But, remember, the Web changes every day, and the URLs might change. If a URL doesn't bring up the page you are looking for, try a search for the company or the topic.

Planning

Most financial institutions, including brokerage houses, mutual fund companies, and comprehensive financial services companies, offer some kind of planning tools to help you plan for finances—and see why you need their products.

Quicken.com

    www.quicken.com

Quicken.com is a comprehensive personal finance site offering tools and links for planning, savings, debt reduction, banking, investments, insurance, and just about anything else. Almost every Web site that offers help on debt reduction links to its easy-to-use Debt Reduction Planner.

Access Vanguard

    www.vanguard.com

The Vanguard Group Web site provides education and tools on investing and other aspects of personal finance in addition to online investing with Vanguard mutual funds and stock brokerage.

American Express

www.americanexpress.com

American Express offers financial services for its clients as well as education and tools for personal finance open to everyone.

Financial Planning Association

www.fpanet.org

The Financial Planning Association is mainly a Web site for members of the Association. However, you can use its PlannerSearch tool to find a certified financial planner in your area.

Strong Funds eStrong.com

www.strong.com

Strong Funds provides planning tools and educational materials on a variety of personal finance topics.

Debt

Just about every financial Web site will tell you that getting rid of credit card debt is the most important step you can take. The following are the sites that can help.

Quicken.com Debt Reduction Planner

www.quicken.com/saving/debt

If you want to find out how to get out of debt online, Quicken.com's Debt Reduction Planner is the most popular. If you have Quicken, use the Debt Reduction Planner on your computer. It has more features, saves the plan for future reference, and can add monthly payments to your accounts.

Debt Counselors of America Web Site

www.dca.org or www.getoutofdebt.org

Debt Counselors of America offers debt counseling, self-help publications, payment plans, creditor negotiation, and much more if you want help getting out of debt. Its One-Pay service pays your creditors while you make one payment to DCA each month—and you can check your transactions online.

Consumer Credit Counseling Service Web Site

www.cccs.org

Consumer Credit Counseling Service is another non-profit organization that can help you prepare a debt reduction plan and negotiate better terms with your creditors.

Online Banking

More and more banks offer online banking. Use the Web sites in this section to see if online banking is for you, and then find out which online bank meets your needs. Go to the bank's Web site to apply and start banking online.

Gomez Associates e-Commerce Web Site

www.gomez.com

Gomez Associates ranks numerous types of e-commerce companies, including banks, brokers, and even pet supply stores. It also offers lists of firms that satisfy different customer profiles.

BankRate.com

www.bankrate.com/brm/rate/ebank_home.asp

Bankrate.com provides a great introduction to online banking along with online banking site reviews.

Quicken.com Banking

www.quicken.com/banking_and_credit/online_banking/

The Quicken.com banking channel provides a list of banks offering online services and helpful reviews.

Your Credit

The Web makes it easy to find the credit card that's right for you. Online credit cards offer online account management as well as discounts when you use your card to purchase online. You also can request copies of your credit report online.

BankRate.com

www.bankrate.com/brm/publ/topcards3.asp

Bankrate.com shows the best deals on cards for several different categories.

Quicken.com Banking

www.quicken.com/banking_and_credit/bankrates/

Quicken.com searches for cards by several categories, a few of them different from the BankRate.com categories.

Trans Union

www.transunion.com

Trans Union is one of the three major credit reporting bureaus. You can request a copy of your credit report on its Web site. After your request is verified, you receive your report in the mail.

Using Other People's Money

When you pay hundreds of thousands of dollars in interest on a mortgage, a better mortgage rate can save you a bundle. With the Internet, finding the right mortgage and the best rate has never been easier.

HSH Associates

www.hsh.com

HSH Associates is one of the largest publishers of mortgage and consumer loan information. You can use its calculators and showcase areas to figure out the type of mortgage you want and what rates are in general. When you're ready to apply, you can buy its HomeBuyer's kit to get a complete list of the mortgages offered in your area.

Quicken.com Mortgage

www.quickenloans.quicken.com/

The Quicken.com Mortgage section shows you mortgages from participating lenders and provides a loan interview so that you can pre-qualify online. If you find a mortgage that you want, you can apply online from this site. But, remember, you only see mortgages from participating lenders, not all the lenders in your area.

BankRate.com

www.bankrate.com/brm/rate/auto_ratehome.asp

Bankrate.com shows rates and fees on auto loans based on the length of the loan that you want.

Protecting Your Money

Insurance is a complicated business, so use the Web to make it as simple as possible. You can learn about the insurance you really need, get quotes, comparison shop, and, in some cases, begin your purchase online.

Quicken Insurance

www.insuremarket.com

The Quicken Insurance site explains the basics about all types of insurance, provides quotes, and sells insurance online. Its Family Needs Planner is one of the most comprehensive life insurance calculators on the Web.

InvestorGuide Insurance

www.investorguide.com/insurance.htm

InvestorGuide provides links to all sorts of insurance information: overall sites, online quotes, online purchases, company ratings, calculators, and more.

The Consumer Insurance Guide

www.insure.com

The Consumer Insurance Guide is packed with news and tips about insurance.

Life-line

www.life-line.org

Life-line is a non-profit organization that educates consumers about insurance. It has an easy-to-use disability calculator in addition to a lot of useful information on insurance.

Quotesmith

www.quotesmith.com

Quotesmith is one site that provides insurance quotes from a large stable of insurance companies.

Insurance Industry Internet Network

www.iiin.com

The Insurance Industry Internet Network provides a lot of information to people within the insurance industry. But you can use it to find insurance companies, agents, and brokers online.

eHealthInsurance.com

www.eHealthInsurance.com

eHealthInsurance.com sells health insurance online. Check its Web site to see if it offers insurance in your state.

Taxes

Taxes are never fun—ever. So, use the Web to make finding forms and submitting your taxes take as little time as possible.

The IRS Digital Daily

www.irs.gov

The IRS site includes a lot of useful information about your taxes as well as down-loadable versions of every Federal tax form.

Find Your State Tax Form Here

http://www.westga.edu/~library/depts/govdoc/tax.shtml

The State University of West Georgia hosts this site with links to the IRS and state Departments of Revenue. From here, it's easy to find your state tax forms online.

Saving Money

Whether you're looking for tips on stretching a dollar, the lowest price when you do buy something, or the best interest rates on the savings you have, the Web is a fabulous resource.

Quicken Excite Frugal Living

quicken.excite.com/saving/frugal

A nice site with tools, articles, and discussion groups to help you use your money effectively and save more of it.

The Cheapskate Monthly

www.cheapskatemonthly.com

The Cheapskate Monthly is a great site for money-saving tips, but it does require a modest subscription fee of $18 a year to get to the best features.

StreetPrices.com

www.streetprices.com

StreetPrices.com searches more than 250 online stores to find the best deals for the products you want to buy. Make sure to compare shipping costs before you make your final decision.

Shoppinglist.com

www.shoppinglist.com

ShoppingList.com lets you electronically search for sales at the stores in your area.

BankRate.com

www.bankrate.com

BankRate.com shows you rates for checking accounts, savings accounts, money market funds, certificates of deposit, and other savings vehicles so you can get the most out of your savings dollars.

Quicken.com Fund Finder

www.quicken.com/investments/mutualfunds/finder

The Quicken.com Fund Finder helps you find mutual funds if you want to use bond mutual funds for part of your savings.

Saving for a College Education

Today's Internet-wired kids can prep for college with a host of online information. Parents can find out how much school is going to cost and figure out how to pay for it.

The College Board Web Site

collegeboard.org

The College Board Web site can help parents plan ahead to save for a college education. It also helps students find the schools they like, register for tests, and apply online.

The Chronicle of Higher Education

chronicle.com

The Chronicle of Higher Education includes data on college costs as well as other useful information for college planning.

U.S. News Online Education Site

usnews.com/usnews/edu

The U.S. News Education section is a comprehensive site for information about college.

The Sallie Mae Web Site

www.salliemae.com

While the Student Loan Marketing Association (Sallie Mae) offers student loans, its web site provides information about all types of financial aid.

Ten Steps to Paying for College (Mapping Your Future Web Site)

www.mapping-your-future.org/paying

The Ten Steps to Paying for College is a chronological guide to the steps you need to take and when in paying for college. The hyperlinks in the text fill you in on all your options.

College Savings Plans Network Web Site

www.collegesavings.org

Hosted by the National Association of State Treasurers, this Web site gives links and information about college savings plans and pre-paid tuition programs.

Saving for Retirement

Saving for retirement is probably the biggest savings goal you will ever have. The government wants you to fund your own retirement, so it provides a variety of tax breaks. If you start investing early, and take advantage of those tax breaks, retirement will be a blast.

Quicken.com

> www.quicken.com/retirement/

The Quicken.com Retirement Planner helps you chart a course for your retirement savings. The retirement section also explains different retirement account options such as 401(k) plans, IRAs, and annuities.

Social Security Administration

> www.ssa.gov

You can request a copy of your Social Security statement online.

Access Vanguard

> www.vanguard.com

The Vanguard Group offers a full range of retirement products. The educational materials on its Web site help you figure out what you need.

Saving for the Rest of Your Wish List

Savings calculators can help you figure out how much you need to save each month for your shorter-term goals.

eStrong.com

> http://www.estrong.com/strong/pc/tools/finance.htm

Strong Funds hosts a nice planning center with tools for different savings scenarios. Savings calculator takes into account inflation as well as your tax rate when determining how much you have to save.

Investing Made Easy

Investing doesn't have to be complicated or take a lot of your time.

NAIC Online

> www.better-investing.org

The NAIC Web site is a good place to learn about fundamental stock analysis. The site provides educational materials, workshops, tools, and software to help you study stock fundamentals.

Investorama

www.investorama.com

Investorama provides a lot of educational material on fundamental investing, along with links to more than 14,000 investment Web sites.

Dogs of the Dow

www.dogsofthedow.com

If you're interested in a simple, yet effective, investment strategy, the Dogs of the Dow has an interesting idea—invest in the stocks at the bottom of the Dow and watch them grow. The Dogs Web site tells you everything you need to know to implement this strategy.

Charles Schwab

www.schwab.com

The Charles Schwab site contains all sorts of investment information along with online trading. Its Investor Profile can help you figure out what asset allocation you should use.

Finding and Researching Stocks Online

The World Wide Web reduces the burden of finding and researching stocks for your portfolio. Here are some of the top sites for this purpose.

Wall Street Research Net

www.wsrn.com

Wall Street Research Net is a comprehensive investment site. It has a simple stock-screening tool. You can link to sites for company data, charts, estimates, research, news, spreadsheets, and much more.

Market Guide

www.marketguide.com/mgi/stockquest

The StockQuest screening tool on the Market Guide Web site can screen by 75 different criteria.

Investorama

www.investorama.com/directory/News,_Advice,_and_Talk

You can sample newsletters, publications, and advisory service offerings by clicking on the links at Investorama.

NAIC Online

www.better-investing.org

The NAIC I-Club-List is a very educational discussion list for investing and investment clubs. The NAIC site also has educational materials and workshops.

The Motley Fool

www.fool.com

The Motley Fool is a great site for beginners and pros alike. It provides investment education and fun. You can find discussions about almost any investment or investment topic on its message boards.

The Silicon Investor

www.siliconinvestor.com/stocktalk/

The Silicon Investor Web site provides data and discussion on all your favorite technology stocks.

Yahoo! Finance

www.yahoo.com

The Yahoo! Finance Web site includes thousands of message boards, online clubs, and lots of other investment resources.

The Value Point Analysis Model

www.eduvest.com

The Value Point Analysis Model determines the fair price for a stock based on 13 criteria. On the Web site, you can analyze a stock by entering data, or view analyses by others.

Equis

www.equis.com

MetaStock is an Equis product. You can download a demo version or just learn about technical analysis.

FreeEDGAR

www.freeedgar.com

FreeEDGAR is the place to go to find and download SEC filings.

Value Line

www.valueline.com

Value Line offers normalized financial data for more than 6,000 stocks.

Compustat

www.compustat.com

Standard & Poor's publishes reports for more than 11,000 companies in North America.

Annual Report Service Online

www.annualreportservice.com

You can request, view, and, in some cases, download annual reports.

Public Register's Annual Report Service

www.prars.com

You can request a hard-copy version of any annual report from the PRARS site.

MoneyCentral Investor

www.moneycentral.com/investor

MoneyCentral Investor offers news, data, and charts for companies.

BigCharts

www.bigcharts.com

The charts on the BigCharts Web site are easy to read. You can get quick charts, or you can customize the charts to your liking. You can email the charts to yourself or a friend on a schedule that you define.

Buying Stocks Online

More and more brokers offer online trading and investment services. Online trading offers convenience and lower commissions. With so many online brokers to choose from, look to the Web to figure out which broker is right for you.

Yahoo! Finance

http://dir.yahoo.com/Business_and_Economy/Finance_and_Investment/

Click **Brokerages@** on Yahoo! Finance for a list of full-service and discount brokers, along with a lot of other useful investment information.

SmartMoney.com

www.smartmoney.com/si/brokers/fullserv

SmartMoney.com reviews several of the best brokers and ranks them on a variety of criteria.

Waterhouse Securities

www.waterhouse.com

Waterhouse Securities is one of the top-ranked online brokerage services.

Gomez Associates e-Commerce Web Site

www.gomez.com

Gomez Associates ranks full service and discount brokers. It also offers rankings of brokers that satisfy different investor profiles.

Quicken.com Investments

www.quicken.com/investments

Quicken.com Investments is a great site for investing. You can create a watch list portfolio while you wait for some stocks to fall to a buy price.

DRIP Central

www.dripcentral.com

If you're interested in buying stocks without a broker, learn about dividend reinvestment plans at DRIP Central.

NetStock Direct

www.netstockdirect.com

NetStock Direct can help you find companies with dividend reinvestment plans and direct stock purchase plans.

NAIC Online

www.better-investing.org/store/lcp.html

NAIC offers a low-cost investing program to its members. NAIC gets you started with a company DRIP and then turns the account over to you.

Investing in Mutual Funds

Mutual funds are great investment vehicles for people getting started with investing, or those with more experience but not a lot of time.

Yahoo! Finance

dir.yahoo.com/Business_and_Economy/Companies/Financial_Services/
Investment_Services/Mutual_Funds/

Yahoo! Finance has a lot of good links to mutual fund information, including two for screening mutual funds. You can also find mutual fund families in its mutual fund section.

Quicken.com

www.quicken.com/investments/mutualfunds

Quicken.com provides good information on mutual funds along with a great tool to find mutual funds to meet your criteria.

Access Vanguard

majestic.vanguard.com/FP/DA/0.0.funds_intro

The Vanguard Web site includes educational materials, a fund finder tool, and a great tool to compare two mutual funds, whether they are Vanguard funds or not.

SEC Mutual Fund Prospectus Search

www.sec.gov/edaux/prospect.htm

You can find a prospectus for any mutual fund on the SEC Web site.

Strong Funds

www.estrong.com/strong/LearningCenter98/

Strong Funds provides some great educational material about mutual funds on its Web site.

Investorama

www.investorama.com/infocenter/funds

You can go from beginner to expert with the educational material on mutual funds on the Investorama Web site.

Morningstar.net

www.morningstar.net

Besides publishing the standard for mutual fund reports, and providing a rating system used by almost everyone, the Morningstar folks have great articles, columns, and educational material on their Web site. Plus, you can send questions to guest mutual fund managers or Morningstar's own experts.

Keeping Financial Records Electronically

Tools on your personal computer and the Internet can track your finances, so that you will always know where you stand.

Personal Record Keeper

www.better-investing.org/computer/prk.html

Personal Record Keeper is one software tool for tracking your investments.

Quicken

www.intuit.com

Quicken 2000 provides tools to track your finances and investments on your computer.

Managing Your Portfolio

Portfolio management is more than just keeping track of what you own. It's constantly improving your investment holdings to maximize your returns.

Morningstar.net

www.morningstar.net

Morningstar provides a quick online portfolio tool as well as one that tracks your transactions. Its X-Ray feature shows you your asset allocation based on your stocks and the allocations within your mutual funds.

Infobeat Finance

www.infobeat.com

Infobeat automatically sends you emails with prices and news about the stocks you're interested in.

Quicken.com Investments

www.quicken.com/investments

You can check out a company's annual revenue and earnings growth rates by entering a ticker symbol, and clicking **Fundamentals** when the company data appears.

Avoiding Scams and Ploys

Cyberspace is as safe as the real world (which might not be as safe as we would like) as long as you follow some simple security guidelines.

The National Fraud Information Center

www.fraud.org

The National Fraud Information Center provides education on all sorts of fraud on the Web and off. You can report complaints and cases of fraud with online forms, so that the NFIC can work with law enforcement agencies to catch the crooks.

The Federal Trade Commission

www.ftc.gov/ftc/consumer.htm

The Federal Trade Commission offers tips on avoiding fraud, as well as legal but tricky schemes.

The SEC Investor Education and Assistance Web Page

www.sec.gov/oiea1.htm

For full descriptions of types of investment fraud and how to avoid them, go to the SEC Investor Education and Assistance Web page.

The National Association of Securities Dealers Web Site

www.nasdr.com

You can find out about brokers and securities firms, including any complaints or legal actions against them on the NASD Web site.

The Better Business Bureau

www.bbb.org

You can look for reports about companies through the BBB offices that are online. But, you have to call the offices that aren't yet on the Web.

Security and Safety

When you use your computer and the Internet for your finances, you should take steps to protect your privacy and your data.

The Federal Trade Commission

www.ftc.gov/ftc/consumer.htm

The Federal Trade Commission also includes a section where you can find out how different organizations use your personal information, and how you can stop them.

Antivirus Software

www.mcafee.com and www.symantec.com

McAfee VirusScan and Symantec's Norton's AntiVirus software can protect your computer from viral infections.

Glossaries

Understanding the lingo is an important step in acing your finances. Check out these Web sites whenever you need an explanation of a financial term.

About.com Glossary

http://stocks.about.com/finance/stocks/msub_06.htm

About.com has several links to glossaries for business and investing. It also offers links to glossaries for technical analysis and trading.

Campbell R. Harvey's Hypertextual Finance Glossary

www.duke.edu/~charvey/Classes/wpg/glossary.htm

Campbell Harvey's finance glossary offers definitions and links to related terms for almost every finance term.

The Cheapskate Monthly

www.cheapskatemonthly.com

One of the member features is a glossary of financial terms.

Glossary

For online glossaries, start with www.about.com. It provides several links to financial and business glossaries.

10-K   Report that publicly traded companies must submit to the Securities and Exchange Commission (SEC), which contains audited financial information about the company's performance for the last fiscal year.

10-Q   Quarterly report that publicly traded companies must submit to the SEC.

12b-1 Fees   Fees that mutual funds charge to help cover marketing expenses. Avoid them!

401(k) Retirement Plan   A retirement plan offered by many companies where you contribute up to 15% of your salary with pre-tax dollars. Your contributions and earnings grow tax-deferred until you withdraw money from the account.

Accountant   A person who can analyze, manage, track, and report on financial accounts.

Actuals   The actual money you spend each month, as opposed to the estimates you made when you built your budget.

Adjustable-rate Mortgage   A mortgage in which the interest rate fluctuates as the interest rate of the financial instrument to which it's tied (such as a 6- or 12-month T-bill) moves up and down.

Affinity Card   A credit card linked to a non-financial organization, so that you can earn some sort of reward, such as free trips or contributions to your favorite charity.

Annual Percentage Rate (APR)   The interest rate that you pay on a loan including the impact of points paid up front.

Annual Report   A publication produced by a publicly traded company for its shareholders that explains what the company does, where it's headed, and details about its finances for the past fiscal year.

Annuity   An investment, usually offered by insurance companies, that has no taxable income until you withdraw your money.

Asset Allocation   A strategy for investing where the critical decision is what percentages you invest in stocks, bonds, and cash.

Asset Class   A broad category of investments, such as stocks or bonds.

Assets   The things you own, including your house, cars, salable possessions, and investments.

Attachment   A file that you attach to an email message. Some email systems do not handle attachments.

Balanced Fund   A mutual fund that balances (at 50–50) its investments between stocks and bonds.

Balloon Mortgage   A mortgage where the entire loan comes due after a certain period of time.

Bandwidth   The amount of data that a network connection can transmit at one time. The more users that share that bandwidth, the slower your response time. Bandwidth bottlenecks can occur with your ISP or with the site that you are looking at.

Bond   A loan that you make to a corporation or the government where you earn interest on your money. When the bond matures, the borrower pays back the loan.

Bookmark   An electronic version of the bookmark you use to find a page in a book. Electronic bookmarks save the URL (Web address) of the Web page you want to keep.

Browser   Software that lets you navigate your way through Web sites and Web pages on the Internet.

Budget   A plan for how you will spend and save the money you earn.

Budget Category   A category of income or expenses that you want to track in your budget, such as salary or utilities.

Business Continuation Insurance   Insurance protection against the death or long-term disability of a key employee.

Byte   A unit of storage on a computer that can hold the equivalent of one character on this page.

Capital Gains Distributions   Taxable payout from a mutual fund to distribute the capital gains realized during the year.

Cash Flow   A view of your finances that shows money flowing in and out of your accounts, and that can identify points where you could be short on cash.

Certificate of Deposit (CD)   A savings vehicle usually from a bank where you commit your money for a certain period of time and, in return, receive interest for the length of the CD.

Charts   Graphs of a stock's historical prices, often used by technical analysts to try to determine where the stock price will go next.

Closed-end Fund   A mutual fund that sells a fixed number of shares and invests the money. The fund price acts like the price of a stock, going up or down based on what shareholders think of the potential future performance.

Closing Costs   Costs to finalize the purchase of a property, including lawyer fees, title searches, and survey costs.

Commission   What you pay to a broker or agent for his help in completing a transaction.

Commodities   Products, such as grain, metal, or foreign currencies, bought on a commodity exchange so that investors can make or lose money on the product without ever taking physical delivery.

Compound Annual Growth Rate   Rate at which your money or a company's revenues or sales grows. Comparable to compound interest at a bank where the bank pays interest on your money, and then pays interest on your money plus the interest that you have already earned.

Cookie   A bit of information downloaded to your hard drive that tracks where you have been and what you've done on a particular Web site.

Credit Bureau   An organization that collects and resells information about people's credit worthiness.

Credit Card   A card you can use to purchase items on credit.

Credit Report   A report that includes information about your use (or misuse) of credit.

Creditor   Someone to whom you owe money.

Database   The electronic version of a filing cabinet.

Day Trading   Buying and selling securities within a short period of time to try to take advantage of short-term price changes.

Debit Card   A card that you use to purchase items where the money is immediately removed from your bank account.

Debt   Money owed to creditors, lenders, or bondholders.

Debt-to-Equity Ratio   The ratio of debt carried by a company to the value of the equity owned by the shareholders.

Default   For computer terminology, default is the option or selection that comes up automatically. For finance, default means failure to make payments on a loan.

Defined Benefit Retirement Plan   An employer invests money and pays a specific amount of money for retirement to an employee based on his or her salary and years of service.

Defined Contribution Retirement Plan   An employee contributes a portion of his or her salary to the plan and invests the money to build funds for his or her retirement.

Derivative   A security derived from underlying securities. For example, an option is a security that gives you the right to buy or sell a stock at a specific price.

Direct Stock Purchase Plans (DPPs or DSPs)   A plan where you can buy stock in a company directly from the company without a broker. Also known as a Direct Investment Plan (DIP).

Disability Insurance   Insurance protection against your inability to work.

Discount Broker   A broker that charges low commissions (and usually provides fewer services).

Discretionary Expenses   Expenses that are not essential, such as dining out.

Diversify   To invest in a variety of securities that generally move in different directions to reduce risk in one's portfolio.

Dividend   A taxable payout from a company's earnings to shareholders.

Dividend Reinvestment   Purchasing more shares in a company using the dividend paid out.

Dividend Reinvestment Plan (DRIP)   A plan where you can reinvest dividends or capital gains directly through the company to buy more shares of stock without a broker.

Dollar-cost Averaging   Lowering the average cost of a company's shares by buying shares with a fixed amount of money on a regular schedule. You buy more shares when the price is low, fewer shares when the price is high.

Download Copying a file from a Web site to your computer.

e-Commerce Buying and selling of products or services using the Internet.

Earnings Estimate An estimate of the earnings for a company by analysts who follow the company.

Earnings Per Share (EPS) The earnings of a company divided by the number of shares outstanding. EPS represents the portion of the earnings to which the owner of one share of stock is entitled.

Economic Risk The risk to your investments from an overall downturn in the economy.

Education IRA A tax-deferred account where you can save some money for college.

Effective Rate The interest rate you pay taking into consideration points you pay as well as the time you hold the loan. If you pay points and hold the loan for a short time, the effective rate is much higher than the interest rate.

Electronic Banking Performing banking services, such as transferring money between accounts or checking bank balances, using the Internet.

Electronic Bill Payment Using software and the Internet to pay bills.

Email Discussion List People exchange information by sending email to an email address that distributes the message to all members on the list.

Emergency Savings Money that you keep in safe investments to cover three to six months of expenses in case of emergency.

Emoticon See *Smiley*.

Encryption Disguising information on a computer or the Internet so that unauthorized people cannot read it.

Equity Ownership in a property or corporation. Shareholders equity is the total assets of a corporation minus the total liabilities.

Equity Income Fund A mutual fund invests primarily in dividend-paying stocks so that investors obtain growth of their investments and some current income.

Estate Plan A plan for how your property will be distributed and managed after your death, often including tax considerations.

Exit Fee A fee that some mutual funds charge when you sell shares in the fund.

Expense Something you spend money on, such as rent or food.

Expense Ratio The operating expenses of a mutual fund as a percent of the net assets of the fund.

Export   Transfer data out of an application into another application or format.

Financial Aid   Money available from various sources to help you pay for your child's education.

Financial Plan   A plan for how you will achieve your financial goals, including paying for college, retirement, and protecting your assets with insurance.

Fixed-rate Mortgage   A mortgage where the interest rate stays the same for the life of the loan.

Front-end Load   A sales fee charged by mutual funds when you purchase shares in the fund.

Frugal Living   Spending very carefully to live well while staying within your means.

FTP   File Transfer Protocol is a standard for transferring large amounts of data from one computer to another.

Full-service Broker   A broker that offers other services in addition to stock transactions, including financial planning, stock research, and analysis.

Fundamental Stock Analysis   A method for analyzing the worth of a stock as an investment by studying the fundamental measures, such as sales, earnings per share, and profit margin.

Gigabyte   One billion bytes, or one thousand megabytes.

Global Fund   A mutual fund that invests in stocks within the United States and the rest of the world.

Good Until Cancelled Order   An order to buy or sell a stock at a specific price that remains in place for up to three months unless you cancel the order or the order is filled.

Grant   Money for college that you do not have to pay back.

GUI   An interface to a computer that uses graphics, point, and click, such as Windows 98.

Health Insurance   Insurance that covers (we all hope) most of our doctor and hospital bills.

Health Maintenance Organization   A health care organization that handles all your health needs generally for less cost than other insurance organizations.

Holdings   The securities that you own in your investment portfolio.

Home Page   The first page you see when you connect to a Web site.

Home-equity Loan   A loan covered by the equity you have built up in your house.

HTML   Hypertext Markup Language makes Web pages look and perform as they do. If you want to see what it looks like, select View Source in your Browser software.

HTTP   Hypertext Transfer Protocol is a standard for finding addresses on the Internet.

Hyperlink   An area on a Web site that has an underlying link to another Web page underneath the words or graphics that you see.

Import   Transfer data from another application or format into an application such as Quicken.

Income   Money that you earn through salary, interest, dividends, or other sources.

Income Distribution   Taxable payout from a mutual fund from the interest and dividends paid by the stocks or bonds held by the fund.

Income Replacement Disability Insurance   Insurance that replaces the income you lost from your line of work, regardles of whether you are able to work in a different job.

Indemnity Benefit   Health insurance benefit where the insurance company pays a fixed amount toward the bill, such as $200 a day for a hospital room.

Index   A standard for measuring some aspect of the financial markets.

Index Fund   A mutual fund where the investments and performance mirror the securities in a market index, such as the S&P 500.

Inflation   The overall increase of prices for goods and services.

Inflation Risk   The risk from inflation eroding the purchasing power of your money.

Installment Loan   A loan where you pay off the loan with a series of payments.

Interest   The amount of money a borrower pays to a lender for the use of the lender's money.

International Fund   A mutual fund that invests in stocks outside of the United States.

Internet   The entire network of computers that connect to each other.

Internet Service Provider (ISP)   A company that provides access to the Internet through its network connections.

Intranet   A network of computers within an organization or company.

Investment Advisor Someone who is registered and provides specific investment advice, but is not required to pass any tests or other qualifications.

Investment Club A group of individuals who pool their money to jointly invest and learn more about investing.

Investment Objective The goal or result for an investment, such as income or capital appreciation.

IRA Individual Retirement Account is an account where you can invest money for retirement with the earnings growing tax deferred.

ISP See *Internet Service Provider*.

Junk Bond A high-risk bond with a low credit rating, but a high yield.

Keogh A retirement plan, similar to a 401(k), for self-employed individuals or unincorporated businesses.

Kilobaud Units of data transfer for a modem. Typical speeds today are 33 kilobaud or 56 kilobaud.

Laddering Putting some money into a five-year CD each year so that you earn the higher interest rates of a long-term CD, but get ready cash each year when a CD matures.

Liabilities The money you owe to others, such as mortgages, loans, and credit card balances.

Life Insurance Insurance to provide for those who depend on your income in case you die.

Lifetime Cap The highest interest rate that an adjustable-rate mortgage can have for the life of the loan.

Limit Order A buy or sell order for a security that sets the price that you want to buy or sell at. The order will not occur unless the security reaches your limit price.

MAGI Modified Adjusted Gross Income is the income used to calculate one's tax liability after certain adjustments are made.

Mandatory Expenses Expenses that you must pay, such as rent, mortgage, or utilities.

Margin Account An investment account where you can borrow to purchase more securities.

Margin Loans The loan that the broker makes against an individual's investments.

Market Order An order to buy or sell a security at the current asking price on the market.

Market Risk   The risk that a particular investment will turn bad.

Megabyte   One thousand bytes.

Megahertz   A measure of computer processor speed and power, which identifies the number of cycles per second.

Modem   A device that enables a computer to transfer data over telephone lines.

Money Market Account   A bank account that invests your balance in the short-term money markets.

Money Market Fund   A mutual fund that invests in the money markets.

Mortgage   A loan to purchase real estate.

Mutual Fund   An investment where an investment advisor or fund manager invests the money of the shareholders to achieve an investment objective.

Mutual Fund Family   A number of mutual funds offered by the same mutual fund company.

Mutual Fund Supermarket   A broker that offers a variety of mutual fund families.

Net Asset Value (NAV)   The dollar value of a mutual fund share, calculated as the total assets of the fund minus the liabilities, divided by the number of shares.

Net Worth   The total assets minus total liabilities for an individual or a company.

Netiquette   The online version of etiquette, including not typing in all uppercase, and using emoticons so that people can tell whether you are being sarcastic.

Network   A series of interconnections.

Newsgroups   An online forum where people discuss a topic.

No-load Fund   A mutual fund that does not charge any sales loads or fees. They will have operating expenses.

Open-end Mutual Fund   A mutual fund that creates or redeems shares as investors add or remove money from the fund.

Operating Expenses   The costs to run a mutual fund.

Option   The right to buy or sell a security at a specific price for a specific amount of time.

Own-occupation Disability Insurance   Insurance that replaces your income if you are unable to perform your current occupation, but won't pay if you able to earn income in some other occupation.

Password   A secret word or series of characters that the user must enter before he can access a computer, file, or Web site.

Payment Adjustment Period   The length of time between points when the lender can adjust the amount of a mortgage payment.

Payroll Deduction   Money removed from the pay you receive for items, such as health insurance, 401(k) contributions, or transfers into savings.

PDF File Format   Portable Document Format is a format for saving files so that others can view them even if they do not have the application that created the file.

Pension   A retirement plan set up by a corporation or other organization for its employees where the corporation funds the plan.

Per Adjustment Cap   The maximum interest rate increase in one adjustment for an adjustable rate mortgage.

Points   Finance charges that the borrower pays up front to the lender.

Portfolio   A collection of investments owned by an individual or company.

Portfolio Management   Adjusting the holdings in your portfolio to improve its performance or reduce its risk.

Portfolio Tracker   An online or software tool that keeps track of investment transactions, such as purchases, sales, or dividends.

Pre-paid Tuition   Programs where you can purchase units of tuition in today's dollars for education in the future.

Preferred Provider Organization   A health care organization that offers better prices when you use the doctors or health care facilities associated with the organization. You can still see health care providers outside of the network for a higher fee.

Premium   A regular payment toward an insurance policy.

Prepayment Penalty   A penalty that some lenders charge if a borrower pays early.

Prequalification   Determining how much a prospective homebuyer is qualified to borrow.

Price Appreciation   The increase in the price of an investment.

Private Mortgage Insurance   Insurance that protects a lender in case a borrower defaults on a loan.

Profit Margin   The percentage of net profit to annual sales.

Rate Adjustment Period   The length of time between points when the lender can adjust the interest rate on a mortgage.

Rate of Return   The annual return as a percentage of the original investment amount.

Realized Capital Gains   The increase in value of one's capital that you obtain by selling a security.

Redemption Fee   A fee that mutual funds charge when you sell shares of a mutual fund. Same as an exit fee or back-end load.

Reinvestment Risk   The risk that interest rates will be lower when a CD or bond matures.

Retirement Account   An investment account where you save and invest money for retirement. Many of these accounts are tax-deductible and the earnings grow tax deferred.

Revenues   The total income from sales, services, or other sources for a company.

Right-click   Click the right button on your mouse.

Rollover   A tax-free transfer of funds from one retirement account to another.

Roth IRA   An Individual Retirement Account where you contribute with after-tax dollars, but can withdraw your money in retirement tax free.

Scholarship   Financial aid that you do not have to pay back awarded for academic excellence, athletic achievement, or for students who belong to an ethnic or other group.

Screensaver   Software that changes the screen display on your computer if it stands idle for a length of time so that an image does not burn into the screen permanently.

Search Engine   A search engine matches keywords to find things you are looking for.

Sector Fund   A mutual fund that invests in a sector of the market, such as computer technology, or health care.

Secure Sockets Layer   The security protocol used on the Internet.

Secure Web Browser   Web browser software that supports SSL.

Service Benefits   Health insurance benefits that pay a percentage of the cost of service.

Smiley   Smileys are punctuation that show a facial expression, such as :) or ;).

Spam   The electronic equivalent of junk mail.

Spider   SPDR, or Standard & Poor's Depositary Receipt, represent ownership in a unit investment trust that mirrors the S&P 500 index.

Stock   A legal document that represents ownership in a corporation.

Stock Screen   A tool for screening out stocks that do not meet the criteria you desire, such as EPS growth rate, debt/equity ratio, or dividend yield.

Stock Split   An increase in the number of shares with a corresponding change in share price so that shareholders' equity remains the same.

Stop Price   A price for a stock that you set at which your broker automatically sells the stock if its price drops that far.

Tax Planning   Considering the tax implications of investment decisions, usually to minimize tax liabilities.

Tax-advantaged Retirement Accounts   Retirement accounts where you receive tax breaks for saving, such as shielding your contributions from current taxes or withdrawing from the account with no tax liability.

Tax-deferred   Income where the taxes are not paid until a date in the future.

Tax-managed Mutual Funds   Mutual funds that manage their investments to minimize the tax liabilities for the shareholders.

Teaser Rate   An extra low introductory interest rate that changes to a higher rate after a certain period.

Technical Stock Analysis   Trying to determine the future price of a security based on the graph of its historical price or trading volume.

Term Life Insurance   Life insurance that provides coverage for a specific term.

Transaction Fee   A fee that brokers might charge to purchase shares in a mutual fund.

Treasury Bill   A U.S. government debt instrument with a maturity of one year or less.

Umbrella Liability   Liability insurance that provides a higher coverage amount or covers additional liability items.

Unrealized Capital Gains   Increase in capital that exists only on paper.

Upload   Copying a file from your computer to a Web site.

URL   URL stands for Uniform Resource Locator, but it is just an address that gets you to a Web site.

Value Investing   An investment strategy that involves finding stocks where the fundamental performance is not reflected in the share price.

Vesting Period   The period of time that an employee must work for a company before he has unconditional ownership of employer pension contributions.

Virus   A software program that is loaded on your computer without your knowledge and can cause damage as it runs and copies itself.

Watch List   A list of stocks that you create to monitor for potential purchase or sale.

Web Discussion Boards   Web pages where you can post messages or view messages from others.

Web Site, Web Page   A Web site is a collection of Web pages. A Web page is one document written in HTML. Clicking on a hyperlink jumps to another Web page.

Whole Life Insurance   Life insurance that covers your whole life instead of a period of time, which also includes a cash value component that builds up over time.

Work-study Programs   Financial aid programs where a student is paid for work in his or her field of study.

World Wide Web   An easy-to-use interface to the Internet.

Yield   The annual return on an investment expressed as a percentage. With stocks, the yield is the dividend divided by the purchase price. With bonds, the yield is the interest rate divided by the market price.

Zero-coupon Bond   A bond that you purchase at a discount that pays the full face value when it matures.

Index

Y-Z